KU-517-499

THE LIBRARY

OF
:R

KA 0003225 5

Studies in Philosophy and Religion

GENERAL EDITOR: P. R. BAELZ

*Regius Professor of Moral and Pastoral Theology
University of Oxford*

Contemporary interest in religion is widespread. The interpretation of man's religious experience raises fundamental questions of knowledge and truth to which philosophical analysis and reflection are highly relevant. The present series will include a variety of writings which explore the significance and validity of the claims of religion to give insight into the reality of the world and God.

Studies in Philosophy and Religion

PUBLISHED TITLES

Ian Ramsey
CHRISTIAN EMPIRICISM

John Hick (ed.)
TRUTH AND DIALOGUE

CHRISTIAN EMPIRICISM

Ian Ramsey
Edited by Jerry H. Gill

SHELDON PRESS
LONDON

First published
in Great Britain in 1974 by
Sheldon Press
Marylebone Road
London NW1 4DU

Copyright © 1974 Margaret Ramsey

All rights reserved. No part of this publication
may be reproduced or transmitted in any form
or by any means, electronic or mechanical,
including photocopying, recording, or by any
information storage or retrieval system without
permission in writing from the publisher.

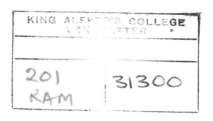

KING ALFRED'S COLLEGE
WINCHESTER

201
RAM   31300

Printed in Great Britain by
The Camelot Press Ltd, London and Southampton
ISBN 0 85969 011 3

For
Margaret Ramsey

Contents

Acknowledgements

The publishers are grateful to Mrs Margaret Ramsey for permission to publish the articles in this book. Thanks are also due to the following for permission to publish copyright material:

The Editor of The Aristotelian Society: 'Facts and Disclosures' by Ian Ramsey. © 1972 The Aristotelian Society.

Chicago Theological Seminary Register: 'On Understanding Mystery' and 'On Being Articulate about the Gospel' by Ian Ramsey in the May 1963 issue.

Department of Higher Education, National Council of Churches, USA: 'Contemporary Empiricism' in the Autumn 1960 issue of *The Christian Scholar*.

The Philosophical Forum, Boston University, USA: 'Biology and Personality' by Ian Ramsey in Vol. XXI (1964).

The Philosophical Quarterly, St Andrews University: 'The Systematic Elusiveness of "I" ' by Ian Ramsey from the July 1955 issue.

The Religious Education Association of the United States and Canada: 'Christian Education: Post Mortem Dei' by Paul van Buren and 'Discernment, Commitment and Cosmic Disclosure' by Ian Ramsey in *Religious Education*.

The Society for Promoting Christian Knowledge: 'Talking of God' by by Ian Ramsey in *Theological Collections 7 Myth and Symbol*.

The Society for Promoting Christian Knowledge and *The Church Quarterly Review*: 'Ethics and Reason' by Ian Ramsey in the April/June 1957 issue and 'Religion and Science' in the January/March 1961 isssue.

The Society for Promoting Christian Knowledge and *Theology*: 'The Logical Character of Resurrection-belief' (May 1957) and 'A Letter to the Editor' (February 1965) by Ian Ramsey and 'The Intellectual Crisis of British Christianity' by Ninian Smart in the January 1965 issue.

Editor's Preface

The idea of editing a collection of Ian Ramsey's more important journal articles grew out of my experience of studying with him at Oxford in 1966, and from my subsequent exploration of the wide scope of his thought. Certain basic features of his approach to philosophy and theology were available only in these essays. Moreover, a number of criticisms levelled against various aspects of his position were herein faced quite directly and, to my mind, effectively. Bishop Ramsey offered both encouragement and suggestions for putting such a book together. I am very grateful that a more complete presentation of the richness of his perspective is now being made available through the publication of these essays in book form.

Working with the writings of creative thinkers and teachers is often less rewarding and exciting than working with them personally. This was certainly true of Ian Ramsey, for his quick insight, unceasing energy, and personal manner enabled him to convey his ideas with great force and clarity. Nevertheless, his writings do mediate a great deal of his personality. Furthermore, they bring a genuinely creative, profound, and honest angle of exploration to the relationship between philosophy and theology. The articles included in this volume provide an excellent testimony to the breadth and depth of Bishop Ramsey's thought. In addition, they speak concretely to specific problem areas.

I am most happy to acknowledge my indebtedness to those whose co-operation has made this book a reality. The editors of the various journals involved were most helpful, as were the authors of the essays included in Part Four. Also, I wish to thank Mr Darley Anderson of the Sheldon Press, who saw the idea for this collection through to completion. Most of all, I am grateful to Mrs Margaret Ramsey for her interest in this project and for her personal kindness. Therefore the book is appropriately dedicated to her.

August 1973   J. H. G.

PART
1

*Contemporary
Philosophy*

Contemporary Empiricism
Its Development and Theological Implications

What is common to present day 'Oxford philosophy' and the logical positivists of the Vienna Circle? How are both to be related to the earlier kind of empiricism practised by G. E. Moore and Bertrand Russell? Must a religious man see contemporary empiricism as a threat to his position? Or can its insights, methods, and techniques be of service to philosophical theology? It is against such background questions as these that the present article is written. We must of course recognize from the start that contemporary empiricism is not to be seen as a 'system'; still less as a group of conclusions. It is rather the label for a certain approach to philosophical questions. In this article I shall try to elucidate this approach by surveying its development over the last half-century. We shall see that some of its features have been retained throughout the whole of this time; others have been modified on the way or even rejected.

THE INTEREST IN MEANING

Of all the features of recent empiricism undoubtedly the most constant and important has been a primary interest in meaning, in meaning rather than truth as such. This arose originally as a natural—and we may think welcome—reaction to the literature of the neo-Hegelians, of which William Wallace may be taken as a convenient example. On pp. 301–2 of his popular *Prolegomena to the Study of Hegel's Philosophy*[1] we read:

> The first part of Logic, the theory of Being, may be called the theory of unsupported and freely-floating Being. . . . The terms or forms of Being float as it were freely in the air, and we go from one to another, or—to put it more correctly—one passes into another. . . . This being is immediate: i.e. it contains no

[1] Oxford University Press, 2nd edition 1894, with reprints as late as 1931.

reference binding it with anything beyond itself, but stands forward baldly and nakedly, as if alone; and, if hard pressed, it turns over into something else. . . . The ether of 'Is' presumes no substratum, or further connexion with anything: and we only meet a series of points as we travel along the surface of thought.

Like the child with the Emperor's new clothes, it was G. E. Moore (1873–1958), the man of plain common-sense, who suspected that discourse such as this might be no more than pretentious make-believe, and he challenged such metaphysical ventures in Hegelianism with the question: What does it mean? More particularly (he said, in effect) instead of discussing, as isolated concepts, such topics as Sensation and Perception, Time, Implicit Beliefs—to take only a few varied examples at random—let philosophical discussion centre rather on the common-sense assertions from which such concepts take their rise. For example, having seen a speck on the side of a distant mountain, we may, in the light of subsequent discovery, say that we then 'saw a man', but did not 'see the man as a man'. 'Sensation' and 'perception' are to be understood by reference to the relations between such phrases as these. Again, have not many puzzles about the 'reality' of Time presupposed some such argument as this: 'We *do* think of Time'; *therefore* 'There must be such a thing as Time'; *therefore* 'Time is a fact'; *therefore* 'Time is real'. Yet there is at least one well-known case where this sequence does *not* provide a valid argument. The fact that 'We do think of unicorns' does *not* entail that 'There must be such things as unicorns'. The moral is that philosophers (F. H. Bradley in particular) ought not to argue about the 'reality' of Time before they know in what common-sense assertions their arguments are grounded.[2] *Or:* how often have people been puzzled about the ontological status of 'Implicit Belief'—whereas the phrase has to be elucidated in terms, e.g. of the surprise we register when, bending low and straining every muscle to raise a large black cardboard sphere, we fall backwards. From our saying 'I thought it was iron' it does not follow that there exists some peculiar process of 'thinking unconsciously'. And so on. In this way philosophy becomes the analysis—the sorting, the illuminating comparison—of common-sense pro-

[2] See G. E. Moore, *Philosophical Studies*, Chap. vi.

positions. In such an exercise the touchstone of meaning and reliability for Moore was an assertion such as 'There is a table in my room', and all questions about the 'external world', 'the self', and 'existence' were to be understood by reference to such reliable assertions as these.

Following out this empirical interest in meaning, we may next mention Bertrand Russell, who gave a much more systematic account of meaningful and reliable language. The touchstone of meaning would not be discovered in assertions about 'tables in my room'. The only words with clear unambiguous meanings were those given by ostensive definition and by reference to 'sense-data'. These were the 'atoms' out of which all reliable 'molecular' language could be constructed.

In one respect this appeal to sense-data seemed promising, for sense-data were immune from error, being by definition common to veridical perception and illusion alike. But the most awkward questions seemed to arise about the relation of these sense-data to the surfaces of physical objects, and very tall stories came further to be told as to how physical objects were no more than groups of such sense-data, some of which indeed might never have been sensed. Empirical philosophy seemed to have become a kind of super-scientific metaphysics, with Russell as the arch-scientist. Further, 'unsensed-data' was a phrase more reminiscent of Wallace than of Russell.

At any rate, the logical positivism of A. J. Ayer, as represented in his book *Language, Truth and Logic* (1936), may be seen as in some ways a reaction against this pseudoscientific metaphysics. Propositions were now said to have meaning if and only if they could in principle be verified by sense experience, or (as a weaker form of this 'Verification Principle' later had it) if and only if sense experience was in some way relevant to them. All other assertions, i.e., those to which sense experience was not in any way relevant, were meaningless; they were indeed literally 'nonsense'. It seemed as if a large part of ethics, and the whole of philosophical theology (if about some 'other world'), fell under this description. But what of logic and pure mathematics? Had these likewise to disappear under the positive axe? The answer was that room could be found for the assertions of logic and pure mathematics when, but only when, they claimed to be about nothing whatever, being purely verbal, merely symbol games, tautologous through and through. It was still true that for a proposition to have meaning, sense experience had to be relevant to it. Mathematics and logic fell into another category. They did not have meaning; they were purely verbal, true by convention, and talked about nothing whatever. Theological assertions found no logical kinsmen anywhere.

It is at this point in our survey that we can rightly mention Wittgenstein (1889–1951), for Wittgenstein can be seen as leading us away from any narrow, hard, and circumscribed account of meaning such as the Verification Principle expressed.

For Wittgenstein the Verification Principle (being itself obviously nonsense, for it could neither be verified by sense experience nor taken as a tautology) was merely a mnemonic, enabling us to formulate the clearest, most precise, and least ambiguous of languages, and it was valuable in so far as its talk about 'verification' and 'criteria' implied that we would only understand a word when we had elaborated a context of use. The Verification Principle in fact specified a particularly simple and straightforward context within which many words undoubtedly gained their meanings. But Wittgenstein would not allow other areas of discourse to be dismissed as 'meaningless'—language was rich in its logical variety, and a major task of philosophy was to display and preserve this variety against all who held that evidence and criteria, if they be not scientific evidence and criteria, are worthless; and against all reductions who would argue that 'x is *nothing but* y', that 'x is *really only* y'. Here are themes explored and developed by Professor John Wisdom, not least in his discussion of our knowledge of 'other minds'.[3]

So we associate Wittgenstein—at least the later Wittgenstein[4]—with a much richer concept of meaning than we find either in the logical positivists or in the early Russell.[5] He rejects vigorously

[3] See John Wisdom, *Philosophy and Psychoanalysis* (1953) and *Other Minds* (1952).

[4] See *Mind*, Vol. LXIV (Jan. 1955), for G. E. Moore, *Wittgenstein's Lectures in 1930–3*, p. 1. The earlier Wittgenstein of the *Tractatus* (1922) shared Russell's view about 'atomic' propositions.

[5] To examine developments in Russell would take us too far afield; but he is correct in claiming that the theory of 'atomic propositions' does not fairly represent his later position such as we find it in, e.g., *Human Knowledge*. See B. Russell, 'Philosophical Analysis' in *Hibbert Journal*, Vol. LIV (July 1956).

and explicitly the view that the meaning of a word is given by reference to some specific image or thing to be called its 'meaning', 'The meaning of a word is no longer for us an object correspond-ing to it.'[6] He is thus against the view once sponsored by himself and (as we saw) by Russell that words whose meanings are given by ostensive definition can be regarded as atoms from which a molecular language is built up: the language being in this way representative of a molecular world. Words rather belong to and are set within the most complicated contexts—they belong to 'systems', verbal systems and social systems; they belong to an area of discourse, and the actions with which that discourse is inextricably knit. As for Verification, Verification is only impor-tant when it gives, in this sense, a full and reliable setting to the proposition it claims to verify. So, to understand a concept of a word, we must set it in its verbal and social context and describe what we find there; always remembering that a particular word may figure in a great variety of contexts; at the same time always searching for some illuminating paradigm case.

It is these themes in Wittgenstein that lead straight to the 'or-dinary language' philosophy associated today with the name of Oxford. On such a view philosophical concepts—such as 'the mind' or 'the good'—are to be elucidated and expounded[7] not in terms of things or qualities they describe, but by reference to the respective occasions, e.g., when people speak of 'knowing', 'thinking', 'imagining', or when they use the word 'good' in sentences about the weather, cars, behaviour, tooth-paste, boys, girls, actors, judges, laws, and so on. So instead of describing memory in a super-scientific sort of way in terms of traces and images and 'mnemic causation', we must (on this view) describe what is the case when people talk about remembering something, how this is related to their past and future behaviour, and so on. Again (it would be said) let us not search for the 'meaning' of the word 'good' in terms of some particular quality—some 'non-natural' quality. Rather study the various kinds of utterance men make about 'a good x' and the varied circumstances in which these utterances are made. In this way the word 'good' will be seen

---

[6] Quoted by G. E. Moore, *Mind*, Vol. LXIII (Jan. 1954), p. 9.
[7] As they are by (say) Gilbert Ryle in *The Concept of Mind* (1949) and R. M. Hare in *The Language of Morals* (1952).

both to describe and to commend a certain pattern of behaviour. Here is the way to discuss the concept of goodness. 'Don't look for meaning, look for use' is a favourite slogan of Wittgenstein. If we recognize a word at all (Wittgenstein implied in this typical aphorism), we already know the meaning. But what we can learn and what philosophy exists to teach us is the *use* of the word, i.e., its logical behaviour, i.e., the logical connections it has with other words in ordinary discourse: recognizing that ordinary discourse may be richly variegated. The highest aim of philosophy must be to generalize about the logical pattern of the most complex discourse, not excluding metaphysical and theological discourse, and to give clues to its logical structure, to search for illuminating paradigm cases, such as the Verification Principle provides in a simple and elementary, even if important, case, viz. scientific discourse.

It is this variety of 'use' which a word may have, and which a philosophical treatment needs to survey, that led Professor J. L. Austin among others to see the *Oxford English Dictionary* as having a very significant part in philosophical discussion.[8]

In these different ways then Anglo-Saxon empiricism over the last fifty years has concentrated on the problem of meaning, and except for the early Russell and some of the logical positivists, this emphasis on meaning has turned our attention not on objects —sense-data or other, which might be said to be the 'meanings' of words—but rather to the contextual setting of words and the patterns of behaviour into which words and sentences are interlocked. If at this stage we wished to formulate any interim conclusions which might have bearing on philosophical theology, we might list them as three:

(i) Let us not look for 'objects' as the meaning of words.[9] Nor would this slogan exclude such words as 'God' or 'the soul'.
(ii) When presented with problematical words, look always at the discourse and behaviour in which such words are set.

---

[8] See e.g. *A Plea for Excuses*, Presidential Address, Aristotelian Society 1956–7, pp. 12–13.

[9] Cp. Berkeley, *Alciphron* VII, ed. T. E. Jessop, p. 293, where Euphranor casts doubt on 'the current opinion' expressed by Alciphron 'that every substantive name marks out and exhibits to the mind one distinct idea'.

(iii) In particular, let us be alert to the empirical grounding of this discourse.

THE CONCERN WITH LANGUAGE

Here is a second feature of contemporary empiricism, which we can likewise trace in outline over the past half-century. For while (as we have seen) contemporary empiricism has been character-ized by an interest in meaning, it has also been characterized—as may already have become evident for the two features can only be separated for didactic purposes—by an interest in language; and we may trace here too, development in its themes, and changes of emphasis.

Let us go back first to Russell, for (as we implied in our earlier remarks) Moore had nothing distinctive to say on this second theme. Indeed, he was disposed on the whole to take language— especially the assertions of common-sense—very much for granted. On the other hand whatever criticism may be made of Russell's theory of sense-data, there arose alongside this theory a view of language as displaying logical diversity, and it was a view to which Russell was also led by his interest in logical and mathematical puzzles and paradoxes. To give an illustration: while Russell may have been wrong in picturing a physical object as a group of actual and possible sense-data; he may well have been right in arguing for a logical difference between the phrases 'the table' and 'that brown object there'. He was certainly right in distin-guishing Class and Member words (for example) as of different 'logical type'. On this view, if a word of one logical type is sub-stituted for a word of another type in a meaningful sentence, that sentence is likely (a) to become nonsensical or (b) to lead by reliable inferences to bogus puzzles. For example: (a) we may say, 'I love a juicy round *orange*'. But we cannot significantly say, 'I love a juicy round *square*'. 'Orange' and 'square' exhibit type differences, and the additional puzzle of 'round square' suggested by the second sentence is only another indication of the diverse status of even the word 'round' in the two sentences. Or (b) we can substitute 'Equator' for 'bridge' in the sentence, 'I crossed the bridge', and it is not evident that nonsense has been generated. But while we can say, ' "I crossed the bridge" entails "I touched it" ,' we cannot say, ' "I crossed the Equator" entails "I touched it" '. Yet any puzzle here is only bogus, arising from a failure to distinguish words whose logical behaviour differs.

Another aspect of the logical diversity of language is expressed in the distinction between logical and verbal form. 'Lions are real' and 'Lions are yellow' may be *verbally* similar, but their *logical* behaviour is vastly different, a difference which Russell expressed symbolically by the difference between:

$$(\exists \ x). \ (x \text{ is a lion})$$
$$\text{and } (\exists \ x). \ (x \text{ is a lion}). \ (x \text{ is yellow})$$

To confound this logical difference is to consider existence as a predicate which (as is well known) Kant thought was the mistake behind the ontological argument. In fact, generalizing, Russell would say that the problems of philosophy are problems about language. They arise—and here Russell and Wittgenstein would agree—when we fail to distinguish what is logically diverse, or when we assimilate too readily phrases which in fact differ in their logical behaviour. If we used language with sufficient logical circumspection, these problems would disappear. So the story can continue with a reference to Wittgenstein, and in this aspect of empiricism Wittgenstein passes easily to Ryle.

Many philosophical errors arise because of false analogies, analogies which are suggested by the actual verbal use of certain expressions, and it must be the task of philosophy to clear up such misunderstandings. For instance, because we speak of a 'green leaf' and a 'good action', because in their actual use these phrases are verbally similar, they may be taken to be *logically* analogous.[10] But we shall look in vain if we expect to find a 'non-natural' quality of goodness, parallel to a sensible quality of greenness. Again, we speak of someone 'knowing Greek' and 'running a mile'—and the similarity of verbal form may tempt us to regard these as analogous descriptions: whereupon—since 'running' describes an activity we can see—'knowing Greek' is supposed to describe some occult activity going on somewhere even when Jimmy is not actually reading his Euripides, where-

---

[10] Here is a point which did not escape A. N. Whitehead, though he developed it in a different way. See e.g. *Process and Reality*, Pt. II, Chap. VII, 'The Subjectivist Principle'.

upon the ontological problems bristle. What sort of activity? Where? If only we were not misled by verbal form!

So for Wittgenstein the task of philosophy must be to put 'in order our notions as to what can be said about the world'.[11] For a definite example of this exercise we may look to Gilbert Ryle. The 'false analogy' he criticizes in *The Concept of Mind* is the analogy embodied in, and suggested by, what he calls the Cartesian myth: the view that there are minds and there are bodies, and that just as all indicative words about bodies describe processes, so all indicative words about minds must do. The whole book—from one point of view—can be understood as a protest against a very common 'category-mistake', a category blunder, assimilating the logical behaviour of categories whose logical behaviour differs. His over-all purpose is to describe the situations which give rise to such mental-conduct concepts as we use, and to display the verbal context in which particular assertions are set.[12]

In some ways the wheel has turned full circle, and the way the contemporary empiricist does philosophy comes in some ways quite close to what Moore did thirty or forty years ago. Eschewing general talk about reality or time or causation, his interest is centred in those particular assertions of ordinary language which lie behind such topics, and which (he believes) can illuminate the difficulties and problems with which such topics bristle. The hope is that, by displaying plainly the rich assortment of relevant assertions and the actions with which they are interwoven, the pattern of reliable discourse will be evident, and such puzzles and problems as have hithertofore occurred will be seen to have arisen from confounding what should be logically distinguished. Empirical practice becomes very similar to what Moore displayed —being in the broadest terms an endeavour to settle by considering particular assertions. But it works against background ideas which have undergone a vast development over recent decades. What has happened since Moore is that (a) we have come to appreciate

[11] See G. E. Moore, *Mind*, Vol. LXIII (Jan. 1955), p. 27, Moore's three articles in *Mind*, January 1954, July 1954, and January 1955, are well worth study. Likewise J. Wisdom, 'Ludwig Wittgenstein 1934–37', *Mind*, April 1952; and the Critical Notice of *Wittgenstein's Philosophical Investigations* by P. F. Strawson, *Mind*, January 1954.

[12] For a more detailed and critical discussion of Ryle see I. T. Ramsey, *The Christian Scholar*, Vol. XXXIX. 2 (June 1956), pp. 159–63.

more and more the vast logical variegation which language displays, and (b) we have come to have different ideas altogether about the 'meaning' of words and sentences. But in all this it has been Wittgenstein rather than the logical positivists who has triumphed.

THE EMPIRICAL ANCHOR OF THEOLOGY

If we now take together the two themes—meaning and language—definitive of contemporary empiricism—we may discover, I believe, two suggestions of importance for reflection about the Christian faith:

(i) *Somehow, in some way, we must contrive to show the kind of situation which illuminates theological discourse,* and this means assertions as complex and diverse as the following: 'Petition lies at the heart of our awareness of God'; 'The Holy Ghost proceeds from the Father and the Son'; 'The inner movement of the Divine life of the Trinity is an eternal separation from itself and return to itself'; 'At death the destiny of the individual soul is fixed for ever'; 'The souls of saints are admitted at once to heaven, and they await the final day with Christ in glory'.

We must make plain the empirical anchorage of theological assertions such as these. It is only in this way that we shall discern the logical behaviour of such theological concepts as 'prayer', 'procession', 'destiny', 'soul', 'glory', 'final day', as are embedded in these assertions, while to be mistaken in their logical behaviour will be to profess absurdities, to generate bogus puzzles, and to perpetuate pointless controversies. Now from the start it is plain that we cannot expect, even in the simplest case, that an adequate logical setting will be given by reference to assertions which relate *only* to public behaviour, assertions which are interwoven with action that is no more the observable activity. For the basic claim of religion is for the 'unseen'. At the same time, theological assertions must have a logical context which extends to, and is continuous with, those assertions of ordinary language for which sense experience is directly relevant. From such straightforward assertions, theological assertions must not be logically segregated: for that would mean that they were pointless and, in contrast to the only language which has an agreed meaning, meaningless.

The logical segregation of theology, however, has not been without its supporters, especially as it has seemed to some to preserve not only contemporary empirical insights, but also the claims of Christianity to be somehow 'distinctive'. As we have seen, words for Wittgenstein were to be set in their context and knit inextricably with activity. So some have argued that theological words need for their meaning and significance no more than their wider context of theological discourse, which further could even secure its distinctiveness by being logically isolated. On this view, we explicate religious language within the charmed circle of the discourse peculiar to and distinctive of some Confession or Church: language knit inextricably with that distinctive kind of behaviour called 'Church-going', 'Kneeling for prayer', perhaps 'Worship'. This is a point of view closely similar to that once expounded by A. MacIntyre.[13] But it is plain that this logical segregation of theology makes theology utterly irrelevant, its words having no relation to ordinary discourse. It is 'pointless' for the same reason that Wittgenstein considered much traditional metaphysics 'pointless', viz., that it had no association with men's ordinary behaviour.

What then may be said? I suggest that without in any way rejecting empirical insights we may do more justice to metaphysics: (1) by taking more seriously and more critically Wittgenstein's doctrine that language is inseparable from 'the actions into which it is woven'.[14] Let us ask ourselves just what sort of language is apt currency for our own activity,[15] (2) by recalling that Wittgenstein was haunted by the double use of 'I' which he found in ordinary discourse. The one seems plainly descriptive; the other seems logically peculiar.[16]

Taking these two points together, consider the kind of situation in which I become aware of myself as distinctively 'I', as being all my observable behaviour and more besides, when in exercising some decisive activity I discern what is more in my activity than the observable movement I display.[17] Here is a

[13] See e.g. his essay, 'The Logical Status of Religious Belief' in *Metaphysical Beliefs*, edited by him.

[14] *Philosophical Investigations*, tr. G. E. Anscombe, 7.5e.

[15] Cp. Berkeley's view that a 'discourse . . . that directs how to act' is 'another use of words besides that of marking ideas'. *Alciphron* VII, loc. cit., p. 292.

[16] See J. R. Jones, *The Two Contexts of Mental Concepts*, Proc. Aristotelian Society, 1958-9, and G. E. Moore, *Mind*, Jan. 1955, pp. 13 et seq.

[17] Here is the basis of what is called 'free will'.

'disclosure' situation which breaks in on us when we survey what Hume would call a train of distinct perceptions, when we survey our public, observable behaviour. The possibility of theology being given an appropriate empirical anchorage depends on its being related to what is objectively given in some such disclosure situation as that in which (subjectively) I become aware of myself. Nor can such situations *ex hypothesi* be wholly described in terms of observables or they would cease to be transcendent, and our subjectivity would be objectified.

My suggestion is that to understand theological language, we must relate it to situations such as these which break in on us, when the straightforward assertions of ordinary language are grouped in a particular way. The paradigm for any theological assertion[18] is the kind of assertion we make about ourselves when we realize ourselves as active in a 'disclosure' which occurs around an enumeration of the observable elements of our public behaviour.

(ii) *We must give to our theology a logical structure peculiar enough to ground it in the kind of situation I have just called a 'disclosure'.* Failure to do this will generate the most pointless and unedifying puzzles, and we must certainly be prepared to discover that some doctrinal controversies are bogus puzzles generated either by such logical errors as type-trespass or more broadly by failing to distinguish, and even assimilating, what is logically diverse.

On such a view, to understand, e.g., the assertion 'The soul is immortal', we would start (I suggest) with discourse about mortality and develop it in such a way as to lead to a disclosure which subjectively disclosed to us everything that sentences containing the word 'soul' aptly express. 'Immortality' is no 'property' of a thing called a 'soul', and there is no *logical* kinship between 'My soul is immortal' and its *verbal* kinsman: 'My flowers are everlasting'. Again, to parallel talk about the omnipotence of God with talk about the all-powerfulness of a newspaper Proprietor,

---

[18] R. B. Braithwaite (see *An Empiricist's View of the Nature of Religious Belief*) endeavours to find a paradigm in the language of morals. In many ways this is a valuable and promising parallel, but in the end we are bound to criticize it as inadequate, not least because, for Braithwaite, Christian assertion seem more important for their psychological usefulness than for their logical ability to express the kind of transcendent situation in which they have traditionally been founded.

is bound to lead to blunders and puzzles. Once again let us rather understand 'omnipotence' by seeing how non-theological discourse about power can become qualified in such a way as to lead to a disclosure whose objective constituent is the empirical basis for using the phrase: 'God is omnipotent.'[19]

Here then, if the empirical possibility of disclosures be allowed,[20] is an approach both sympathetic to, and benefiting from, contemporary empirical insights, while being of real value to theology. It is an approach which forces on theology no systematic metaphysics. Rather it goes to theology interested in the whole range of theological discourse, and its only aim is to map the logical relations exhibited by this discourse, so that we may see more clearly, more reliably, less ambiguously, how it performs the task which its initiators gave it when they theologized about their religion.[21]

Let us at the end recall William Wallace: 'Religion and philosophy', he says, 'coincide: in fact, philosophy is itself a divine science, is a religion. . . .' Here is the grand synthesis of Hegelianism and Christianity. But it was a synthesis which preserved only the palest version of the Christian faith: its historical basis was denied; its distinctive character compromised. The 'essence of Christianity', continues Wallace, is 'not the annals of a life once spent in serving God and man, but the words of the "Eternal Gospel" . . . the "revelation of reason" through man's spirit'. What mattered was only the 'revelation of reason' and the 'Eternal Gospel'. It was in reaction to claims such as these that there arose the 'irrationalism' of Kierkegaard and Barth.

But contemporary empiricism, broadened to include 'disclosures', introduces a more generous account of rationality,

---

[19] For further detail I venture to refer the reader to my *Religious Language* and *Freedom and Immortality*. There I use the term 'qualified model' to indicate the logical structure of a word such as 'omnipotent', and how this differs from such a phrase as 'exceedingly powerful' which has a purely descriptive logic. On this view, the phrase 'omnipotent', while not without a descriptive element, behaves more like an imperative, and for this reason its *verbal* parallels are misleading.

[20] As I urged in *The Christian Scholar*, loc. cit., this is the crucial issue between the 'believing' and the 'unbelieving' empiricist today.

[21] In this way, we may learn their 'commitment', a concept which Wittgenstein did not hesitate to use in a not dissimilar connection. See Moore, loc. cit., Jan. 1954, esp. p. 7.

endeavours to map mystery,[22] and displays a deliberate concern for the empirical basis of the Christian faith as expressed in its language of Bible, doctrine, and liturgy knit with appropriate activity. We may recall that contemporary empiricism began in protest against neo-Hegelianism. It may even yet revitalize 'theological thinking' as it has revolutionized philosophy.

[22] For a disclosure is subjectively and objectively 'mysterious' precisely because it is not exhausted by observables it includes and around which it arises.

The Systematic Elusiveness of 'I'

I propose to begin by distinguishing what are *prima facie* two kinds of elusiveness—the one associated with the name of Hume, and the other with the name of Ryle. It might seem at first as if only Ryle's account justifies the phrase '*systematic* elusiveness', but my contention will be that the views of Ryle and Hume, in whatever ways different, are similar in sharing a common assumption. It is that common assumption which I shall presume to criticize; and it is in setting forward an alternative that I shall try to develop an independent account.

In Book I of the *Treatise of Human Nature*, Part IV, Section 6, Hume gives us his classic account: 'For my part, when I enter most intimately into what I call *myself*, I always stumble on some particular perception or other, of heat or cold, light or shade, love or hatred, pain or pleasure. I never can catch *myself* at any time without a perception. . . .' That perhaps would not be too bad, but, Hume continues, he 'never can observe anything but the perception. If any one upon serious and unprejudic'd reflexion, thinks he has a different notion of *himself*, I must confess I can reason no longer with him. All I can allow him is, that he may be in the right as well as I, and that we are essentially different in this particular. He may, perhaps, perceive something simple and continu'd which he calls *himself*; tho' I am certain there is no such principle in me.'[1] In short, any simple and continuing self eludes Hume's gaze. So as to illustrate better its presuppositions, let us put Hume's argument like this: A certain situation is described by the words: 'I am looking at a bus.' This may be (it would seem) symbolized by 'I r B'. But if so, then we might suppose that in being aware of this situation we were aware of I, and of r and of B; so that in all situations, besides the varying 'perceptions', which 'I' refers, of which we were constantly aware. But, says Hume, 'when I enter most intimately into what I call *myself* . . . I never can observe anything but the perceptions'. There is

[1] *Treatise*, ed. Selby-Bigge, p. 252.

never an I. No matter how many acts of reflection I indulge in,
then a constant self always eludes me in the sense that there is no
'constant perception'. *But what do we conclude from this?* Even
Hume hesitates to say. In the Appendix to the *Treatise*, where he
is expressing his own misgivings, he first of all makes it plain, and
quite rightly, that his conclusion could never be more than the
assertions that 'we have . . . no idea of [a continuing self] in that
sense', viz., as an 'impression'. As we have said, a constant self
always eludes us in the sense that there is no constant perception.

At the same time, with characteristic honesty, he admits, 'I am
sensible, that my account is very defective,' and confesses a little
later that a person 'alone finds personal identity, when reflecting on
the train of past perceptions, that compose a mind'. The 'ideas'
of these 'past perceptions' are 'felt to be connected together'. His
difficulty is that he 'cannot discover any theory, which gives me
satisfaction on this head'. In other words, Hume confesses that
experience, as and when it involves what he would call a 'feeling'
of 'personal identity', cannot be treated in terms of his theory
of distinct ideas and impressions. In more contemporary language, 'self-awareness' is, for Hume, logically problematical. Its
logical mapping has yet to be done. What sort of fact is it? How
oddly has it to be described? These are questions I am trying to
face in this paper, and to that extent I am taking up Hume's
problem where he left it.

At this point it is convenient to move to Ryle's account as though
he were proffering an answer to these questions. What would he
say about 'self-awareness'?

Ryle expounds his view by reference to 'higher order actions'.
This is a phrase he introduces by remarking that 'some sorts of
actions are in one way or another concerned with, or are operations
upon, other actions. When one person retaliates upon another,
scoffs at him, replies to him or plays hide-and-seek with him, his
actions have to do, in one way or another, with certain actions
on the part of the other; in a sense to be specified later, the
performance of the former involves the thought of the latter. An
action on the part of one agent could not be one of spying or
applauding, unless it had to do with the actions of another agent;
nor could I behave as a customer, unless you or someone else
behaved as a seller. One man must give evidence if another is to

cross-examine him; some people must be on the stage, if others are to be dramatic critics. It will sometimes be convenient to use the title "higher order actions" to denote those, the descriptions of which involve the oblique mention of other actions.'[2]

Diagrammatically we may represent higher order actions by bracketing, e.g. (B boxing C) or (Y selling Z) would be actions of one order: A applauding (B boxing C) or X acting as a customer of (Y selling Z) would be actions of the next highest order. The point is that there is here 'oblique reference' in the same way as, if y = f (x) and x = Q (t) then y is 'obliquely' a function of t and we might say that y was a second-order variable of t. In less formal language highest order actions are said, you remember, to involve 'the thought of' other actions.

Now against that background Ryle's suggestion is that self-elusiveness is *systematic*, because with any of our own operations of any order there immediately arises the possibility of an operation of a higher order. So when we are concerned with *our own* operations, there arises the systematic possibility of an infinite series of operations, and this means that at no given time *we* ever completed our *self-description*. *We* can never completely describe *ourselves*. But this fact, Ryle would say, is no occasion for mystery or awe. 'I' is elusive, but as *systematically* elusive the elusiveness of I is no more than the elusiveness of an infinite series to a term by term enumeration. There is no more to it than that. The elusiveness of the self is just the point that we have never completed our self-description; but no new mysterious fact claims our attention; no words of an odd logic are demanded. For what eludes us at any one moment becomes perfectly tractable the next . . . so where is the mystery? There is nothing odder here than in any occurrence of delayed appearances.

Let us look at this argument in more detail. It points out that if we try to describe ourselves completely 'now', we perform a higher order action 'now'. So that what we attempt will never be done, simply because an extra fact is systematically added at every attempt. Every time we attempt self-description, we add a fact to be described. But here (says the argument) is nothing mysterious. It is an elusiveness only tantalizing till we see what is happening—like trying to count the pennies in a line when, as

[2] *The Concept of Mind*, p. 191.

I am enumerating the last penny another is always added. But is it? Let us look at this penny story further. The penny which eludes me for a moment I count the next moment. There is nothing but a temporal delay. On this view of Ryle's the self eludes me for no other reason than that the next moment eludes me, and as it is a necessary feature of time that there should be a temporal flow, so also does *this*-moment elusiveness become *next*-moment presence. Ryle himself notices that 'I' and 'now' have indeed similar logical placings. Thus the 'extra autobiographical fact' which eludes me at any one time, becomes available immediately afterwards. The total situation of which I am *then* aware, embraces entirely the highest order action I just performed. The penny I count in the line is the same penny which eluded me just now; the review which could not be done yesterday is precisely this which is done today; the diary entry which eluded me is exactly this which I am now making. The elusiveness of 'I' is, for Ryle, on all fours with the daily elusiveness of a diary, and there is nothing more mysterious about the self than about diaries and reviews. Diary entries, reviews, and 'I' have the same logic.

To begin our criticism let us notice that despite their differences, behind both Hume's account and Ryle's, is the same assumption, viz. that any situation which becomes the 'object' of a higher order action is unchanged in the process. Hume expressed this assumption in terms of 'perceptions', when he avowed that experience, i.e. 'all the perceptions of the human mind', can be adequately treated in terms of objective 'ideas' and 'impressions'. As we have seen, he was himself already doubting its adequacy, especially in relation to self-awareness. I do not think that Ryle, on the other hand, ever explicitly states the assumption, but I have tried to show that nevertheless it is implied by his argument. *What now of this assumption?*

I would like to mention two difficulties, and in this order:

1   With this assumption what do we make of the subject-object distinction? (This question we will develop by reference to Ryle.)
2   With this assumption, what account do we give of what Hume calls 'personal identity'?—the problem about which, as we saw, Hume had second and puzzling thoughts.

1   Let me develop my first question as follows: Consider the

situation when a person B is trying to solve a chess problem C, and A endeavours to describe all about B except the fact that he, A, is describing B. Then there is the lower order action: (B solving the chess problem C)—as A understands it—followed by the higher order action: A describing (B solving the chess problem C). We need not go into details here, for I think we would all be prepared to admit that there is for A—from his standpoint—nothing puzzling about these two formulations. B and C are identical terms in each expression and no new facts keep arising which make possible a systematically endless description. But consider now *self*-commentary. By analogy we might suppose that it could be properly represented as: I describing (I solving the chess problem C). Certainly at first sight this seems to be 'simply a special case of'[3] the former, with 'I' substituted inside the brackets for 'B'. It might further be said, as I think Ryle would certainly continue, that the only puzzle which arises does so if, and in so far as, I seek after total self-commentary at any moment, when my higher order action of describing would itself need to be included, and so on *ad infinitum*. The only comment then is: *either* do not aim at self-commentary at all *or* if you do, just '*accept*' the odd quest which it is. That would seem to be Ryle's view.

But steady: *is* our second example 'simply a special case of' the first? Is 'I describing (I solving the chess problem C)' simply a 'special' case of 'A describing (B solving the chess problem C)'—assuming of course that the question is not begged by use of the two words 'simply' and 'special' being put together in the curious way they are. Let us emphasize that if it is not, we have no right to have 'I' within the bracket; for whatever in detail 'I' *there* stands for, *if the cases are parallel*, it would have to be in principle some matrix of events as '*objective*' as those which characterize B. That this is so is indeed evident from one of the sentences that Ryle himself uses, viz. '*I* was laughing at *myself* for being butter-fingered.' The grammar is reliable enough to show, by the distinction of 'I' and 'myself', that the facts cannot be described by having in place of these two variables, either two 'I's or, for that matter, two 'me's. Rather is there one 'I' and a class of events which are (in some sense) 'mine' and which are the objective

---

[3] Ibid., p. 195

residue of *past* actions when these have become included within a *later* 'higher order action'. Only in this way, I suggest, can we preserve the subject-object distinction, without which we would talk the most absurd nonsense. To *objectify* the *subject* is to deny ourselves the possibility of ever talking sense. It is the opposite mistake, though with the same result, that the mystics commit when they subjectify the object.

Here then is my first difficulty. If we assume that what eludes us now, becomes in the next minute wholly tractable, then since, at this next minute, an earlier situation has been completely object-ified, what account can we then give of the subject-object dis-tinction which is the permanent presupposition of all living and talking alike? What account can we give of our 'subjectivity' 'now'?

2 Now for the second difficulty: On the assumption common to both Hume and Ryle, what becomes of 'personal identity'? Going back to Hume let us portray 'I am looking at a bus' as 'I r B'. When now we make ourselves aware of this situation by creating a higher order activity, Hume, we saw, and Ryle for that matter, would suggest that the formula for such a higher order activity would be 'I r (I r B)'. This is the common assumption. But with this move, as we have seen, arises Hume's difficulty. For there is no constant 'I'. No easy account, such as the formula suggests, is possible of 'personal identity'. Let us now take the difficulty a little further. Hume confesses that, try as he will, he 'never can observe anything but the perception'. This is to confess that try as he will, all the terms within the bracket are always in all attempts 'objective'. In the sense that they all have the status of 'perceptions', and as our discussion of the first point suggested, we would readily sympathize with that contention. But this means that our higher order action must always be portrayed not as 'I r (I r B)' but as 'I r $(I_n r_n C)$' where $I_n r_n C$ are in different ways 'perceptions'. The formula is meant to make it plain that any attempt by 'I' to discover 'I' replaces 'I' by some fact I_n and so on without end. So the problem of 'personal identity' is now raised in this way, viz. How are we to talk of 'one self' if all we have is an infinite series of perceptual terms? How can '$I_1 + I_2 + I_3 + \ldots + I_n + \ldots$' elucidate 'I'? The answer is what the mathematical form of question might well suggest: only if, taking a hint from infinite series, 'I' has an altogether different

logic from any of the terms. May not 'I' with this peculiar and curious logic witness to some sort of invariant in any higher order awareness? Let us admit with Hume that 'I can never catch *myself* at any time without a perception'; let us also admit that I 'never can *observe* anything but the *perception*'. Nevertheless, may it not be the case that the awareness which always includes 'a perception', and in which nothing but perceptions can be 'observed', may yet in some way or other be the awareness of some invariant for which an 'I' with an odd enough logical status could be proper currency? Is there indeed in self-awareness, some area which is *observationally elusive*? Further, if 'I' witness in part to this elusive area, would this not give to 'I' the peculiar logic it possesses?

Rejecting then the assumption that a highest order action at one moment can be publicly exhausted at the next; claiming that only by such a move can the subject-object relationship be preserved; claiming further that 'personal identity' is somehow given in an awareness which is *not* exhausted by observation language what can we say positively about our logical mapping of 'I'?

So we are back where we started. We are claiming that self-awareness is logically problematical; that the self-awareness which characterizes any highest order action as it occurs, is in part observationally elusive. How can this claim be defended? Which raises two questions:

1 How can we display a fact which in part is observationally elusive?
2 How can we appropriately talk about it?

Let us face these last two questions in turn.

1 In the first place we plainly cannot give a straightforward account of what is observationally elusive, in observation language. All we can do is to evoke or induce by some tale or other, the sort of situation for which part-elusiveness is claimed. All we can do is to tell a story and hope that it works, viz. to evoke a situation which, as it occurs, displays the inadequacy of observational description. Let me venture to give five such stories of the very many which might be told.

(*a*) Recalling that source book for philosophical examples—*Alice in Wonderland*—let us in particular recall the story when Alice's size is subject to a curious sequence of changes. Such a story would be used in the hope that the very curiosity of the sequence would apprise our patient of that part of Alice's self-awareness which in all the changes *she*—Alice—would have said remained the same. Something besides rapidly varying observational language would have been wanted to describe all that happened.

(*b*) Alternatively, we might read the familiar nursery rhyme about the old market woman, who, sleeping on the way back from market, had 'her petticoats cut all round about' by a pedlar. She, on waking, says: 'Oh, deary, dear me, this is none of I.' Then she argues: 'But if it be I, as I do hope it be, I've a dog at home and he'll know me; If I be I, he'll wag his tail, and if it be not I, he'll bark and wail.' Off she goes home, and the dog begins to bark. The result is that she cries: 'Lawk a mercy on me, this is none of I.'

The fun of course is that anyone should suppose their self-awareness to be exhaustively described by 'objective data', and if our patient laughed, we should have good hope that the experiment had worked. We should have good hope that he had realized that in self-awareness is something which *cannot* be so reduced without absurdity. Here is a point not unlike that which Dr Waissmann makes in his paper on 'Language Strata'[4]—that it is never impossible for the person himself to say, 'But I have toothache,' even when all the experimental tests have proved negative.

(*c*) As another example, let us take the case of Sally Beauchamp, and her multiple personality. I do not know enough details of the Sally Beauchamp case to tell the full story, but I think for our purpose it is sufficient to know (what Broad tells us) that: 'Sally Beauchamp . . . claimed to be aware of most of the things of which B[5] was aware, when the latter was in control of the body and the former was not'. If this statement is meaningful and correct, then the awareness *Sally* had of the events B_1 owned, would be different from B_1's awareness of those same B_1 events as they occurred, and despite the same 'objective field', there would, in the two cases, be a characteristically *different* self-awareness in each case. To recognize the possibility that in *two* cases of *self-awareness* all the objective factors could be the same,

---

[4] *Logic and Language*, ed. A. G. N. Flew, Series ii.
[5] *The Mind and its Place in Nature*, p. 374.

yet the self-awareness be different, will, I hope, help to elucidate from another direction the curious empirical fact I am trying to commend. In one good sense, a sense which Sally could use, there is not 'double personality'.

(*d*) As another example, let us take the case of the 'perfect mimic'. The case would offer many empirical difficulties if it had to be specified completely, but for our example, I think we might suppose that two people could appear on the stage in similar clothes, with similar features, the same height, the same coloured hair, the same voice, and so on, and we would have to suppose that there could be no sort of record which would establish the 'identity' of either of them. Clearly from the point of view of the audience no test could be specified to distinguish between them—I am assuming that something or other could be done even with regard to their spatial position. The point of the story is this. Supposing one of the people on the stage was I. Then I should claim that *I* would know which was *I* and which was the *perfect mimic*, though in an ideal case, others might never discern the difference. The empirical story would, of course, have to suppose (to be the ideal case) that neither could see the other's body—perhaps both would have to be blind. But if we had to complicate the story like this, it would be evident that this patter was not going to be successful, and rather than build the story with an increasingly complicated structure, it would be best to move to another one altogether.

(*e*) Certainly then, let us give at any rate *one* more example. Ask anyone to recall, in rapid succession, varying situations of veridical and illusory sense perception. The more, and the more varied, these were, the better. The hope would be that such an exercise would use the commonly recognized differences between each situation to emphasize all the better, that part of our self-awareness which is an *invariant* in all the situations.

2   If we admit that these examples, or some like them, may evoke a self-awareness which is in part elusive to spatio-temporal, perceptual, public, observation-language, the next question will be: How do we appropriately talk of what, from the standpoint of observation language, is elusive? How do we portray what, in that sense, is not altogether 'objective' but which has yet features that are objectively tractable accompanying it, and the whole of which constitutes our highest order awareness at any given time?

Let us begin by assuming that our highest order awareness has a subject-object structure, and that, as such, it can be symbolized as 'I r O'. For our present purpose and for the sake of argument—but no more—let us suppose that O is tractable without residue in observation language. *Then* what is elusive is portrayed by the symbol 'I r', which is then claimed as an invariant *not* to be worked by ordinary subject-predicate grammar, and never to be worked in 'objective' terms. So do not misunderstand me. I am *not* pleading for a 'self' which inhabits an altogether distinct world, and which is nevertheless talked about as though it were here all the time—a permanent 'self' untouched by the vagaries of space and time, but if such, also untouched by arguments and meaning alike. I am claiming no easy objective pictures for 'I' or 'r', indeed, precisely the contrary. In fact 'I r'—so far—is just a symbolism recommended for that part of any highest order awareness which is not satisfactorily dealt with in language relating to 'objective particulars'.

It is just as though I had introduced 'I r' like the concept of 'sum' in relation to an infinite series when we have given nothing but examples of longer and longer sequences of terms, and where we had not developed the logic of infinite series. All I have done is to say: Here is your fact and here is your phrase, which is not to be given a logical placing in spatio-temporal language. So I am quite ready to grant that to date my recommendation is disgustingly small and negative. But let me at any rate defend and elaborate it a little further and first by developing it in relation to the two difficulties we mentioned earlier.[6]

(i) The recommendation might be said to be one—is it not the only one?—on which what Whitehead calls 'extreme objectivism'[7] can be avoided. Without the assumption that 'I' and 'r' have a problematical logic, we seem to be in a 'purely objective' world, though it might perhaps equally well be called either 'objective' or 'subjective' as it pleased us.

(ii) What now of our second difficulty—the problem of personal identity? Part of the defence of my view would be that while it involves an assumption which is *extra* to that of Hume, it is an assumption which, had he accepted it, would have solved his

[6] See p. 20.
[7] *Process and Reality*, 22, p. 1.

puzzlement. Whatever 'I' stands for, whatever its logic, it will not relate to anything like a 'perception'. True. But as no number of terms 'I₁', 'I₂', etc., standing for 'perceptions' ever adequately describes a higher order action; so personal identity will have for its empirical defence that part of self-awareness which is observationally elusive—that part which is an invariant—and when we recommend 'I' thereto, we are recommending, for an account of personal identity, a symbol with a *logical status all of its own*, different from *all* the levels into which observational language can be separated. At the same time, because 'I r O' describes 'one fact', then no matter how odd the logical status of 'I', it must be capable of being used with any or all the levels of observational language, different altogether though its logical status may be. *The problem of personal identity, self-elusiveness, and the systematic elusiveness of 'I' are all alike to be related to the inadequacy of 'objective' terms and relations, worked by the ordinary subject-predicate model, to account for a highest order situation—what we have called 'I r O'—as it occurs.*

That could be the conclusion. Before concluding, however, let us face two other problems, which further and better help to develop the view I am putting forward. One of these problems we have reached already, the other may well have troubled you as being very close to the surface, if it has not actually raised its head. Let us first take the problem we have reached already.

(*a*) Even if you agree that a case has been made out for the logical uniqueness of 'I', you may well object that I have done very little positively to show how 'I' is united with observational language. Are there indeed any words which do something to treat of the *whole* 'I r O' situation and which, therefore, by implication, do something to suggest links between 'I' and observational language? *Are there any words whose logic is odd enough both to give 'I' a public anchorage, and also to give observational facts their elusiveness?* I think there are at least two, but I will spend most time on the first.

1 Let us recall Hume's discussion, with which we began. It was (he said) our *'feeling'* of personal identity which could not be adequately treated in terms of ideas and impressions. Is it not then significant that Ryle also notices a peculiarity about the logic of *feeling*? Situations where feeling predominates, might then be

useful clues to the total situation which 'I r O' symbolizes, and useful clues precisely in so far as 'feeling' has the curiously ambiguous logic which troubles Ryle.[8] 'Feeling' is certainly a word which has both subjective and objective references and we might therefore use it as does Whitehead (and *pace* Bradley) to call attention to the curious empirical fact and linguistic point I am trying to make. It might constitute a sixth story. At any rate let me say a little more about it.

Ryle reminds us that the word 'feeling' can have an objective reference and work very much like a perception word, e.g. we can feel the ship, we can feel grit (in our eyes), we can feel the accelerator (in the car).

> In our ordinary use of them, the words 'sensation', 'feel' and 'feeling' originally signify perceptions. A sensation is a sensation of something and we feel the ship vibrating, or rolling, as we see its flags flying, or hear its siren hooting. We can, in this sense, feel things distinctly. . . . As we see with our eyes and hear with our ears, so we feel things with our hands, lips, tongues or knees.

So far feeling has an *objective* reference like any other perception word. But then there is a difference because in other situations the word 'feeling' is used with a curious reference to the *subject*, and in this way there is *no parallel* in the use of perception words.

> A person whose foot is numbed may say not only that he cannot feel things with his foot, but also that he cannot feel his foot, whereas, a momentarily blinded or deafened person would say that he could not see or hear things with his right eye or right ear, but not that he could not see his eye or hear his ear.[9]

I think this is the same point as that which is behind Ryle's later remarks in which again the *subjective* reference of feeling is emphasized. He points out that in some cases of feeling we do not speak of feeling X where X is somehow 'externalized', but rather we talk about having, e.g. 'a gritty feeling'.

[8] *The Concept of Mind*, pp. 240 ff.
[9] Ibid.

. . . if a sufferer is asked just what he feels, he does not satisfy the questioner by replying 'a pain' or 'a discomfort', but only by replying 'a stabbing feeling', 'a gritty feeling', or 'a burning feeling'.

Hence we see that feeling words are not always the names of moods nor do they always work like perception words.

The point we would make is this, viz., that it is this *very peculiarity* about the logic of 'feeling' which makes the word fit so well what is being urged as something which is both subjective and objective. It is precisely the puzzle Ryle discovers in the logic of feeling that might be said by Whitehead to justify the sort of use that he at any rate—and certainly I—would make of it. 'I' and 'feeling' are close logical kinsmen: with similar logical placings.

2   The second word, which we will mention only briefly, is 'action', or 'activity'. Ryle and I, and no doubt many others, would agree that action-logic is not event-logic, and that not the least mistake of most free-will arguments has been to overlook this. But then to mention yet again an earlier point, ought we not to be specially cautious of working highest order *actions* as though they could be adequately understood in terms of just another set of spatio-temporal *events* which presently 'come of age'? At any rate, I will all the more strongly suggest that the logical peculiarity of 'action' might well be related to the peculiarity of 'I'-logic. So here is another word, by which links might be forged between 'I' and observational language.

(*b*) Let me now mention the second problem which, I said, has been hovering around. Does our viewpoint commit us to what Ryle calls 'privileged access'? Certainly it does, in so far as it claims an awareness wherein 'myself' can be distinguished from 'others'. But there are two blunders we need not make, and which I do not think we make, and whose evasion relieves us from any of the criticisms Ryle brings against this notion:

1   We do *not* suppose that this privileged experience can be properly described in language which denies its very claim. We do not suppose that 'I' can be worked perfectly in terms of object-words—a suicidal supposition indeed, and one which is very rightly an important target for Ryle's attack. On the contrary, to protest against this has been our constant theme.

2   Nor need we blunder by supposing that the awareness which

is '*self*-awareness' (and for convenience we have generally used that phrase) is not also 'other-awareness'. Nothing is properly called an 'awareness' which has not a subject-object structure; nor, as we have previously remarked, quoting Whitehead in support, must this subject-object relation be taken as equivalent to the subject-predicate relation which, as a relation between '*objects*', would repeat the first blunder at the second move. The awareness I am talking about may be privileged, but it is not wholly private; still less (however we contrive to talk about it) must we make it wholly public.

And now a brief historical retrospect to lead to our conclusion. If it be thought that I have made too much of the curious empirical fact of self-awareness involved in a highest order action, let it be remembered that, e.g. Descartes and Berkeley amongst others, have claimed 'self-awareness' as an empirical curiosity.

Descartes, in his 'cogito', centred his metaphysics on a highest order action, seeing his 'thinking' as a fact which, while empirical, was also very odd. Let us certainly applaud Descartes' flash of insight and readily support him in so far as we would say that this 'I', given to each one of us in reference to a curious 'self-awareness', is a clue to the status of metaphysical words. Let Descartes be notable for more than a blunder.

Again, Berkeley's doctrine of notions, connected as it is with the awareness I have of my own activity, and distinguished as it is from his theory of ideas, becomes a plea not to work the self-awareness which accompanies highest order actions in terms of the subject-predicate logic appropriate to 'ideas'. The logic of notions is Berkeley's way of emphasizing the empirical peculiarities of self-awareness, and in the doctrine of notions is Berkeley's venture after an empirical metaphysics.

Summarizing then, we may say that the systematic elusiveness of 'I' relates to the *fact* that self-awareness, as characterizing highest order 'actions', or feelings' of personal identity, cannot be adequately dealt with in terms of those elements to which a highest order action *objectively* refers and which become available for treatment later. In Hume's words, we do indeed '*feel*' personal identity *now* when reflecting on a 'train of *past* perceptions'; but Hume's error was to suppose that its empirical anchorage could be no other than those 'past perceptions' alone. From the point of view of *language*, the systematic elusiveness of 'I' makes the claim that 'I' systematically eludes all observation language; it is a claim that 'I' has a logical status all of its own and is not a 'perception' word. Perhaps indeed, and my remarks about Descartes and Berkeley are meant to point in this direction, we have here a starting point for an empirically based and suitably chastened metaphysics. But that would be another story.

Biology and Personality: Some Philosophical Reflections

It will be generally agreed that Descartes provides an obvious starting point for any philosophical reflections on biology and personality. But to mention Descartes is to remember that from the turn of the present century philosophers have been increasingly critical of his mind-body dualism, which has for long expressed the popular, and Ryle would say the 'official', view of personality, and which has given medicine its sailing orders for some 300 years. At the same time, it is hardly fair to father on Descartes some of the more extreme interpretations and expositions of his view.

For Descartes well realized that his separation of minds and bodies was difficult to reconcile with the apparently obvious fact that all of us are unities, and we may most fairly see his talk of animal spirits and the pineal gland as no more than the best he could do to meet a difficulty he neither wished to avoid or deny.[1] But those who took over Cartesian philosophy as a basis for their physics and biology either overlooked these difficulties or excused themselves from dealing with them. It was enough that henceforward both physics and biology could develop free from ecclesiastical interference.

But in the present century, both philosophers and biologists have underlined difficulties in Descartes' position.

Let us take first the biological difficulty. It is well known that there are recent developments in medicine which fit uneasily (if at all) into the Cartesian scheme. The recognition of a class of psycho-genic disorders, of psychosomatic illnesses of which asthma is perhaps the best-known, introduces a category of illness which spreads untidily across the neat Cartesian separation of minds and bodies. Further, if a duodenal ulcer can benefit from psychiatric advice, or even an understanding talk, if we come to

[1] Cp. his letter to the Princess Elizabeth, June 1643, and the comments by James Ward, *Psychological Principles* (C.U.P., 1918), p. 10.

see quite unexpected medical virtues after all in the bedside manner—what (from the other side) of the depression which benefits from biochemical or electrical treatment? Such developments in medicine suggest 'personality'—not a 'mind' nor a 'body'—as the basic category for the study of human behaviour. They suggest, as it is sometimes expressed, man as a unity, man as a whole. Now at first sight, this is the very same conclusion to which many and diverse philosophers in the present century have been led.

We may first recall James Ward, who believed that Descartes' dualism of minds and bodies arose because of a primacy he gave to, an emphasis he laid on, cognition, and Ward's own reaction to Cartesian dualism was to say that experience was 'not primarily cognition but also, and above all, conative activity'.[2]

Then there was Ward's pupil, G. F. Stout, who in *Mind and Matter* argued that 'mind and body are not primarily apprehended as distinct *things*. . . . What we are primarily aware of is the individual unity of an embodied self.' It is here, argues Stout, that the personal pronoun properly belongs. 'I see the moon' does not equal 'My body (or my mind) sees the moon'. If there are (as undoubtedly there are) times when we say, 'My body walks', this is to distinguish those occasions explicitly from *ordinary* walking, e.g. in the case of sleep-walking.

Now it is in this succession that I would place my colleague Gilbert Ryle, and a number of others who, it seems to me, can all be seen as contributing to a revival of philosophical interest in personality. But this common interest will lead in due course inevitably to our problem: can an adequate account of personality by given in spatio-temporal terms?

We are all familiar with Ryle, who in *The Concept of Mind* shows what bogus puzzles and insuperable difficulties we invent for ourselves when we misconstrue language about human beings, by taking the mind-body picture—popularly expressed as the 'ghost-in-the-machine'—as a guide for talking about our thinking and behaviour. 'Men are neither machines nor ghosts in machines,' says Ryle, 'they are men.' Talk of persons as persons, not as compounds of minds and bodies.

This interest in the personal recurs, for example, in Stuart Hampshire's *Thought and Action* and in P. F. Strawson's

[2] *Psychological Principles*, p. 28.

Individuals when Strawson does what he calls 'descriptive metaphysics' by elaborating the peculiar features of language about
persons who are sometimes talked of as material objects, e.g. as
weighing 140 lbs or lying outside on the grass, but at other times
in ways characteristically personal, e.g. as smiling, or thinking
hard, or believing in God. He acknowledges and with great skill
explicates the primitiveness of the concept of a person. Here is a
primary concern with persons, and as Strawson himself admits,
the concern might go further. He himself says, 'We may still
want to ask what is it *in the natural facts* that makes it intelligible
that we should have this concept?'[3] It is a question to which we
will return. But meanwhile let us note that the late Professor J. L.
Austin with his emphasis on performatives might also be viewed
as registering a new interest in the personal. For in introducing
us to this feature of language which had hitherto remained
unnoticed, viz., that some assertions have what he called 'per-
formative force', so that in saying some sentences we do something more than saying the words (e.g. when the minister asserts
in a marriage: 'I pronounce that they be man and wife together'),
Austin from another point of view highlighted the significance
of some first person assertions.

At this point it might seem as if contemporary medicine united
with much contemporary philosophy in stressing the significant.
Has it any significance beyond its being a particular question:
in what way is human personality supposed to be significant? Has
it any significance beyond its being a particular complex pattern
of overt behaviour? Are we more than organisms of particular
biological and social complexity? Certainly other contemporary
developments in biology seem to be denying that we are. They
seem to be denying to personality any distinctiveness beyond
what can in principle be expressed in terms of observable
behaviour in spatio-temporal terms. We need do no more than
summarize these other scientific developments, which in this way
attribute only a limited significance to human personality.

Take first the crucial case of cybernetics where important and
revealing comparisons are made between the human brain and
electronic calculating machines, on the basis of which man's
behaviour is illuminatingly compared to that of an exceedingly complex computer. So striking are some of the performances of these

[3] *Individuals* (italics mine).

machines that people begin popularly to say of such a machine that it 'thinks', 'answers', and even 'reasons logically'. Are men then machines which are distinctive merely because, on the whole for complexity and cheapness, they compare favourably with standard computers?

Again we may recall how developments in neuro-surgery seem to revolutionize our views of experience and personality. If the temporal lobes of the brain are stimulated in conscious patients, we have the most vivid and detailed memory reports. 'It is just as if I were hearing him reciting this very instant,' the patient remarks as he repeats the words of a poem he cannot have heard for years. Again, I understand that there are sites in the human brain where if a subject is stimulated, he enjoys an extremely pleasant sensation, so pleasant that he pleads with his doctor to continue stimulating. Or what of frontal leucotomy? The behaviour of a patient after his frontal lobes have been removed, differs significantly from his previous behaviour. By contrast with that behaviour, there is now a tendency to be governed by momentary impulses, to ignore social conventions of etiquette and morality, and to aim at satisfying what are more-or-less primitive desires.

The memory may be scientifically improved beyond all expectation; that pleasure sensations may be vastly increased at will; that frontal leucotomy may lead to a zest for life which sits loose to all conventions—let none of us deny this. But the crucial question which is already formulating itself is: is personality *wholly and exhaustively*, and even if only *in principle* treatable by science?

Next, there are the recent developments in molecular biology, which attempt to understand the simplest forms of life in terms of the molecular structure of the units of living matter—of what is called the DNA molecule, the molecule of deoxyribonucleic acid. This is a molecule which is pictured as one of those iron spiral staircases which we still find in some old houses and libraries. This DNA molecule is regarded as the building unit of living matter and it enables us to see (we are told) how, with a molecule of sufficient complexity and of this structure, genetic development can be understood. Already it seems clear that there is in principle no ultimate gap between living and non-living matter—and that the possibility of matter being organized in the forms we call 'living' was logically implicit in the molecular properties of all matter from the start. What, then, is distinctive about human personality except its particular complex molecular organization?

Finally, there was a day when it was commonly allowed that there was an intimate connection between moral insight, responsibility and the religious life. Wrong-doing was closely, and perhaps sometimes too easily, assimilated to sin; and sin was the province of the priest. But sin is now (it is said) rather the province of the psychiatrist or the biochemist. 'It's not me, it's my glands', or 'Don't blame me, its all due to a spectacular rise in my blood-sugar concentration', says someone caught in some offence or wrong-doing. In sexual temptation, don't talk of the devil, talk of testerone. Does 'moral behaviour'—once supposed to be so distinctive of personal behaviour—now do no more than name the new frontier areas of biochemistry and psychiatry?

Here in outline is the full perspective of contemporary scientific accounts of personality; and it focuses on the crucial question as to whether human personality at least in principle can or cannot be given an exhaustive analysis in scientific terms. Is man just another animal or organism, distinctive only in having a particular biological complexity and social behaviour? Does 'personality' speak of no more than a special brand of organism with some distinctive overt behaviour? This is the question which from all directions biology presents to the philosopher: and it is a question which (as we saw) the philosopher is raising for himself.

The question is no new one—it is of course in principle at least as old as David Hume. So let us first recall Hume's attempt to give an account of the self and personal identity in terms of distinct perceptions—the subject matter of science. When Hume tried to do this, he confessed himself to be completely bewildered: 'Upon a more strict review of the section concerning *personal identity*, I find myself involved in such a labyrinth that, I must confess, I neither know how to correct my former opinions nor how to render them consistent.'[4] As he says on the next page: 'Having thus loosened all our particular perceptions, when I proceed to explain the principle of connection, which binds them together, and makes us attribute to them a real simplicity and identity, I am sensible that my account is very defective, and that

[4] *A Treatise of Human Nature*, Pt. ii, Everyman edition, p. 317.

nothing but the seeming evidence of the precedent reasoning could have induced me to receive it. If perceptions are distinct existences, they form a whole only by being connected together. But no connections among distinct existences are ever discoverable by human understanding.' No account then of the self or personal identity is possible in terms of distinct perceptions, for no account can ever be given, merely in terms of distinct perceptions, of how the distinct perceptions are 'connected together'. Yet, as Hume admits presently, when we reflect 'on the train of past perceptions that compose a mind', these 'are felt to be connected together'. Personal identity for Hume in some sort of way is given in feeling, and Hume's 'diffidence and modesty' amounts to saying that he can give no account of this feeling in terms of distinct perceptions alone.

We may readily grant that to remind ourselves of Hume's difficulty is not by itself to prove that the problem is insoluble. But at least Hume shows us that something else besides 'distinct perceptions' will be wanted, something else besides the topics of scientific discourse, if we are to do justice to the 'feeling' we have of being ourselves and of being the same person.

Taking up from Hume, we may note however that any and every account of scientific discourse is concerned with what he called 'distinct perceptions', with 'objects' of one sort and another. But this very possibility of talking about 'objects', demands logically that there shall be at least one 'subject'. The very concept of an object presupposes a subject, as the very concept of a subject presupposes an object. To use the one concept without the other is to be logically inadequate and incomplete. The very subject/object distinction is a presupposition of all language, as it is a presupposition of all our talking about experience. Here then are logical grounds why the sciences in terms of new 'object' alone can never give a complete account of our subjectivity, indeed of any part of our subjectivity that is basically subjective. Plainly the sciences can tell us a good deal about our personal organs, e.g. lungs, heart, kidneys, and so on, and in a vague sense of the word these would be said to be part of 'ourselves' and might be thought to belong very specially to our 'subjectivity'. But in the way I am using the word 'subjectivity'—about which I shall say more presently—they are no more definitive of our 'subjectivity' than are our clothes, our houses, or our environment, though like these they may express our individuality and sufficiently well isolate us from other human beings.

The same conclusion may be reached from another direction. To suppose that scientific discourse could in principle be the whole story about ourselves is to suppose that second- and third-person language is logically primitive and ultimate. But in fact all second- and third-person language requires a first-person setting and con-context for logical completeness. 'The car does 50 miles to the gallon' may seem to be a clear independent ultimate assertion, but in fact it carries with it (however much this may be overlooked) a necessary social and verbal context and more importantly from our point of view and as a minimum, it presupposes a speaker who might make his existence known by uttering some sort of first-person introduction such as 'I am telling you, "the car . . ." ' or 'I can vouch for it—"the car . . ." ' and so on.

No doubt the question will now be asked: But what is it that this first-person language is supposed to refer to? Recall Strawson's question about the 'natural facts'. What are the 'natural facts' which lie behind characteristically first-person assertions? Now at this point we may profitably look at the kind of answer which Professor Ayer would give, the kind of account he would give of self-knowledge. We may do this profitably because with so very much of his account I entirely agree. In fact it might be said not so much that I disagree with Ayer, as that I would wish to continue the story beyond the point where he leaves off.

I begin by agreeing with Ayer that 'I' is a referring expression. I further agree that *NO* set of descriptions can be given which are logically equivalent to this referring expression. There are no logically necessary descriptions of myself, though some descriptions are always wanted in order to talk about myself, and in practice as distinct from being a matter of logical necessity, one or two of these descriptions may do the trick of picking me out from my fellow man. So far, as I say, I agree with Ayer and would underline all he says in *The Problem of Knowledge* where in the following passages he makes the points which I have been making now.

> The fact that I answer to certain descriptions may enable me in practice to be recognized; but . . . (this) . . . is a contingent fact; I might not have answered to them, even though I do. One may,

therefore, be tempted to infer that I must be something different; a substance that merely happens to have the properties so described. Furthermore it does not seem necessary that two different people should always be descriptively distinguishable. If, for example, history were cyclical, I should have my exact counterpart in every cycle: assuming that the whole process had no beginning or end, so that we were not differently related to a uniquely describable point of origin or termination, every description that I satisfied would also be satisfied by my counterparts; merely by the use of predicates there would be no way of differentiating between us. Even so, we should not be identical: the very posing of the question implies that we are not. If it were contradictory to speak of different things as being descriptively indistinguishable, the suggestion that history might be cyclical could not significantly be made. But while it is a fanciful suggestion, which has no likelihood at all of being true, it does not seem to be unintelligible. That I should have such counterparts would appear to be logically possible. But in that case it will follow that people can differ otherwise than through their properties. . . . [5]

Professor Ayer rightly concludes that his discussion has proved:

That we are not restricted to individuating by description. We can discriminate further by the use of *demonstratives*, taken in their actual context. That I differ from my hypothetical counterparts is shown by the fact that in using the word 'I', I point to *this*, while they do not. In the same way I, alone among us, am living *here* and *now*. Descriptions of time and place will not divide us: for *ex hypthesi* each of us will stand in the same spatial relations to objects of exactly the same kind and in the same temporal relations to exactly similar events. It will be true of each of us also that he says that his use of the word 'I' points to what he indicates by saying 'this'. But the reference will be different in every case. It is a *difference which defies description*, just because it is not a difference of properties, not even of spatio-temporal properties unless these are made to include a reference to some point which is demonstratively identified. The use of a demonstrative on a given occasion *shows* what is being referred to: but if we are asked to say *what* is being referred

[5] *The Problem of Knowledge*, p. 210

to, we can reply only by giving a description; a description which normally does individuate but conceivably might not.

As I have said, I am largely in agreement with Professor Ayer in all he says in these paragraphs, but the possibility of more being wanted has already shown itself. For what does Professor Ayer mean when he says that 'in using the word "I" I "point to *this*" '? What is '*this*'? What do I 'show' in this way? How can the pointer point at the pointer? What do I point to as the reference of 'I' who point?

Now I am not so stupid or naïve as to suppose that Professor Ayer must answer this question by using some descriptive expression. Certainly he, and certainly I, would reject outright the possibility of such an answer. I entirely agree with Professor Ayer when he says that 'because referential expressions are not used to describe properties they must be used to describe something else'. I agree that 'they do not owe their meaning to their describing anything at all'. As he says: 'I call them referential expressions just because their use is demonstrative and not descriptive.' He continues: 'In an actual context, *one can as it were, produce* what they refer to: but if we have to identify it by description, then we can do no more that instance some of its properties; for there is nothing else to be described.'

It is at this point however that I begin to move beyond Ayer. Notice that he says that in an actual context one can only 'as it were' produce the reference of 'I'. Now what is 'as it were' production? What is production that is only in a curious sense production! Is Ayer, and I would say rightly, here acknowledging that the way in which we 'produce' I is altogether different from the way in which I produce an object along with a demonstrating expression? Later in the same paragraph he remarks that if we ask what is 'it' that has the properties, this is to ask a question which is questionably sensible:

What is the sense of this question? What possible ways could there be of answering it? In favourable circumstances one can produce the object that one is referring to; and that is one form of answer. Or one can give a description of it which is necessarily a listing of its properties. No other possibility remains.

Now, what I want to suggest is that another possibility *does* remain. We certainly do *not* describe 'I': but no more do we 'produce the objects that one is referring to', otherwise it is an 'object' indeed, and our apparent success is utter defeat. The answer is that *we* do no production at all, but let the *subject disclose itself*.

These reflections bring us almost full circle back to Hume. My suggestion is that each of us becomes aware of what is distinctively himself when surveying a set of 'distinct perceptions' there breaks in on him a self-awareness, a self-affirmation of such a kind that he recognizes the distinct perception to be 'his'; becomes aware at the time of what it is to be himself, the same self; becomes aware of his personal identity. It is in such a disclosure, as and when it occurs around 'objects', that we have the empirical basis for all distinctive first-person utterances. Further, let it be noted, such a disclosure does not occur in spite of, but only because and in so far as there are, objects of which relevant descriptions can be given. The disclosure of ourselves occurs around a certain set of circumstances or other, which then constitutes, by way of descriptive terms, a descriptive approximation of what it is that has been disclosed to us.

We may now perhaps see what is behind C. D. Broad's distinction between regarding the self as a 'unity of *system*' or *series* and a 'unity of *centre*' respectively. Rightly criticizing the inadequacies of so-called 'bundle theories' of the self like that of Hume, Broad comments that one of their difficulties is that while they would make the self a unity of series, it is in experience a 'unity of *centre*', and he further argues that while we can understand how a unity of centre comes to be seen as a unity of system or series, it is difficult to know how a unity of series can be misunderstood as being a unity of centre.[6] By using this contrast Broad is able to make a point which chimes in with what I have said about self-disclosure. The interpretation we would give of Broad's comment is this. Suppose someone asks us to elucidate what we mean by saying that our self-identity, what we are distinctively and uniquely is disclosed to us. We might say to them, picture a series of events which consists of events occuring haphazardly one after another. They would see merely one event after another in a

[6] C. D. Broad, *The Mind and its Place in Nature*, Chap. IV, pp. 212 et seq., and Chap. XIII, pp. 584 et seq.

spatio-temporal sequence. But now (we say) suppose this group of events is in fact arranged like this . . . and we proceed to draw a group of points on the rim of a wheel. At some point or other in the exercise may not the viewer then 'see' another sort of unity altogether—may there not be disclosed a 'centre'? May not a disclosure occur which embraces all these separate events in a 'unity' which transcends them? Does this not echo the unity which is the self? If this experiment has worked, then (it might be said) I can help you to see what I am talking about when I speak of 'self-awareness' in your case or in mine. For I am talking about a series of events of which descriptions could be given, but which when surveyed together, similarly disclose in a sort of 'unity', ourselves and our self-identity.

In this connection too, I believe that the fact of memory is significant. It is plainly possible for us to picture some merely 'imaginary' past event, and no one would say that I could 'remember' that. Now I suggest that we only use the word 'remembering' of some past event when, taken with present events, it precipitates a disclosure, disclosing ourselves in virtue of which we can say of the past event, 'I was there when it happened'. At the same time we can now see why any such claim to remember needs always testing. For in countless ways an event (not present) may spark off a disclosure, and whether we can legitimately say that it is something we 'remember' depends entirely on how well this claim coheres with other claims I would make about the past and present. My point is that to talk of memory at all demands a disclosure, but that memory only becomes knowledge when it has been checked for coherence, consistency, and the rest.

Here then is the broad basis for saying that no account of myself in terms of scientific discourse will ever be adequate for it does not (and logically *cannot*) exhaust the subjectivity which is disclosed to me in self-awareness. There is a further logical point which can be usefully made here, and here I may perhaps quote from what I have written elsewhere. Considering the assertion 'I exist', we may remark that it

> is entailed by all kinds of scientific assertions. 'He has a heart beating', 'He has a blood count of X', 'He has a digestive system characterized by all that the bio-chemistry of fats, proteins, carbohydrates, and enzymes can teach us', 'He has

such and such reflex actions', 'He has such and such brain potentials': 'I exist', is entailed by all these, when said of me. But 'I exist' entails of these. We cannot necessarily *deduce* from 'I exist' any of these *particular* assertions. Yet the affirmation of my existence is that which gives all these varied assertions their concrete reference; is that which unites them all.[7]

We may at this point take the matter one stage further in a way when relevance will soon be seen. It is possible now to make one more move and to claim that not only may descriptive events be so ordered as to disclose a *subject* which while it includes them also transcends them, but that descriptive events may also be ordered so as to disclose an *object* which in a similar sort of way transcends them objectively and that indeed such a transcendent object is associated with a transcendent subject in the same situation. We become aware of it as we become aware of ourselves.

Without doubt this is best seen in the case of Duty, where we become aware of ourselves and indeed of our responsibility and freedom as and when we respond transcendentally to the claims of what has become a transcendent, moral challenge. This may be, in Professor Ayer's sense, 'as it were produced', or in my phrase 'disclosed', when for example a discussion of *prima facie* duties is so developed and complicated that it becomes (as it may in some cases, however few) a disclosure of Duty, which is unquestionably what I 'ought' to do at that time. It is in becoming aware of such an overall objective moral demand that in such circumstances I become aware of myself, my freedom, my responsibility. The example most often quoted in this regard is the well-known story of David and Nathan[8] and the logical exercise Nathan performed was that of calling up by a parable such a description of events which might, alongside David's behaviour, produce a disclosure of a transcendent obligation in relation to which David would 'come to himself'. And he did.

Broadening these reflections we may say that the traditional arguments for God are not to be seen as tight deductive arguments proving the existence of some object—'God'—as in Euclidian

[7] Ramsey, *Religion and Science: A Philosopher's Approach; Church Quarterly Review*, Jan. 1961, p. 89. See also *Religion and Science: Conflict and Synthesis* (London, S.P.C.K., 1964), pp. 73–4.

[8] 2 Sam. 121–7a.

geometry we can prove the existence of the nine-point circle. Rather are the arguments for God's existence to be seen as talk, discourse, designed to evoke a disclosure in relation to whose disclosed object we use the word 'God'. Further, in one way or another the arguments will give us more or less help as to how we can best use this word 'God' which they recommend.

Without now going into details, we can at least draw a parallel between the word 'God' and the word 'I'. Again, to quote what I have written elsewhere:

> Now what I suggest is that the word 'God' must be seen as a logical kinsman of 'I' in having, at least in these two respects, a similar logical behaviour. 'God exists' entails no particular verifiable assertions. Theology can provide no verifiable deductions. But this does not mean that it has no empirical relevance. On the contrary, like 'I exist', 'God exists' is a phrase which is in fact entailed by and so linked with verifiable language, while entailing none of it. The latter point used to be expressed in old-fashioned language by people who said 'The world is not necessary to God.' As to the earlier point, namely; that scientific assertions entail 'God exists' as some entail 'I exist': this used to be expressed as 'God is necessary to the world.' Further, the basis for 'God exists' is an affirmation which arises around the universe in a moment of disclosure in a moment of worship, indeed in prayer. It is thus like the basis for 'I exist'. Here, in worship, scientific assertions are integrated with, yet distinguished from, the theological assertion of God's existence.

Here then is the answer—a more far-reaching answer than perhaps we might have expected—to Strawson's question: what are the 'natural facts' which lie behind the logical primitiveness of first-person expressions? Here, in Stout's phrase, is that 'individual unity of our embodied self' to which the personal pronoun most aptly belongs. Persons are what is disclosed to each of us when we 'come to ourselves' in recognizing a world that has likewise, in some way or other, 'come alive', 'taken the initiative', 'declared itself' in a personal sort of way. On this basis, and by way of conclusion, I will now formulate some outline reflections on the contemporary challenge of science to personality.

I do not want to spend long on my first point. Psychosomatic medicine may not be the end of the story. While what might be called theological medicine may be hazardous in the extreme and more likely to stimulate prejudices, not to mention superstitions, the *possibility* obviously arises that *if* (as we have argued) persons are not restricted to the observable behaviour they display, what are loosely called spiritual ministrations *may* have more than the psychological value they understandably (I hope) possess. The priest may have a ministry of healing which is not only a matter of a smile above a clean collar. But to treat of the problems, possibilities, and difficulties in this area would take us too far afield.

That developments in neurosurgery may provide us with the most striking and startling possibilities of modifying our observable behaviour, I do not deny. But I would at the same time emphasize that they will also provide us with the most novel moral perplexities as well with circumstances in which we have to learn again, so to say, how to practise moral behaviour. In short, we shall have to learn new occasions of moral disclosures. But what is quite evident is that these developments never necessarily take from us the status and privilege of 'being ourselves' or of displaying 'responsible' behaviour: for this builds out from all and every scientific circumstance. The possibilities that arise in neurosurgery merely exemplify the old phrase—new occasions teach new duties.

Further, with regard to cybernetics it might be said that from the first it is a downright *logical* blunder to speak of machines 'thinking' or 'answering', or 'reasoning logically'—for it is in terms of these phrases that we characteristically distinguish machines from persons in the language game we all play. It is the kind of point Peter Winch makes against too scientifically-minded psychologists or sociologists. But I hope I have done something to show the kind of basis in fact which we have for making this logical distinction, the sort of fact which justifies it.

Again, in the case of glandular secretions, let us recognize that the possibility of such an 'explanation' of our overt behaviour, does not make our activity something about which we must necessarily be morally neutral. Indeed, there are two cases here: (a) If a person who is a *prima facie* offender has exerted no personal activity at all—then the shoplifting (say) is mainly an event which happens to, and centres on, his arm. He has failed to be a house-trained citizen. He must be biochemically adjusted accordingly. *But all this is only as a preliminary* to his rediscovering the possibility of genuine moral activity. (b) If the *prima facie* offender *did* display some personal activity—then moral training will be as necessary as biochemical treatment. Both features will be needed in any adequate therapy. In fact, glandular trouble *would* be remedied, psychiatric treatment *would* be successful *precisely when and because* it permitted of responsible moral activity, allowed the agent to rediscover himself in responding to a genuine moral challenge.

Finally, developments in molecular biology certainly hint at the possibility of a 'new manhood', and an altogether new outlook on an altogether new world. But thus to explain some features of 'life' in terms of molecular biology, to 'explain' what is or will be by all over appearances distinctively human, is not at all to deny that we also possess other features of 'life'—pre-eminently a 'subjectivity' of which we are aware and which can be associated with any and all scientific stories however novel and however various. The future man may be vastly different from ourselves: but around vastly different organisms and brain structures disclosures could still arise. And as for neurosurgery, because our overt behaviour is vastly different it does *not* follow that we are different 'persons' except in a very superficial sense. Let it be granted that our social responses change enormously when we are tired or when we are presented with a different environment. 'A cruise will do you good, and make you feel a different person', the shipping poster tells us, and it may well be true. Colleagues may appear very different at a dinner party than at a committee. In one sense of the words, people *are* 'different persons' in the Assize Court, or on a Mediterranean cruise, at a Committee, or at a City Dinner. But in one sense—the sense in which we know our subjectivity in disclosures—they are not different persons at all. An eminent neurosurgeon, Sir Geoffrey Jefferies, once said to me that while the overt behaviour of his patients often changed after an operation—on *no* occasion had any of them ceased to be 'ultimately' the same person. It is that sense of 'person' which I have been trying to elucidate, but it would be another task and admittedly a tricky philosophical exercise to specify the kind of criteria to which Sir Geoffrey would ultimately have appealed.

At any rate my conclusion is that the metaphysical distinctiveness of human personality given to each of us in what I have called a 'disclosure', cannot, even in principle, ever be completely eroded by scientific discoveries. To do that would be to objectify the subject, and to deny the very presupposition of all language and all experience, even scientific language and experience. What contemporary discoveries in science show, however, is that the situations in which this subjectivity is realized may soon be vastly different than any we have known before—but disclosures of subjectivity will still be logically possible, they will always be morally significant: and scientific 'explanations' of the self or human behaviour will never exclude other 'explanations' in a different logical key, especially if the 'natural facts' about our-selves are not as restricted as some narrower empiricists would wish to believe. That they are not so restricted has been my central point in this paper.

Ethics and Reason

Professor Ginsberg's lecture[1] is concerned with the relation between the empirical and rational elements in ethics, the relation between 'experience' and 'reason' in moral behaviour. If this distinction seems bewildering, the reader can take heart from the candid confessions he will find on pages 7 and 11. Not only are 'the words "reason", "rationalist", "rational", like the word "positivism", highly ambiguous and emotion-laden', but 'even in the more technical philosophical discussions' the terms are 'far from clear'. Can we find any other way, then, of describing Professor Ginsberg's endeavour; can we find any clearer way of expressing his theme?

When I say to someone, 'You ought to do so-and-so', or when I describe some situation as 'good' or 'valuable', Professor Ginsberg would rightly distinguish at least four questions that we could ask in regard of such an assertion:

1 How far does it gather together certain instincts, attitudes, feeling, or desires?
2 How far does it arise from a 'direct and immediate apprehension' centred on the particular situation in question?
3 How far does the assertion follow from general principles which have somehow or other been 'intuited' or seen as 'self-evident'?
4 How far have I reached my assertion as a result of a reasoned argument not only about the possibility and suitability of various 'means', but even about the particular 'end' in question?

It is such questions as these which any discussion of the relations between reason and experience in ethics inevitably raises. Those who have been called 'rationalists', those who have wished to emphasize the place of reason in ethics, have been those who have

[1] *Reason and Experience in Ethics* (August Comte Memorial Trust Lecture). By Morris Ginsberg. Cumberlege.

concerned themselves either with question 3 or (more generally) with question 4. Some 'rationalists' have even gone further and urged that 'the knowledge of right and wrong' is *itself* 'capable of influencing, if not necessarily determining, action' (p. 9). The 'empiricist', on the other hand, eager to emphasize the close dependence of ethics on 'facts' of one kind and another, would be concerned certainly with question 1 and (quite often) with question 2 as well.

No moral philosopher has been, or indeed could have been, entirely 'rationalist' or 'empiricist', and, as Professor Ginsberg shows by reference to Lord Russell, 'those who hold that reason has nothing to do with the choice of ends' may nevertheless, before they finish, have evolved 'a rationalism of their own'. Professor Ginsberg points out that though Russell thinks 'that the ends of action are given by desire, and that the basis of moral judgements is to be found in emotions of approval and disapproval and the feeling of enjoyment, he claims, nevertheless, that it is possible to build up a theory of ethical propositions which are true (or false) in the same sense as if they were propositions of science'. In short, if Lord Russell's interests begin with question 1, he concludes by giving an answer to question 4, and indeed such an explicit answer as would say that ethical argument is at its best scientific. There is, of course, no necessary criticism of Russell here; what the example shows is how difficult it is to divide moral philosophers into 'rationalists' and 'empiricists', and criticism, if criticism be deserved, would centre on that distinction and not on Russell.

In this kind of way, then we have to recognize from the outset that while the four questions we have formulated show the kind of issue that Professor Ginsberg's lecture is concerned with, the questions are by no means separate. Indeed, the whole lecture argues for a particular view of their inter-relation—certainly the inter-relation of questions 1 and 4. Much less is said about questions 2 and 3.

Professor Ginsberg spends some time, at the beginning, with a form of rationalism which, while having a necessary basis in facts, has nevertheless, and indeed for that very reason, been suspect. This is the view that moral assertions are given to us as scientific generalizations of one kind or another, a view with close similarities to that of Russell's which we have mentioned above. Against

such a view, Hume and Poincaré (to take the two examples Ginsberg gives) both claim that no one can legitimately argue from
'judgements of fact', to 'judgements of value', from 'is' to 'ought'.
Or, as Poincaré says, from the 'principles of science' we 'will
never obtain a proposition which says, "do this", or "do not do
that"; that is a proposition confirmed or contradicted by morality'.
There is on the one hand sociology and the natural sciences;
on the other hand ethics, with no logical bridge across the gulf.
Now if one begins with an absolute distinction between 'facts'
and 'values', if we begin with such a dichotomy, we certainly *never*
will legitimately argue from one to the other. But is there, after
all, any very plain demarcation? Does not every *situation* have
both its 'facts' *and* its 'values', so that no matter how differently
these can be talked of or treated, there must, *since they belong to
the one situation, be some kind of connection between them*? There is
a road accident, and the doctor living nearby leaves his game of
bridge to minister to the wounded. Here is an exceedingly complex group of facts: a pattern extending over drawing room and
road, cards and bandages, coffee and blood. Each in its own way
exerts a certain 'value-claim' on us. But to the doctor (supposing
he leaves, not with a thankful relief to be saved from a boring
game, but in response to a genuine 'call of duty') the maximum
value claim is exerted by certain complex sub-group centring on a
'person' on the road, rather than the bridge-party. On the other
hand, if the doctor were playing bridge because of its therapeutic
value on a player-patient who (as a scientific fact) might have a
relapse if the game were suddenly terminated, then the maximum
value-claim might lie elsewhere. And so on. . . .

In ways like this, and within *one situation* values and facts are
inextricably linked. Whether we 'ought' or 'ought not' depends
very much on what a thing 'is' or 'is not'. *Is* and *ought*, science
and ethics, while being distinguishable, are also connected. In
short, I have myself never been over-awed by Hume's claim
which was the outcome of an empirical theory of knowledge where
'facts' were supposed to be no more than cosmic tiddly-winks
with 'values' housed somewhere else if (and the alternative is
significant) housed anywhere at all. To separate 'facts' from
'values' may lead to a high view of ethics: it may equally lead to
no ethics at all.

I am a little alarmed, then, when Professor Ginsberg uses the phrase *sui generis* of ethics, which might well imply a logically unbridgeable gulf between facts and values. This, however, I am glad to say, he for the most part denies allowing only to Hume the point that rational enquiry cannot 'create morality or derive the moral from the non-moral', where the important words are 'create' and 'derive'. No one can ever reasonably expect to begin with purely indicative assertions and end with moral ones. But this does not mean that the kind of assertions ethics deals with are not *in part* indicative and *in part* valuational. I agree whole-heartedly with Professor Ginsberg when he says that there can be no criticism of ethics which takes moral judgements as it finds them, 'to elicit the assumptions latent in them, and the categories employed by them, and to discover whether any fundamental principles can be formulated, whereby actual morality might be made more coherent and systematic'. Further, since moral judge-ments relate to and talk about certain specific situations, i.e. certain groups of facts, then 'a knowledge of the relevant facts is of the greatest importance for the study of morality'. It is obvious, though that is not to say that it is not often overlooked, that if anyone is to make a moral judgement about a situation it is of the first importance for him to know the 'facts' of that situation as clearly as ever he can. Often 'we need fuller knowledge than we possess of human needs and potentialities, and in particular of the ways in which the means to their fulfilment, including the modes of distribution, are likely to affect the ends and ideals aimed at'. Far too frequently are the facts involved in moral decision 'taken for granted' and Professor Ginsberg takes as a special example the morality of sex. He shows that even the intuitionists (and he takes Dean Inge as an example of them) cannot get away with certain psychological and sociological cir-cumstances. After all, intuitions terminate in the facts of certain situations; and no intuition belonging to a situation S^1 can be unaffected by the fact (if fact it be) that S^1 belongs to and is part of a wider situation S^2, which includes more 'relevant' facts. Professor Ginsberg's conclusion of this discussion is, it seems to me, immensely important: 'I am not suggesting that ethical differences would necessary all disappear when the relevant facts are better known. But I have no doubt that the area of disagree-ment would be reduced and that, at the very least, there would be a better chance of discovering what the disagreements are about.' Here is implied both the possibility and necessity of checking 'intuitions'.

So far then, Ginsberg has been urging that ethics must, more than has sometimes been realized, gather together by the help of biology, psychology, sociology, and the rest, more and more details of the situations whose 'facts' are also value-bearing—in this way ethics must have a strong 'empirical' bias. On the other hand, Ginsberg believes that when this empirical gathering together has been done, ethics will be sufficiently 'rational' to detect some conformity, some similarity of pattern, between all the situations it calls 'good', all duties which it claims 'ought to be done'. But this of course is to bring us at once up against the variability of moral judgements from age to age and from civilization to civilization. Allowing for all the variety and variability of moral judgements, can we ever hope to detect rationally a uniform pattern that we could legitimately call, for example, moral improvement or moral development?

Ginsberg believes that we can, and most of the second half of this lecture is concerned with enumerating 'five closely related but distinguishable criteria' by which moral systems can be compared. In other words, the more the pattern of a moral judgement exhibits features in accordance with these criteria, the 'better'— the 'more developed'—will it be. The five criteria are as follows:

1 Any morality is so much the better the more it sees 'goodness (as) self-sustained and independent of external sanctions'.

2 Any moral judgement is the better the more it can be 'universalized'.

3 A moral system is all the 'higher' if it can allow for what Ginsberg calls 'comprehensiveness', but what we might call 'flexibility' or 'synthesis of opposites'. His point is that 'the higher systems find room for spontaneity and control, self-fulfilment and self-denial, personal and social good. Richer in content, they are more sensitive and differentiated in response.' They hold together 'conflicting claims and diverse interests . . . rebel and innovator'.

4 Any moral judgement is the better the more it belongs to a system showing 'coherence' and 'systematic connectedness'. At the same time, Ginsberg is anxious not to overstress the importance of systematic connectedness so far as to look for

logical unification in a deductive scheme. There can be, as Mill said of Comte, 'an inordinate desire for unity'. But after all, there has to be a broad consistency and a measure of coherence between various moral judgements.

5 A moral system which shows 'capacity for self-criticism and self-direction' is better than one which does not. A moral system is all the better the more 'impartial investigation of the facts and critical scrutiny of the ends to be pursued is allowed to shape public policy'.

Professor Ginsberg rightly notes that 'advance as estimated by one of the criteria . . . does not necessarily imply advance in the direction of the others'. For example 'a system may be internally coherent, but narrow and exclusive, and thus fail in universality. Again, a system may be comprehensive in the sense of covering a wide variety of needs and interests, but rely on coercion and other external sanctions, and thus fail to satisfy the criterion of differentiation.' Even so, for Ginsberg it is important that the various criteria can be rationally elucidated at all, and in their very emergence is a justification of what he calls later 'the rationalist assumption'. This assumption 'is that such comparison and evaluation of the forms of life is logically impossible, and that despite the diversity of moral codes, general principles are discoverable which are implicit in all of them, and which come to be recognized as universally binding in the course of development'. In this connection, he notes that reason has also a three-fold function in relation to 'ideals'. These it can 'clarify and define', 'show their relations to each other', and formulate 'the conditions . . . upon which they depend for their realization'. Once again, we come back to an earlier theme when we recognize how much of this work is at the same time 'factual', requiring, as it does, the aid of the social and natural sciences.

So Professor Ginsberg can claim both a certain sympathy with Comte and an important difference from him. In so far as Comte believed 'that ethics has to be firmly rooted in our knowledge of human nature and human history', and in so far as he held that morality must be 'self-authenticated'—depending on no external sanctions, Ginsberg would go with him. But he would criticize Comte in so far as he does not allow for any distinctiveness about value judgements (I think it is better to put the matter in this way

c

rather than to speak of the *sui generis* character of ethics) and—
something which is another aspect of the same point—is guilty of
precisely that form of argument from indicative to moral assertions
which Hume and others would rightly attack.

Looking back over the lecture, and besides the various points
that we have already raised, there are for the Christian moralist one
or two questions of perhaps special significance which I might
here set out:

1   We can surely agree that *moral judgements* must inevitably
benefit from the knowledge that sociology and the natural sciences
can supply. At any rate, such knowledge is certainly a *necessary*
condition for making a reliable moral judgement.

2   But equally certainly such knowledge is *not* of and in itself
sufficient. Will it be enough, in making a moral judgement, to see
the sociological and psychological details of a situation clearly?
No: for a moral judgement is distinctive in being concerned with
the *values* which these facts, whose relevance is revealed by the
social and natural sciences, exhibit. But those who grasp the *same*
facts, will they inevitably intuit in the particular situation the same
value-claim? It seems to me that the presupposition of any ethics
which is 'rational' in any sense whatever, depends on an affirmative
answer being given to this 'empirical' question. In this sense
Comte would be both a good rationalist and a good empiricist
when he suggests that 'if we were more intelligent we should
also be more moral, and if we were more moral, we should also be
more intelligent'. But this does *not* imply that we would give an
affirmative answer to another related but different question:
Does an appropriate *moral response* follow from every recognized
value-claim? On the contrary, the Christian has always recognized
the situation so notably expressed by St Paul: 'The good that I
would, I do not.' And the question 'Why?' is fearfully important.
Even the irreligious must presumably take account of the disturb-
ing influence exerted by all kinds of 'non-rational' factors, and
no discussion of the place of facts and reasoning in the moral life
can overlook this stubborn feature of everyone's behaviour.

3   Has morality need of 'supernatural sanctions'? Both Comte
and Professor Ginsberg would say 'No'. 'A command, whether it
emanates from God, society, or ourselves, has to be justified, and
the justification cannot lie in the mere fiat of anyone's will. . . .
There is no doubt an element of virtue in submission or abne-

gation. But to emphasize this element is to ignore the other and possibly the more important, of liberation and fulfilment.' For my own part (though the story would be a long one) I would in the end agree with Ginsberg, and I would further admit that Christian ethics have sometimes been interpreted in a way that is open to the kind of objection he makes. But to deny that morality has need of 'a supernatural sanction' does *not* deny that morality has some close links with religion.

What if a situation, besides having 'facts', was not wholly exhausted even when these facts were seen to be 'value-bearing'? Then, just as the social and natural sciences might give us important truth about the universe on which moral 'insight' could build, so it might be argued that what ethics tells us about the situation could be set within an even wider scheme. The kind of principles which Professor Ginsberg would find implied by moral judgements, might even prove to include religious ideas, the kind of system we detect may prove to be in pattern theistic. In this way, without at all invoking theology in a way which Professor Ginsberg would reject, morality might nevertheless and inextricably be bound up with religion.

4 Certainly, I think Professor Ginsberg's view suggests a somewhat novel answer to the old question, 'What are Christian ethics?' In brief, this answer would say that for Christian ethics those situations which the Bible and Christian doctrine speak of, and which centre on the facts of Jesus of Nazareth, are brought alongside any particular situation as it has been portrayed in terms of the natural sciences, sociology, and the rest. In other words, Christian ethics would supplement the factual aspect of any situation we judge. Here would be a supplementary basis of 'fact', and from the whole we would intuit a certain value-claim.

Further, as for 'principles', Christian ethics might claim that the resulting moral judgements not only fit the general kind of five-fold pattern Professor Ginsberg elucidates, but a pattern which also involves categories of a theological kind, though I recognize that this theology could not then be sanctions-theology. Nay more: such a Christian ethics might well provide *some* kind of answer to the problem we raised under question 2—it might well inform moral behaviour with that power which *enables* appropriate action, moral *responses*, to follow moral *judgements*. Indeed, in so far as the Christian faith is based (and in however complex a fashion) on certain 'facts', its power to influence action would, I should say, be that much stronger than the power which might be exercised, for example, by a fable. But that is to touch on other questions, affecting morality and religion, which contemporary philosophy is raising.

PART
2
The Meaning of God Talk

Theological Literacy 1
On Understanding Mystery

It is by this time well known that contemporary empiricism represents a challenge to Christian belief. What needs to be said, however, and indeed emphasized, is that this challenge needs often to be welcomed, first for setting squarely before us problems of crucial importance which otherwise we might not notice or even seek to bypass if we did; and second, since contemporary empiricism encourages us to loiter over our language, to be alert to its variegations, to see how we use that language in various ways to do different jobs of work, this approach is likely to be a great help as we turn to that most complex and peculiar language in which in a vast variety of ways a religious man expresses himself. I believe that contemporary empiricism may revitalize our faith and our doctrine and make what seem so often to be the dry bones of theological discourse live. At any rate, those are the convictions which lie behind this lecture, and they will prepare you I hope for what follows, not least because I begin my lecture precisely with one of those valuable challenges of which I have just made mention. In a recent paper on the *Hiddenness of God and Some Barmecidal God Surrogates*, Dr Robert C. Coburn, of the University of Chicago, rightly remarks that the concept of God is 'both exceedingly complex and exceedingly peculiar'.[1] A particular example of this complexity and peculiarity occurs, he would say, in those 'innumerable pieces of religious discourse' where talk about God displays two features not obviously reconcilable. On the one hand, talk about God is about 'something with quite determinate humanly intelligible characteristics'. God is for instance 'a supremely powerful, perfectly righteous, all knowing person, who created and controls the spatio-temporal order in a providential way'. The particular puzzle arises, however, because talk about God is *also* of 'something whose characteristics

[1] *Journal and Philosophy*, LVII, Nos. 22 and 23, 27 October and 10 November 1960, p. 689.

are totally beyond our grasp, something ineductably unknow-able and wholly incomprehensible'. Here, says Coburn, is 'a very fundamental problem'. How can we just talk of God as being both hidden from and open to our comprehension? How do we combine mystery and understanding? How do we understand a mystery?

Now it is true, as Coburn reminds us, that some believers would give and have given short shrift to the question. There are those who have in Coburn's words, 'italicized God's hiddenness at the expense of his openness and then retreated into holy silence'; those who have held, in the words of another philosopher, Thomas McPherson, that religion 'belongs to the sphere of the unsayable'.[2] And at the other extreme, are those who have produced, say Co-burn, 'a more or less readily understandable but somehow re-ligiously uninteresting "philosopher's God"', and I think we ourselves might go even further and say religiously scandalizing philosopher's God. Now Coburn recognizes that the sanction of the Church, however, has most often been accorded to those whose views have avoided both these extremes, those who have somehow tried to reconcile God's hiddenness with God's openness. But the broad argument of Coburn's paper is that these attempts 'are easily as perplexing as the difficulty of difficulties they ostensibly surmount'. Can I hope for better success? At any rate let me try.

Two points become clear from Coburn's discussion, though I shall put them largely in my own way. First, if religious language is used literally, if religious language is descriptive through and through, then the only possibility of mystery arises from there being some inaccessible facts. This indeed is a sense of 'mystery' which even scientific inquiry could and does allow. Lord Rayleigh and others in 1892 no doubt spoke of the 'mystery' of the atomic weight of nitrogen, when samples of nitrogen prepared in differ-ent ways, and in each case with every possible precaution, yielded different values for the atomic weight of nitrogen. But this mys-tery disappeared once Sir William Ramsay discovered the pre-sence in atmospheric nitrogen of the inert gas argon. When Ramsay and Rayleigh announced the discovery of argon in August 1894 the mystery had disappeared. Here is mystery used

[2] Sechis 'Religion as the Inexpressible', in *New Essays in Philosophical Theology*, ed. A. N. Flew and A. Machtyre, Chap. VII.

as a synonym for temporary ignorance about the facts. In this case we might speak of a two-year mystery. Now I think it is quite clear and for two reasons that this sense of mystery is of no help whatever for religious belief. First, to preserve ultimate mystery, we should have to talk of facts which were permanently inaccessible. But what could be meant by talking of facts which are permanently, indeed logically, inaccessible to everybody? If any facts are logically inaccessible they will never, logically never, be talked about. And the sooner we cease trying the better. The alternative is to suppose that the mystery of religion will sooner or later, like the mystery of the atomic weight of nitrogen in 1894, lie open for everybody to see, believers or not. But then the topic of religious belief is no more than observable facts and, being in no sort of way transcendent, is in no sort or way religious. So let us agree with Coburn that religious language can hardly be literal and do its job of understanding mystery.

Now the second move. If, however, religious language preserves a reference to mystery by somehow not being used literally there are at least two different difficulties. First, it is objected, if religious language is not used literally, what becomes of its factual claims? What sort of fact is it that can only be talked about in some slanting kind of way? What sort of fact is it which eludes direct statement? It is 'far from obvious', claims Coburn, that 'the notion of facts which elude direct statement' makes sense. Indeed, I think Coburn would say that all these attempts to avoid the literal use of religious language, if they are intelligible at all, either compromise factual claims or prove unavailing by having to make in the end the very kind of link between language and fact which they set out to avoid. Or perhaps both. As for the first alternative, which makes no pretence to possess factual claims, claiming that religious language merely expresses this or that way of looking at things, we may readily agree that of all religions Christianity cannot give up its factual claims by regarding its Bible or doctrines as, say, no more than encouragements to or mnemonics for a worship which then will be no more than the family at play, a sort of make believe with jolly social possibilities. This is something not too far from C. B. Martin's picture parody of what he thinks worship is.

On the other hand, suppose a more subtle attempt to preserve the factual reference is made by supposing religious language to be used metaphorically. Now on such a view, an assertion like 'God is a person' might be supposed to work to take Coburn's own example, like 'Mrs Q is a duck' or, as I heard someone say the other day, 'General de Gaulle is a mule'. The trouble is that if those metaphorical assertions claim to be in any sort of way a 'statement of fact' we must still suppose, says Coburn, and rightly, that they fulfil both what he calls the 'referring condition' and the 'descriptive condition'. In short, without going into all the complexities, God, like Mrs Q or General de Gaulle, must be somehow identifiable, and there must also be a number of literal descriptions, however few, which God shares with persons, as Mrs Q presumably shares either her waddling or her cackling with the ducks, and De Gaulle his stubbornness with mules. But, says Coburn, and I think we are bound to agree, 'God can neither be indicated demonstratively nor described in such a manner as to be uniquely related to a demonstratively identifiable particular'. Second, does anybody know of any literal description which God satisfies and shares with all of us? It is clear, I think, without pursuing the matter further, that we shan't answer Coburn's difficulties, we shan't meet his challenge, unless we are able to elucidate a 'notion of facts which elude direct statement', unless in other words we are able to broaden Coburn's empiricism in some intelligible way. So our problem becomes: What can be meant by claiming that something is mysterious if, as we agree, it is not to be understood in terms of the inaccessibility of facts, and yet has got to have some sort of factual reference? In other words, in what sort of situation do mystery and understanding meet? What sort of 'facts' elude in principle exhaustive description and yet permit us some measure of understanding! What is my recipe for a wider empiricism?

My answer begins with, though plainly it must not finish with ourselves—each one of us. None of us need doubt that an enormous amount can be said about himself in descriptive language, that an enormous number of facts in Coburn's ordinary sense can be predicated of all of us. These are the facts about our age, our height, our hair, our eyes, our health record, and so on—all those facts indeed in which passport officers are interested and which are the very bread and butter in the lives of immigration officers and insurance agents; and there are those facts about our behaviour responses, our complexes, our learning abilities, in which the psychologists will be interested. There are also the facts about our social life and our families and our budgets in which the sociologist and economists are interested; facts about our digestion in which the biochemist will be interested, and so on. Further, it is to these experts that I go to clear up any 'mystery' about my age, or my behaviour, or my purchasing ability, or my digestion. For it is all a matter here of further inquiry and greater competence, of knowing more facts, of greater expertise. But is each of us then in principle no more than what the passport officer, the insurance broker, the psychologist, the sociologist, the economist, the biochemist, and so on, can report about us? Are we no more in principle than what is referred to by such a very variegated cluster of important and true and far-reaching assertions? The answer in principle is 'No'. Why? Well notice what the claim that it *was* sufficient in principle would imply. It would imply that a first-person assertion about myself could be replaced without loss by that admittedly enormous but nevertheless finite cluster of *third-person* assertions, assertions about objects. But if that were ever true, it would objectify the subject and it would deny the very subject-object distinction which is the basis of all talking, all language, and all experience. Now it is true that 'He has blue eyes' is subject-predicate in character, but a mere glance at it makes it evident that nevertheless it is a third-person assertion through and through, even though it is subject-predicate in character. And as a third-person assertion it is wholly about objects, despite its subject-predicate structure. Indeed, its logical incompleteness can be recognized the moment we reflect that every third-person assertion is enclosed in invisible quotes. So that 'He has blue eyes' needs setting within a wider sentence frame such as 'I have written for your consideration: "He has blue eyes" ', *or* 'I am telling you: "He has blue eyes" ', *or* 'I am saying: "He has blue eyes" '. Now, I am not denying that, on occasion, we all of us use first-person assertions which give 'I' no more genuine self-reference than you give to 'He' when you use it of me. And undoubtedly that kind of point would make the whole story very complicated. But for our purposes, all that need be recognized is that there is a subjectivity which each of us realizes for himself which is not, and logically could not be, exhausted by any number of third-person descriptions, however various they were. Here, then, is a 'fact'—my own existence as I know it, in its full subjectivity—which eludes, and in principle, any exhaustive direct description. How then is it revealed, and how do we come across it? 'Revealed' indeed is the right word, for in fact it is disclosed to us, it breaks in on us at some point or other as the descriptive story is ever more fully built up. Here is something whose possibility I think we may recognize from various illustrations. For example, we must all have played those party games where clues are given and the winner is the one who 'sees', from the fewest clues, what is being talked about. On the basis of the fewest clues, the disclosure occurs; the winner sees the point of the story. Let us see how the same game goes in the case of self-disclosure. Suppose B comes up to A one day and says: 'I am looking for a man who is age 23, black hair, blue eyes, 5' 9", weight 162 lb., Passport EA 24607, suffers from chronic catarrh, can't eat shell fish, earns $7,800 a year, has a wife and two children, and so on.' Now A could perfectly well understand all that B said and never, as we say, realize that it was himself. Even though the description fitted every time and even though with the help of the passport officer, the bathroom scales, the mirror, a doctor, a sociologist, an economist, a biochemist, and so on, the picture was better and better filled in, at no point would we be *compelled* to conclude 'It is I'. It could always be no more than an interesting character study of my perfect double. If, however, at some point we declare, 'It's I', it means that at that point, as those pictures are enumerated, the light dawns, we jump to it, a disclosure occurs, and we recognize the inquiry to be for ourselves; 'Thou art the Man.'

That which each of us knows, when he most significantly comes to himself in this way, is nothing at which we can satisfactorily point, it is nothing which can be 'indicated demonstratively'. There is no demonstratively identifiable particular which is I. Whatever particular fact is selected for rough and ready identification purposes, e.g. as on the passport, colour of eyes, height, even what is called in those documents 'distinguishing marks'; whatever fact is selected, it is not logically impossible for somebody else to share it—even the so-called 'distinguishing mark'. As A. J. Ayer himself admits—a point to which I return presently—there is no particular which could unambiguously identify a person. On the other hand, what each of us realizes himself uniquely to be is something which facts in Coburn's sense may contrive to disclose.

But my argument has been that what they disclose is something which is all of these facts and more, and it is *not* a more that will ever be covered by more of the facts. For it is a subjectivity for which no set of third-person descriptions, of what are technically public 'objects', no matter how many or varied, can ever be exhaustive currency. Here is a fact that eludes direct statement. But it is a fact as indisputable a fact as my own subjectivity.

Let me elucidate this subjectivity a little further. There might be, in principle, circumstances when, from the point of view of my identifiable description, my existence to you may be exceedingly problematical. We might imagine, for instance, that by some extraordinary freak of space and time, when I am leaving this room, I suddenly disappear and at the same spot appears General Robert E. Lee of the Civil War. Now from the point of view of descriptions, I should certainly be an exceedingly great puzzle. Even if I said, 'But I am Ramsay', the identification difficulties would be immense. But the important point is that, all the time, no matter how bewildered you were, I have *no doubt whatever at any time* that I am the same person.

Contrariwise, suppose, to give another example, that someone believed that a completely satisfactory set of identifiable characteristics had been listed, guaranteed to isolate me on any occasion. He would certainly have made a great mistake. Because there would always be in principle the identical twin, he who is born an identical person in some counterpart earth which the course of evolution has thrown up. Or as A. J. Ayer himself points out, there is always at least the logical possibility that history could quite literally repeat itself.

I need neither complicate the examples nor take them further. My point is that in the disclosure he has of his own subjectivity, each of us has a notion (and it is a 'notion' in a sense very close to that technical sense in which George Berkeley used the word) of what eludes direct statement, or what eludes expression in descriptive terms. Each of us in his own subjectivity has a paradigm of mystery, and it is irreducible mystery because the subject will never be exhaustively objectified.

Now with that background, let us pass to the case of God, in order presently to say how we shall understand mystery, and talk intelligibly about the mystery of God. My suggestion will be that the mystery of God arises and is safeguarded precisely because God discloses himself in situations which objectively match those of whose subjective features I have just been speaking. Indeed, I would suggest—and let me emphasize, since my task at the moment is primarily one of giving meaning to religious assertions that on the face of it are questionably intelligible, I need no more elucidate a visible possibility—I am going to suggest that such awareness of our own subjectivity, of our own subjective transcendence, arises along with and matches an awareness of objective transcendence, a cosmic disclosure, when the universe, as we'd say, 'comes alive'. We may recall, for instance, that David in the presence of Nathan came to himself *subjectively* when there bore down on him objectively, through the parable or model that Nathan used, a moral challenge.

In this way, and to this degree, but no further, I can agree with those who, following Kierkegaard and other existentialists, stress the significance of what is called 'the realization of one's existence as a self' or (another favourite phrase) 'choosing oneself' or rather 'receiving oneself', 'coming to oneself as an inward action of the personality', and I agree when these existentialists go further and argue that this significant and 'authentic life' will be matched by 'a word from God'.[3]

Suppose, then, that this is the situation in which language about God is grounded, the kind of fact that subjectively and objectively eludes any exhaustive descriptive account, which eludes direct statement, which combines hiddenness and openness. How do we contrive to talk about it? To what conclusion do these suggestions lead about that 'peculiar and complex language', which occurs in 'innumerable pieces of religious discourse'?

My broad answer will be that a religious assertion which embraces the comprehensible and the incomprehensible, which does justice to and is currency for both the hiddenness and the openness of God, which speaks of a disclosure in part mysterious, does so by incorporating words or phrases whose logical behaviour I called elsewhere that of 'models' and 'qualifiers', respectively. Let me illustrate and develop that distinction by reference to two examples: (1) 'God is a necessary being', or its synonym, 'God necessarily exists'. (2) 'God is infinitely loving'. Now in these examples, I call 'being' and 'loving' models; I call 'infinitely' and

[3] Cf., e.g. Reidar Thomte, *Kierkegaard's Philosophy of Religion*, pp. 48–9, and *The Witness of Kierkegaard* (ed. C. Michalson), p. 127.

'necessarily' qualifiers. Why and how I call them that, I will explain. It will always be tempting to someone who is all too literate in theology to suppose that the assertion 'God is a necessary being' has a *logical* behaviour precisely like its many *verbal* kinsmen, for instance, 'Churchill is a remarkable being'. Similarly, it will be supposed that 'God is infinitely loving', works like its verbal synonym, say, 'Wendy (or Jim) is wonderfully loving'. In this way it will be supposed that 'necessary being' describes some brand of existence, that 'necessary existence' takes its own place alongside the 'shadow existence' of a Labour Cabinet in Britain, the 'crowded existence' of a city artery at the rush hour, 'future existence' on the moon and so on. Now if that parallel is made, objections cluster fast and furious. Some like Professor J. N. Findlay would remark that 'necessary' can characterize nothing but propositions like those in mathematics and symbolic logic, and can never characterize things so that 'necessary being' is a mere noise.[4] Others will emphasize that every existent we know is contingent—it could have been different. So God must exist as we can suppose nothing else to exist. The implication is that talk about God as a necessary existent is absolutely vacuous. Those are certainly difficulties into which we get when we either neglect the function of qualifiers and say in isolation 'God exists' or 'God is loving', or misread their logic regarding them as descriptive of some sort of quality, some brand of existence, some brand of love. What is the alternative? The alternative, I would suggest, is that we look at the assertion 'God is a necessary being' as we ought to look at *all* assertions about the mystery which is God. First we shall look for one word on which everyone will agree; one word which can be understood descriptively, something to give an intelligible route into the disclosure of mystery, something to enable us to be as articulate as possible about it afterward. Here is the model. It is like all models at least in this regard, viz., it is something about which we are reasonably clear by which to understand something which is very problematical.

Now in the sentence 'God is a necessary being', the model word here is 'being'—and I take it in its universally admitted sense, to describe anything, say, a melon or a house; there need be, on this

[4] See his contribution in *New Essays in Philosophical Theology* (eds. A. N. Flew and A. MacIntyre).

view, nothing esoteric about 'being'. Now suppose we start with a melon on a dining table on a particular evening. Clearly, this is not a necessary being. It may be indeed the first time we have had melons for twenty years. So the qualifier 'necessary' will direct us, starting here and now with this melon, to seek situations displaying less and less contingency. For instance it might be said that while a melon obviously would not always grace a college dining table, meals would. But there are times when there are no meals on the table. So when we talk about a college, and in that context 'Here's a melon' is more contingent than 'Here is a meal', which is itself more contingent than 'Here's a table'. But is not the dining hall more necessary than the table it contains? The city though might exist without the college; the state without the city. But the country could be here without this state, and so on. In this way, the qualifier 'necessary' pushes us along and along, to generate an ever broadening perspective, to embrace and to pass beyond more and more models for being. It is the party game again. And the hope is that as this pattern is developed and increased, at some point a disclosure will occur, the universe will 'come alive'. In the words of David Hume and despite all his criticism of the argument from design, 'something will immediately strike us with a force like that of sensation'.[5] Now if this disclosure occurs at the level of the word 'country', if we 'see' and 'jump to it' when we have got that far, people will begin to speak of 'my country, right or wrong', or across the water they will start to sing 'There will always be an England'. And they may well then make a religion out of their patriotism. But the religious man would claim that as and when the disclosure occurs, 'God' is the word appropriate to what is objectively disclosed, where 'God' is a word about which this can be said, that the assertion 'God necessarily exists' stands as an ultimate posit, or presupposition of all the tales I have told of any being. Put differently, just as we move by an informal inference, that is, by an inference within a particular context, from 'Here is a melon' to 'Here is a meal' to 'Here is a dining hall' to 'Here is a college' to 'Here is a state', and so forth, the claim is that in the same sort of way our inference will culminate in 'There is God', when God is the end of our inference spread. With that sort of logical map work, that kind of placing for the word God, we could then say that God declares himself

[5] *Dialogue concerning Natural Religion*, Pt. III (Cleanthes).

to us as each of us to ourselves when each of us knows his own subjectivity. We speak of there being 'one God', as some, like Gilbert Ryle, would speak of 'one world'. Here is some final key concept, one ultimate presupposition. I would suggest, incidentally, that it is by reference to a disclosure as the ground for belief in God that people have said that 'God is the one true subject', or that 'God is not one object among others'. We do not demonstrate God any more that we demonstrate ourselves. He is no object any more than we are wholly objects. We know God in his disclosure of himself.

In order to show that there are countless routes to disclosures and that qualifiers may proceed by either inclusion or exclusion, let us now take a house as a candidate for necessary being. This may seem very plausible because as the builders say, 'All contingencies have been overcome; here is the bill'. But this house, which is of wood, might have been of brick, or it might not have been there at all. Once it wasn't. Still, someone might say, there has always been a hill there. But there was not before the Ice Age. Well, wasn't there at least soil? But perhaps not this soil—only perhaps certain basic elements like carbon, nitrogen, oxygen, or phosphorus; or it may have been just some fundamental particles, or whatever the infinite divisibility of space might yield . . . and that means (you see) endless possibility of playing the game forever. So we see how we might continue the tale, develop whatever model we choose for being, and in whatever way the word 'necessary' suggests, until we reach the point at which a disclosure is evolved, when everything collapses into immediacy, if I may pilfer a phrase from Hegel. Thus the logic of 'God is a necessary being' can be most reliably expressed as

$$\text{necessary (being)} \rightarrow \downarrow \text{ 'God'.}$$

Here 'necessary' has the logic of an operator, a directive, an imperative, so that the assertion is not altogether unlike

$$n \rightarrow \infty \left(\frac{n}{n+1} \right) \rightarrow \downarrow \text{'1'}$$

I do not think that I need now spend long on the elucidation of 'God is infinitely loving'. Here is another assertion with both descriptive and imperative force. 'Loving' is the model: bearing, enduring, hoping, trusting, redeeming, caring for, and so on, which 'infinitely' would develop along the lines of 1 Cor. 13.7. Beareth *all things*, endureth *all things*, always unwavering, unyielding, untiring in reconciliation, we must build out that picture till it discloses God. When we know what the phrase 'infinitely loving' refers to, we know God. Our position indeed concurs with what P. T. Geach says rightly about Aquinas. For Aquinas as indeed for me the phrases 'God', 'the Power of God', 'the Wisdom of God', and so on, all have the same reference. The logic of God is as odd as that.

In this way, then, God is known as disclosing himself, and religious discourse works to 'show' God in this way. Religious assertions thus in part conform to the logic of descriptives, but in part, because of the qualifiers they control, they also display the logic of directives and imperatives, and they are inexpressible in descriptive language. Indeed, the qualifiers gear into models, they intersect with models, like operators or directives gear in the terms in which they relate. Suppose you are in some hall and there at the back is written on the wall the word 'Exit'. Now 'Exit' is in part a very good descriptive word. But supposing you see the word 'Exit' on an absolutely blank wall, with blanks on either side, you remain rooted to the spot. Before you can do anything, there needs to be an arrow added or some doors below. So it is with 'loving' or 'being'. Qualifiers have to be added if they are going to take us to God, if they are to prepare us for a disclosure.

Which leads me, by way of conclusion, to the first of five corollaries.

1   'God is loving', 'God exists', are therefore logically incomplete, as we might say of any third-person assertion about ourselves that it was logically incomplete. Qualifiers are needed for logical completion, so that we more aptly say that God is infinitely loving, God necessarily exists. We don't even say that God is our Father. When we are wise we say that God is our Father Who art in Heaven, and there is qualification enough in that phrase. The first need of a religious assertion, if it isn't going to generate bogus puzzles and unnecessary difficulties, is to be logically complete.

2   It is to models that we must look when we want to be articulate about the mystery to which with the qualifiers they point, which with the qualifiers they enable us to reach. But the fact that we have but models which never exhaust the mystery, models which inevitably provide only partial understandings,

means that sooner or later, inferences from those models become precarious. We then need to balance one model with its associated context against another model with its associated context. Contrariwise, we will always look for more and more adequate models for talking about that mystery which is God. These will be discovered as and when we grade our models and discover super models. Let me illustrate that distinction like this: It is as though we might have talked usefully about something in terms of an ellipse one day, a parabola another, a hyperbola another, a circle another, a pair of straight lines another, a point another. We might then discover a double cone as a super model. Here will be a far more reliable way of talking about what hitherto we have only talked about piecemeal. What we have talked of will be better talked about as a double cone. Similarly, what is talked of in terms of power, wisdom, love, models of one order may be better talked of in terms of the concept of person—a model of a higher order. And, again, we shall be the more reliably articulate about the mystery; the most coherent our discourse is, the more we complete cross-plottings from one model to another. For instance, in the case of God, the models of King and Judge and Power may all lead us to talk of 'protection'. And further and most importantly, at the outposts of our discourse we must connect that discourse with facts and observable behaviour in the world around us. In this way there are various criteria which will test the reliability of our theological understanding about a mystery.

3   Not all qualifiers will be a single word. For instance consider those models contained in such sentences as 'God is a Potter', or 'The Lord is My Shepherd'. Now here the logic is somewhat different and not straightforward. To say 'God is a Potter', or 'The Lord is My Shepherd', we must suppose that God in fact disclosed himself, that the world became alive around the Potter's bench, or the Sheep-fold. But mystery may now be safeguarded, not this time by incorporating a qualifier as a word, though that might be possible, but more usually as in the psalms and hymns, by qualifying with other models in the single discourse. Mystery is now safeguarded by recognizing that to talk adequately of the God who is disclosed on any occasion will need language culled from and growing out of all the models which arise in all the vast variety of circumstances God has been disclosed. So Jesus is spoken of as shepherd, prophet, priest, my husband, friend, and

king. In this kind of way, we see piling up of models, each qualifying the next. This is a rather more rough and ready way of qualifying: by the jostling of models. Here is another less orderly, and more haphazard way of being articulate about a mystery. But it emphasizes from another direction the need to balance one model against another and to be literate only with the greatest circumspection.

4   Having once mentioned Kierkegaard, another reference at this point may not be entirely misplaced. In so far as I have appealed to a disclosure, to something which breaks in on us, to a situation in which we pass beyond any and all the models we have developed to date, when (as *we* say) we 'jump to it', there is involved what might be called logical leap, just as there is a logical leap between seeing '$1 + \frac{1}{2} + \frac{1}{4} + \frac{1}{8} + \frac{1}{16} \ldots$' and saying '2'. So, like Kierkegaard, and Lessing before him, I too can talk of a leap. But for me there is no special reason whatever for thinking of that leap as a leap across what Lessing called a 'grim broad chasm'. For me, it can be pictured not only just as well but I think rather better and more consistently with the rest of our language about God, as a leap into the arms of a loving Father, as a jump to an embrace, an embrace which cannot be wholly and aptly described in terms of muscular grippings with appropriate organic sensations.

5   Let me finally illustrate my theme by reference to angels in reflections which take their cue from Coburn. The word 'angel' is, of all words, probably that one where there is almost an equal danger of making it too intelligible on the other hand or too incomprehensible on the other. To some people the word 'angel' disappears in a fog of mystery and to others the word is so intelligible to be crude. For instance, the angels which walked up and down Jacob's Ladder did not fly (said the boy in his scripture examination) because like his hens they were moulting. 'And how do angels get their jackets over their wings?' asked the down-to-earth coal miner in Warwickshire after listening to a lecture on religious Symbolism. Here you see are people taking angel as a descriptive word and the logical 'Are there angels?' is on logical all fours with the question Are there pygmies? or, are there Himalayan snowmen? But the wings on angels' backs are not supposed to be descriptive of what we see on hens in the farmyard. The wings on an angel's back have the logical function of qualifiers so that the picture of an angel symbolizes a particular encounter with God, and

models it in terms of personal interchange. Because talk of an angel is talk of a personal interchange, we never speak of an angel whose model is like a businessman carrying a briefcase. In other words, the concept of an angel has to be grounded in a situation which discloses God through some particular kind of quasi-personal encounter. What these philosophical reflections suggest is that 'The Angel of the Lord' is a rather more reliable, because logically more complete, phrase to use of these situations. We have to be especially cautious in talking about angels, lest being too articulate, we cease to be religious, like the boy in the scripture examination. To ask whether there are angels is really to ask whether God can be known in particularized circumstances.

Let me now complete my paper by brief reference to another philosopher who, liked Coburn, writes in a very lucid and challenging fashion—Paul Ziff of the University of Pennsylvania. In a paper called 'About God', which Ziff gave to a New York symposium in 1960,[6] he gives his own account of the mixing of the intelligible and the incomprehensible in discourse about God. It has to be understood, he says, by reference to what he calls the Unproblematic Conditions and the Problematic Conditions which characterize God. To quote:

> Some unproblematic conditions are the conditions of being a being, a force, a person, a father, a son, a creator, spatio-temporal, crucified, just, good, merciful, powerful, wise and so forth. I class these conditions as unproblematical, because it seems clear to me that each condition is in fact satisfied or readily satisfiable by something or someone; furthermore, each condition is satisfied or readily satisfiable in a fairly obvious manner.
>
> Some problematic conditions are the conditions of being omnipotent, omniscient, eternal creator of the world, a non-spatio-temporal being, a spirit the cause of itself and so forth. I class these conditions as problematic for this reason. If someone were to maintain that a traditional conception of God is unintelligible, I should think he would base his claim on the prior claim that such conditions as these are fundamentally unintelligible.
>
> All such conditions seem to involve some extreme form either of generalization or abstraction.

[6] *Religious Experience and Truth* (ed. S Hook).

Omniscient, he says, merely generalizes 'the condition of being informed or learned'. Non-spatio-temporal being is an abstraction from the condition of being a spatio-temporal being. He believes that such terms as these are like the high abstractions of a scientific theory which of course is only asking for trouble, as Ziff not surprisingly soon discovers. You will have noticed, though, that this distinction between problematic and unproblematic conditions can in fact be alternatively and further analysed in terms of what I think is the more fundamental distinction between models and qualifiers. But this means that on my view Ziff is wrong in supposing that we have two brands of conditions, for models and qualifiers have not the same logic as this supposition implies. It is not a case of what Ziff calls two conditions differing only in respect to the degree of generalization. The difference between models and qualifiers is something far more radical than that. So I think that the distinction between models and qualifiers not only illuminates Ziff's distinction, I think it also shows where the problem as he expresses it, is bogus, and his account mistaken. But it is true, as he suggests, that the problem of uniting the intelligible and the incomprehensible is the problem of relating what he calls the unproblematical and the problematical conditions which for me becomes the problem of uniting models and qualifiers which I hope I have done something to illuminate here.

The overall lesson to be learned, then, is that if we want to understand language which claims to talk of a mystery, if we want to understand some piece of distinctive religious discourse, we must first pick out the words which are most straightforward and most obviously descriptive. We then look at the other words to see which of them act as qualifiers behaving logically like an imperative to direct us to a disclosure. Every complete religious assertion will thus use words descriptively and also specify a technique by which we may move from 'what is seen' to 'what is seen and more', from the expressible to the point where the expressible becomes part of the inexpressible. Religious assertions will certainly scandalize if descriptive assertions are taken as an ideal of understanding, or if the function of qualifiers is neglected, or if the function of qualifiers is neglected or their logic misread.

The broad conclusion may be expressed alternatively by saying that we must recognize two sorts of 'understanding'. One arises when we use words descriptively; the other arises when we use words which, in Berkeley's phrase, direct us how to act, when we engage in activity directed towards that with which we are descriptively familiar. We are thus like a musician who, on the one hand discursively understands his 'score', but who also in keen devotion gives himself to the playing of it, responding to the disclosure which it has evoked. Theological literacy demands both kinds of assertions.

Now for a brief summary: The problem of understanding mystery is, I said, one of those problems with which contemporary empiricism usefully challenges us. Our response must be (*a*) to elucidate some meaning of 'facts which elude direct statement' and (*b*) to say how this sort of fact can be expressed in language. A case could be made out for such facts, I said, if we considered an illustration which discloses my first-person subjectivity and contrast this with a similar disclosure of objectivity. As currency for such a disclosure, I considered expressions which incorporate models and qualifiers, and I tried to show the ways in which we can then be articulate about a mystery and how we may use the distinction of models and qualifiers to solve the problem of understanding mystery as it is put to us by Ziff. In the next lecture I hope to show how this kind of reflection broadens into the realms of the Gospels and Christian doctrine.

Theological Literacy 2
On Being Articulate about the Gospel

We saw in Lecture 1 that it is to models we must look for the possibility of being articulate, and reliably articulate, about that mystery to which models with their qualifiers point, the mystery to which qualifiers hope to lead us. But that is not the only way in which models and mystery may be supposed to be connected. A disclosure, in the sense I am using that word, may clearly occur without being explicitly generated by qualifiers, as when we suddenly find ourselves in the presence of mystery. Even so, we shall only be articulate about what has been disclosed as and when we somehow relate the disclosure to a model or models which can thereafter be developed. It is still true that if ever we wish to talk of a disclosure, it is to models we must go.

I would like to illustrate and broaden out those reflections by reference to the titles of Jesus. First, let us notice about titles in general that they often incorporate a descriptive phrase specifying some criteria by which in practice a person is normally identified. For instance, we may recall a number of titles given to people in English history, for example, Ethelred the Unready, William the Conqueror, Richard the Lionheart, the Iron Duke, and the Lady with the Lamp. Here, in each case, is a descriptive title merely labelling a particular characteristic of the person in question: the unreadiness of Ethelred to repel invasion; William's part in the Norman conquest of Britain; Richard's courage in the Crusades; the fact that the Duke of Wellington surrounded his London house with iron railings; Florence Nightingale's habit of going around the sick beds of the Crimea nightly with her lamp. Here are titles purely descriptive giving information which might very likely lead to the virtual identification of the particular Florence, Arthur, Richard, William, Ethelred, as the case may be. Here are titles which build up what might be often historical know-all.

Now it seems to me that very often all the titles of Jesus have been given that kind of logic. It is supposed that the point of entitling him Messiah or Son of David or High Priest or Lamb, and so on, is just to single him out more satisfactorily, to afford a more exact characterization, to give him, so to say, a rather better sheet of biographical data calculated to satisfy the most exacting public relations officer. No doubt there are some titles of Jesus whose logic is no different from that. There immediately come to mind titles like 'the Carpenter', or 'the Son of the Carpenter', and perhaps even 'Son of Joseph'. But my contention is that the most significant titles of Jesus are those which incorporate and provide models which are grounded in a disclosure, on the one hand, and enable us to be reliably articulate about the Gospel, on the other. In the first case the point of learning the titles of Jesus would be to extend the theological syllabus, so to say, to contribute to biographical know-all. Nor need we think any the worse of it for that. But in the second case the point of the titles would be to provide a better understanding 'of the disclosure of God' in Christ, and this very different point would be matched by their having an appropriately different logic.

Let me illustrate: Begin by recalling that the Gospel, the good news, arises from a disclosure of God in Christ. That is the disclosure to which, I am saying, the most significant titles of Jesus may be expected to point, and it is about this disclosure that they will enable us to be articulate. Granting that, we may distinguish at least four ways in which the titles of Jesus fulfil those two tasks.

1   The first occurs when and because a particular title of Jesus serves to single out and to spotlight some disclosure which is universally acknowledged among Christians and therefore centrally significant; for that very reason it provides a model or models which thus dominate vast areas of Christian discourse. Probably the most obvious example is the use of the phrase 'the Resurrection and the Life'[1] as a title of Jesus. Such a title implies that the disclosure of God in Christ may be seen, had been seen, preeminently in the Resurrection, in a resurrection-life. Here is a title of central importance incorporating a dominant model. Indeed, so prominent is this model of the resurrection and resurrection-life in Christian theology that the claim has been made by some Christians that the whole of Christian doctrine might be

[1] John 11. 25.

built out from this single starting point. There are some, in other
words, who would trace all Christian discourse back to the resurrection, just as others might articulate the Gospel around a dominant model of salvation and take as their central title of Jesus,
'Redeemer'. Here, then, is the logically most primitive kind of a
title, being one grounded in a disclosure so generally recognized
among Christians as to be considered by some to be pre-eminent
and incorporating so dominant a model as can claim to preside
over the whole spread of the Christian Gospel.

2 Second, there may now seem to arise the obvious possibility
that all the words and phrases that Jesus himself used, in a first-
person assertion on some revealing occasion for instance, 'I am the
Good Shepherd',[2] might provide titles with that same logic and
having that primitive status. But such is not the case. While at
least to some of those present on the original occasion this model
of the Good Shepherd may have had disclosure grounding, that
disclosure will not be automatically preserved in the written word.
From another point of view this is merely to recognize that the
model of the Shepherd which this title incorporates has a much
less dominant status than that of resurrection or Redeemer. In
short, the titles and their models in this second group will somehow have to take on what so far they do not possess, namely,
disclosure point, before they can enable us to be reliably articulate
about the Gospel. And how will the titles in this second group
take on this disclosure point? One possible answer is that the
developed discourse from the title 'Shepherd' at some point or
other might connect with other situations in such a way as to
secure a disclosure grounding. For instance, the Good Shepherd
model, though it may be grounded in no disclosure, at least leads
to articulated discourse, which speaks of the Good Shepherd
laying down his life for the sheep, of there being other sheep
which are not of this fold, of the possibility of their being eventually one flock under one shepherd, and so on. Now that articulated discourse from the model of the shepherd happens at one
point at least, namely, in the phrase 'laying down his life', to
make a sort of tangential contact with the Crucifixion narratives;
and in this way a disclosure may be generated between the two,
just as disclosures are often generated by combining similarity
and differences in a rough and ready way. Here is (we might say)

[2] John 10. 14.

the point behind a 3–D viewer when two pictures, very similar, but slightly and importantly different, come together to create 'depth'. Something like this, I suggest, occurs with this second type of 'title', which perhaps represents the great majority of the titles and name-phrases used in the Gospel narratives themselves. Indeed, it is perhaps not too rash to suppose antecedently that only those titles and name phrases would commonly be used in the Gospel narratives for which in the major events of the Christian dispensation or in the life of the church, a disclosure context could be found—which means that there is a possible variation of this second type of model which perhaps deserves a separate mention. Let me give an illustration. It is well know that such may be found in the Fourth Gospel, in particular where we have discourse of the form 'I am X', when X may be, say, 'The Bread of Life'[3] or 'the Vine'.[4] My point would be that this is not primarily, perhaps not at all, to record what Jesus said, it is not designed to increase the stock of theological know-all, but to give models with the possibility of disclosing God in Christ, a possibility which is actualized when, in this particular case, the models are brought not alongside the crucifixion this time but alongside the Eucharist. But you will notice, I hope, the possibility of an interesting difference from the earlier example of the Good Shepherd, a possibility which makes this case deserve a separate mention. In this case, the Eucharist, the Holy Communion, *may* already be for the contemporary Christian a disclosure situation, whereas the Gospel narrative about the Crucifixion as a crucifixion—just that—may not be. If so, our revised plan of articulation would be this. Here is the word 'vine' finding tangential contact, so far like the earlier case, with the Eucharist through the wine of the Sacrament called by our Lord himself (Mark 14.25 and parallels) 'the fruit of the vine', or through the bread of the Sacrament, 'eating this bread' likewise, and thus finding in the Eucharist an immediate grounding in a disclosure *without having to create it.* Thereafter, the model, like all models, can be developed to enable us to be theologically articulate, and on this particular occasion to be articulate about the church and Christian duty and the Christian life. 'Ye are the branches of the vine, expected to bear much fruit, not to be withered and cast away. . . .' Or, 'As bread

---

[3] John 6.   [4] John 15.

gives life, and sustains the flesh to which it is converted nutritionally, and the flesh fills up the body, so those who eat this bread, who share in this Eucharistic disclosure, will build up the body of Christ, the Church', and so on. My point is that to regard the titles of Jesus in this light is to insure that talk about the church and the Christian life has a genuine basis in God's disclosure in Christ; and from the other side, it insures that the Eucharist, the service of the Holy Communion, is expertly articulated in relation to life and behaviour.

Another instance of how a title incorporates a model which gains its essential disclosure reference, by spreading its discourse until it makes connection with a situation whose disclosure character is already granted, may be seen by reference to the transfiguration. I am supposing, of course, for the sake of argument that the transfiguration story is already granted as evocative of a disclosure; I am supposing that the transfiguration story may be to many evocative of a disclosure when the reading of the crucifixon might not be.[5] Now if the transfiguration be evocative of a disclosure, titles may be used of Jesus which incorporate models which sooner or later establish links with that situation, as when Jesus is spoken of, for example, as 'the Radiance of the Divine glory'. In this way the titles of Jesus may be used to give a logical pattern to that discourse which is Gospel preaching; providing, as they do, models, they will be rightly understood only when they are taken back into disclosures, on the one side, and built out into implications for Christian thought and life and behaviour, on the other.

3   The next group of titles includes those which incorporate a model which already has a disclosure setting, even though it is one which is outside the Christian dispensation. Messiah, for instance, is a title which works in this way. And presumably such a title as 'High Priest', if it were used by a devout Jew, would work likewise. Now here, it seems to me, we have some degree of logical parallel with the cases of the Eucharist and the transfiguration. Messiah or High Priest discourse thus provides promis-

---

[5] If this is challenged, I would not wish to pontificate. All that lies behind my examples is the sense that, while it is all too easy to read the crucifixion narrative as 'mere matter of fact' without disclosure point, if the transfiguration story makes any impact on the reader at all, it is likely to be one exhibiting the mystery and the depth of a disclosure.

ing possibilities of Christian articulation. But it is very important to notice that we have no more than promising possibilities. Unless, somewhere in our development of Messianic or High Priestly discourse, the *inadequacy* of the model is expressly made evident, there will be no chance of a genuine *Christian* Gospel arising from these titles, imbedded as they are in the Old Testament. It was absolutely essential, if we may so say, for our Lord to cap Peter's description of the title of 'Messiah' to him with that of 'Son of Man' which, as I have shown elsewhere, is on our Lord's lips a virtual synonym for the word 'I'.[6] Likewise, I think it was absolutely essential for the writer to the Hebrews to contrast the once-for-allness of our Lord's work with the repetitive character of the High Priest[7] and to contrast the blood of bullocks and goats with that of the crucifixion.[8] In this way a model, such as the Messiah or High Priest, grounded in a divine disclosure, enables us to be articulate about Jesus, but it is essential to display the point of strain if the discourse is to be reliably Christian. So Christian discourse, making use of the title of High Priest, emphasizes that the blood of the crucifixion is not to be regarded exactly as that of a bullock or a goat, that the crucifixion is not repeated annually. In this way, a difference superimposed on a large similarity then evokes a new disclosure. We may call it a second-order disclosure, recognizing that our basic language was already grounded in a disclosure in the Old Testament. So we begin to have an idea of how there may be logical pointers towards the distinctiveness and the uniqueness of the Christian dispensation. All this emphasizes, of course, that to be reliably articulate about the Gospel needs, as a prior condition, that the full disclosure basis of every model is realized. Talk about Jesus as the Messiah or High Priest will not, merely as such, even begin to enable us to be reliably articulate about the Gospel. For this, such titles must already have had a disclosure setting, and in these two cases must soon also possess a new one. Yet I fear that for very many people a disclosure setting is what these titles are never given in the Old Testament, let alone in the New. People may know all details about temple worship; they may know all about Old Testament ideas of Messiahship. But not for many

[6] See *Religious Language*, pp. 137–44.
[7] Heb. 10. 10; 9. 24–7; and *passim*.
[8] Heb. 9. 11–14, and *passim*.

does Messiah discourse or talk about a High Priest have the dis-closure setting it must have even to begin to be illuminating about Christian Gospel, let alone to be able to complete the job.

The reader is not likely to think, I believe, that I underestimate the difficulty of the task of bringing some kind of logical order into that variegated discourse which is Christian teaching and preaching. So let me single out at least one further complexity. We have seen how the title 'the resurrection and the life' might be given a fully adequate Christian setting from the start. But for some it *might* conceivably be a case of this third type of title. Suppose, for instance, a divine disclosure had already occurred, as it plainly did for Moses, around the phrase 'I am'.[9] Then we should have a disclosure attached to the phrase 'I am', to which phrase a title of Jesus is subsequently annexed to give the asser-tion: 'I am the Resurrection and the Life'. The oddity of this annexation might well then generate a second-order disclosure, enabling the Jewish reader to see the point of the Christian resur-rection narratives when the Christian title phrase would now lead to distinctive Christian articulation. Such articulation would not be about that immorality or eternal life to which with great difficulty the Old Testament moved and which might be linked, later than sooner, with the Mosaic theophany. It would now be about eternal life in Christ Jesus our Lord, something as distinc-tively Christian as that. The example may seem intricate and complex, but at least it suggests that the language of the Bible is rich and complex enough to benefit from a variety of logical insights.

4   Finally, in this matter of titles, I might mention a sort of natural parallel to the Old Testament case we have just noticed. A title may be used of Jesus which has its model grounded in a natural disclosure of a cosmic kind. For instance, suppose some-one has waited through a weary night, cold and tired—like air-craft observers in England in the days of the last war. He sees the first promise of dawn, the bright and morning star, the herald of a new day. The universe breaks into life, a disclosure occurs, we 'see' and respond. Here, as will be recognized, is one of the best-known natural models in terms of which the Gospel has often been made articulate. Think of the advent message: 'the night is far spent', 'the day is at hand', 'the Lord is nigh'. Or the

---

[9] Exod. 3. 14.

Benedictus speaking of 'the dayspring from on high' which 'hath visited us', 'to give light to those who sit in darkness and . . . death and to guide our feet into the ways of peace'. Here is articulation going back to a natural disclosure. We even recall the incorporation of cognate discourse in familiar hymns. As and when the passing of an eclipse evokes a disclosure like that which occurs at the dawn of a new day, so that we come again to life as the cold darkness gives way to the light of the sun and then, and only then, when we have in fact witnessed a total eclipse ourselves, or have enough imagination to put ourselves in that position, can we sing significantly, as expressing the Gospel, 'lo! the sun's eclipse is o'er'.[10] Once again my point is that this line in the hymn does not merely provide us with a colourful metaphor; it is not just a display of literary spaciousness but a Christian articulation which we only understand as speaking of the Gospel when we give the phrase a full and adequate mapping. In this connection it is interesting and important to recognize that just as, for example, the Messiah model from the Old Testament had to receive its Christian baptism anew, so in this hymn the natural model of the sun emerging from an eclipse must give rise to sun discourse which speaks *inter alia* of the redness of the setting sun, whose redness is then linked with the blood of the crucifixion, so that discourse is now created which, beginning with a grounding in a natural disclosure, takes on a distinctively Christian point: 'Lo, he sets in blood no more/Lo, the sun's eclipse is o'er!' How intricate, but how worthwhile, the plotting of the logic of a hymn may be. It is even possible that some of the most appalling hymns may yet conceal a complex logic which once revealed enables them to be reliably articulate about the Christian Gospel. Make no mistake; I do not say, of course, that every hymn writer consciously and deliberately followed the kind of intricate logical pattern that I have tried to put before you; nor am I suggesting that we need to explicate the intricate pattern for those parishioners or members of our churches to whom a hymn already makes its point. But I do say that here is the kind of intricate pattern which some of us have got to trace when we are challenged to state a case for our faith, and to elucidate the significance of what to many of our contemporaries is the mere verbiage of our message.

[10] See Charles Wesley's Easter hymn.

No doubt during this discussion, many of you will have been recalling Vincent Taylor's *The Titles of Jesus*, and it may help to make my over-all point clearer if I set it in relation to what he himself says of the titles of Jesus. After surveying some fifty phrases of great variety, Vincent Taylor writes: 'The question, who Jesus is, is approached best by considering how men named Him, for it is by His names that He is revealed and known.'[11] What I have been trying to do is to show what a complex logic has to be given to the names of Jesus; nevertheless, if they *are* to *reveal* Christ rather than merely to extend his biographical data sheet, if they are to tell us more about him than just who he is, I have suggested that the titles of Jesus, if they are to have this fuller significance, must be seen as incorporating models grounded in disclosure whose articulation possibilities extend to a wide area of Christian life and behaviour. We miss the point if we suppose that the various titles of Jesus merely provide us with so many extra descriptions, extra theological know-all.

Again, Vincent Taylor says, on page 70:

Originally, Messianic, the title [The Son] reveals the Messianic idea in eclipse. Doubtless, one and the same meaning is not always to be found whenever the terminology is applied to Jesus. Sometimes the meaning is Messianic, but for the most part, and even in the words of the Divine Voice at the Baptism, it is Messianic with a plus. And the plus is a significant thing. When the Fourth Evangelist writes, 'these are written, that ye might believe that Jesus is the Christ, the Son of God' (John 20:31) all that is left of Jewish Messianic teaching is the language. And when St. Paul says that 'in the fullness of time God sent forth his Son' (Gal. 4.4) we have passed far beyond the idea of a divinely commissioned national deliverer to the thought of One who comes to our world from the depths of the being of God.

So I too have earlier reminded you that if the title of Messiah is to be given any distinctively Christian position, the inadequacy of its discourse must somewhere, somehow or other, be made evident, and this at a point where a second-order disclosure may then supervene. Once again, I have just tried to supply

[11] Vincent Taylor, *The Titles of Jesus*, p. 1.

a logical mapping for the conclusions which Vincent Taylor reaches as a New Testament scholar.

Vincent Taylor continues:

> When we attempt to say just how much is to be read into this terminology, we are baffled; but the reason is undoubted. The situation is not one in which a clearly defined label, with a meaning known to all, is being used in its application to the man Jesus. The reverse is true.
>
> A man revered, loved and worshipped is described by a terminology which bends and cracks under the strain, because it is being used to describe a unique person, and therefore to serve an end for which, humanly speaking, it was not intended from the standpoint of its history. Divinity is felt before it is named, and when it is named, the words are inadequate. And this situation obtains throughout the long history of Christology. First the perception, then the halting words, and then the despairing attempt to find better words. When at length the decisive word of Nicaea is spoken, all we can say is that this is the best that men can do. And if it should be given to modern theology to speak better words, more accordant with the thought of our time, we may be sure that our constructions will run but lamely after a knowledge of Christ which antiquates them almost before they are framed. Christology is the despairing attempt of theologians to keep pace with the Church's apprehension of Christ.

We may be a little nervous about terminology's being said to 'describe' and about his metaphor which speaks of words bending and cracking under the strain. For this they will only do, I think, if they have ever been supposed to be adequate *descriptions*; and I confess that I suspect that this idea that titles are somehow better or worse descriptions also lies behind Vincent Taylor's view, as he expresses it in another place—that there might be some kind of permanent progress in getting better titles. Are better titles more perfect descriptions? If I am right, they are not. Every model grounded in a disclosure and having articulation possibilities may be welcomed at all times. But this is what, on the whole, Vincent Taylor is saying. All that Nicaea or any of the Councils did was to try to do some cross-plotting to bring order and coherence into the discourse that had been derived

D

from the various models used to speak of the person of Christ. They did their best. But their phrases demanded for their very intelligibility a passage back to Christ, no matter how complex. Their phrases needed (and need) that contextual routing if their discourse was (and is) to be a genuine contribution to the Gospel, if their formulas were (and are) to be genuinely Christian.

Vincent Taylor says elsewhere in his book that the Christological titles 'sum in a name what is in reality a process of thought'. A little later he continues: 'The names form the teaching and express what was believed and taught'. My own interpretation of those remarks would be that the names are models, from which are indeed to be articulated all our teachings. The model which a title incorporates does 'sum up', as it presides over a process of thought. But to make their point, to express 'what was believed', those titles and their models must by this very summation point to a disclosure as that in which all articulation will find its basis, and I have suggested four possible ways in which this could be possible.

Before leaving this first section, let us consider, because of its general interest, one more question which Vincent Taylor raises. He points out that with one exception, namely, that of the Redeemer, Christians never have added other names to the titles of Jesus. Why? Why has the church never added other names to the traditional titles of Jesus? Now behind his discussion of this topic Vincent Taylor seems to imply some sort of logical finality and ultimacy about the traditional names. For me, this would obviously imply some finality about the associated models. But surely no veto can be placed on the logical possibility of other titles for Jesus. Whether or not a new title is valuable will entirely depend, according to me, first on its disclosure grounding and second on its articulation possibilities, by reference to which it makes better or worse contact with the world around us.[12] What we undoubtedly recognize about Vincent Taylor's examples of the poverty of recent names, for example, the Elder Brother, or The Master (to take but two of the examples he gives) is that, while they have undeniable links with the world around us, their disclosure possibilities seem very minimal. That is, I suggest, the reason why they fail to attract Vincent Taylor, as it is certainly

[12] As we shall see in particular by reference to the doctrine of the Ascension.

the reason why they fail to attract us. Recalling what I said earlier,[13] it is significant that in this same group he puts 'The Carpenter', which is, I have suggested, so much a down-to-earth title as to be perhaps no more (and no less) significant than any piece of biographical data. But granted all that, why should we ever suppose that logically speaking we have exhausted all possible insights and all articulation possibilities? Yet that would be presupposed by any idea that there could be no new names for Jesus.

It might perhaps help to clarify my own presentation as well as to set it in a wider persective if, in rounding off this section, I indicate where my views echo those of another theologian, Karl Barth, no matter how vastly different may be our standpoints on the reasonableness of the Christian faith. Reflecting on Barth's answer to the question as to where our certainty about Christian faith rests, it is, he says, 'in reference to the Living Jesus Christ himself'.[14] And what do I say?—that it is to be found by reference to the disclosure of God in Christ which here and now can and must be the basis for all Christian talking. As for theological literacy, Barth remarks:

> Even what we have tried to say in development and confirmation (of our views) . . . must not be understood as a substitute for the guarantee which is given in and with Jesus Christ himself, but only as an attempt to explain and concretely to describe it.

I would say: 'only as an attempt to develop various models'. Barth continues:

> None of the lines of presentation along which we have explained the superiority of Jesus Christ and the certainty awakened by it, can pretend to be this superiority or to give this certainty in itself. . . . Our own explanatory and confirmatory argumentations can be effective, illuminating and helpful only insofar as they point to Him, and He Himself places Himself behind (them) . . . Himself awakening, establishing, creating and maintaining certainty.

Plainly, I like this emphasis on 'lines of presentation', which I

[13] See p. 77 above.
[14] *Church Dogmatics*, IV, Pt. 3, first half, 274.

would interpret as different patterns of discourse developed from various models. I, too, could say that argumentation is illuminating and helpful only in so far as it points to God's disclosure of himself in Christ, and I gladly say with Barth that as currency for what Christ himself declares in a disclosure 'even the best theology can only stammer after him [for example] . . . Jesus the Victor'.

About that very title, 'Jesus is Victor', Barth has said earlier in the book: 'I have chosen as the title for this subsection the statement', and then he significantly makes an important change, 'or rather the challenge Jesus is Victor', for, he emphasizes, 'the statement . . . is really to be heard and read as a challenge'. Notice that it is not to be read as a statement, as a characterizing description like William 'the Conqueror' or the 'Iron' Duke. It is to be read, and I agree, as evocative of a disclosure which is articulated in victory discourse. 'Jesus is Victor' is, says Barth, 'the first and last and decisive word to be said in this respect'. I would interpret this as saying that, for Barth, it is considered to be that model which best presides over our articulated discourse, and to which Christian discourse leads back; it is for Barth the model which best expresses the 'decisiveness', the challenge, of God's disclosure in Christ.

No more with Barth than with Kierkegaard would I want to give the impression that my position is identical with his. But I thought it useful to notice where our views come alongside each other and have significant echoes. Both of us emphasize the exploratory tentative character of all discourse developed from models; the reference to the discourse is primarily to the disclosure to which the models point; and the discourse will always find its relevance by contact with our empirical situation.[15]

In order to make clearer the practical pastoral implication of what I have been saying, I now pass in a second section to a topic—the ascension—where our articulation of the Gospel is hazardous in the extreme and where it is very hard to be theologically literate in the way that the man in the Chicago Loop can understand. Certainly to very many believers and unbelievers the ascension is altogether enigmatical. As is well known, the Gospel speaks with neither a single nor a clear voice. Further, such

---

[15] It is perhaps worth saying that where we would differ is in the different views we would take of the 'authority' of certain models.

uncertainty and variation are matched by the fact that no one seems to know how or when the commemoration of Ascension Day began. I do not think any of the designations, for example, 'Επισωσομένη, that we can discern in the early history of liturgy have ever been satisfactorily explained. From early days to our own times, Ascension Day has had its difficulties.[16] Two days after Ascension Day last year, the London *Times* made these comments in an article:

> There is perhaps no point in the Church calendar at which the failure of communication is more obvious or more unfortunate. To the man in the street, the day means very little and even to many inside the churches it appears to make but a limited appeal. . . . Its highly symbolic picture language [can be so easily taken] to mean almost the opposite of what the Church is in fact trying to say.

'Failure of communication', 'the day means very little', 'highly symbolic picture language'—there is probably no festival about which we need to learn how to be more reliably articulate. Unless we have some idea of how we are using language here and to talk about what, many will suppose that this is just another of those theological extravaganzas, those large-scale pretences, if you like, that constantly compromise our witness and apologetic and scandalize our agnostic friends. As Professor H. J. Paton remarks in his book *The Modern Predicament*: 'The currency of theological thinking may have its own inflationary spiral.' As a particular warning he says: 'One of the strongest tendencies of modern times is to reject or belittle the historical facts and yet to construct a dogmatic theology very similar to the old.' This is the way that some essays in theological literacy strike our agnostic brethren. Now what I hope to do in this second section of the lecture is to show that we can reliably articulate about the ascension by regarding the word 'ascension' as a model born in a moment of insight, in an occasion of disclosure, and that a full defence and apologia for ascension theology will depend on our making that disclosure origin clear, on the one hand, and also, on the other hand, our showing how the model comes to have an empirical

[16] E.g. in one of the earliest Ascension Day sermons (late fourth century), Epiphanius complains that the greatness of the festival is not duly appreciated.

fit as and when ascension discourse has application to life and behaviour.

Let it be granted from the start that no one is ever likely now to have a detailed picture of what happened on that first Ascension Day. But that there must have been something to distinguish that parting from all the other partings is obvious, or the occasion would not have been especially remembered at all. What could that significant difference have been? Granted that our Lord appeared to his disciples many times after his crucifixion and his death, and many times had parted from them, it follows, as is well recognized, that a mere parting is not the point of the ascension. It was not just another disappearance, another parting, but such a parting as was full of significance; such a parting as had the distinctive point of a disclosure. How can we be articulate about this point? The first answer would be that here was a promised assurance of power, and at once the aptness of this answer is evident. In making a promise, a person affirms his existence, so that we speak, in the context of a promise, of a man being 'as good as his word'. A promise, in fact, registers more than rule-bound behaviour. Promises are well-recognized examples of disclosures.

Now normally we are articulate about a promise-disclosure in terms of its fulfilment; a promise embodies a pattern which is later empirically verified as the promise is kept. From this point of view we can perhaps see why the ascension is often absorbed in Whitsunday, and consequently has a very uncertain status of its own.

But Whitsunday had its own cosmic disclosure. Could we then be more specifically articulate about the disclosure of Ascension Day? Whitsunday aside, can we be further articulate about the promise-disclosure? Then we recall that not only was a promise made but also it was a promise made on parting. We had, so to say, nearly forgotten the distinctive feature of the ascension story from which we began. How could the disciples do justice to a parting-disclosure that was associated with a promise of power? How, then, were they to be articulate about this disclosure? I suggest that there were two ways by which the model of ascension became the basis of articulation. First, this situation had certain features—partings associated with empowerings—which were echoed by other situations in the Old Testament from which the model of ascension was readily derived. Second, the model of ascension may have impressed itself because it was already embodied in some of the most significant natural disclosure situations which the disciples had known. There was, in other words, the possibility of giving either a natural or a revealed defence of the ascension model, and it may be noticed that parallels to these two possibilities may be found in the third and fourth sections of our discussion of the titles of Jesus. Let me now discuss these two possibilities in a little more detail.

There were, in the Old Testament, the well-known stories of Enoch and Elijah, respectively. Enoch walked with God and then was not, because God took him.[16] A parting, a taking-up and, as the Epistle to the Hebrews would suggest,[17] Noah is empowered to succeed Enoch as a hero of faith. Here was another parting associated with a later empowering, one like that which the apostles had known. But there was an even closer fit in II Kings, chapter 2, Elijah and Elisha were walking together, and Elijah, we read, was taken up by a whirlwind into heaven. Elisha before this had been a ploughman with twelve yoke of oxen, and, in the words of Ecclesiasticus,[18] we might well have expected his discourse to be confined to the stock of bulls. His heart might well have been centred on turning his furrows and giving his heifers their fodder. But Elisha was now someone of whom the sons of the prophets which were at Jericho could say that the spirit of Elijah rested upon Elisha. After the taking up of Elijah, Elisha had been empowered with a power and vitality not his own. Noah and Enoch; Elisha and Elijah—in each case a parting and an empowering. Here were stories which matched and echoed the disciples' own situation and their own stirrings of heart. But now we must notice, for this is the important point, that these were stories whose dominant theme, whose crucial centre was an ascension. This was the model they purveyed; and so it was in terms of this model of ascension that the disciples began to understand what had happened on their own occasion; to understand and to plot a mystery for which in the end all talk will be inadequate. How did they do it?

It was soon discovered that the ascension model contained many

[16] Gen. 5. 22–4.   [17] Heb. 11. 5–7.   [18] Eccles. 38. 25, 26.

possibilities of articulated discourse, many possibilities of explication as well as being grounded, as it must be for theological
literacy, in a disclosure setting.

But there is one major difficulty to be faced before we look at
some exercises in articulation. Do I suppose that the model of
ascension had any basis in fact, or was it merely a dominant
image? Meanwhile, it might be said that, if our congregations
and the man in the Chicago Loop are going to be affronted by the
geophysical features of the ascension, they are hardly likely to
welcome, or to think the matter is made more reasonable by
introducing further talk of whirlwinds and ascensions in the
Old Testament. Nor are we more, but much less, likely to have
detailed pictures of what happened to Enoch or between Elisha
and Elijah than we are to have details of the first Ascension Day.
To meet these and similar difficulties, let us begin by reminding
ourselves that the primary and most significant features of all
these situations are partings followed by and associated with empowerings, and that the importance of the ascension model is
that it registers a union and interlocking of those two themes
within a disclosure. To answer the question raised above and to
face these various difficulties, all we then need suppose, but admittedly *must* suppose if we are not going to be disingenuous and to
make a hollow pretence, is what were *some* observable features of
those various situations for which talk of an ascension was appropriate currency. *What* in detail and for certain these features
were, I doubt whether we shall ever know. Certainly I, myself,
do not know. But as the disciples looked back on this parting
associated with an empowering, I am suggesting that besides
there being obvious echoes of the Enoch and Elisha disclosures,
there must also have been some observable features of some kind
which fit the Old Testament theme of ascension and enable the
disciples to be articulate about that Christian occasion they themselves have known.

Is it possible to say anything more about these observable features? I think we may be helped a little if we begin to consider
what we called the natural disclosure which might lie behind the
ascension model. Even the man in the Chicago Loop may recall
partings he has known, whether in the street, at the railway station,
on the dockside, or at an airport. A friend goes farther and farther
away as he walks, or more rapidly as the train, the ship, or the

aircraft departs. Details of clothes and face get less and less distinct. They either merge into the street and its buildings or they merge into the vehicle, and the vehicle into its background, until all disappears. But just at that point, when all seems to disappear and be lost, does it not sometimes happen that there breaks in on us, there comes a disclosure of a constant presence? We know our friend, we know him to be present, as we have not realized him before. It is a proximity and a presence which physical proximity and presence have somehow kept from us. Further, in all these situations there is an element of 'ascension'. Even if it is not obvious,[19] it will always exist, if only because all our perspectives point to the centre of our visual field, so that those leaving us seem always spatially to 'rise'. We may perhaps begin to see how naturally Jesus could be understood as disclosing himself as he parted, and in parting, ascending. We may well broaden the argument and recall that very many of our most significant experiences, other 'natural disclosures', are associated with the theme of ascension, even when this is understood quite literally as the climbing of stairs or a ladder. It has been said that 'the act of climbing or ascending . . . arouses an ambivalent feeling of fear and of joy, of attraction and repulsion'[20] which is typical of the religious man. Here is the *mysterium tremendum et fascinans*— our sense of the holy. It occurs when, climbing the spiral staircase in the lighthouse, we are fearful and yet thrilled. The boy wants to run up; he also wants to come down: repelled yet attracted, dismayed yet empowered. Or still more striking is that combination of terror and fascination that combines to make mountain climbing that high religious pursuit which it is. Many students must think it significant that the dean's room is often at the top of a staircase. So it is often around the image of climbing or ascending that our most profound and impressive and memorable experiences occur. Certainly it would not be surprising if the last memory which the disciples had of our Lord on earth was epitomized in the idea of an ascension. Only, if we are not to be

[19] As in the case of aircraft.

[20] Mircea Eliade, *Images and Symbols*, p. 51. Professor Eliade also remarks that 'Julien Green notes, in his Journal for the 4th of April, 1933, that "in all my books, the idea of fear or of any other fairly strong emotion seems linked in some inexplicable manner to a staircase"', and so dramatic events—love, death, crime—often happen on a staircase.

disingenuous, it must be true that amongst all the complex features of the situation on that day, there were some which could
provide the basis in fact for an ascension model by which the
disciples could begin to understand and talk about that whole
situation in its overwhelming significance.

I now return to the question we deferred some time ago.
Granted that we have seen how the ascension model fits the disclosure; granted that we have reason to think it could have *some*
basis in fact—how can the ascension model, then, help us to
articulate Christian discourse? Let me give two examples of how
articulation is made possible.

First, whatever we think of mountain climbing or ascending
stairs, whatever novels we read or like, all of us must recognize
the aptness of the ascension model in phrases which speak of our
hearts being 'lifted up', our hopes 'raised', and so on. We may
drop our eyes in shame and shyness, but to lift the eyes always expresses trust and joy. So to talk of the events at Bethany in terms
of the ascension model is to talk of something meant to inspire
and to raise us. It is to create a context of inspiration which makes
it possible to use of Ascension Day such phrases as you will
find in the appropriate Collect in the liturgy of the Church of
England: 'Grant that we may in heart and mind thither ascend,
and with him continually dwell.' What I am saying is that if that
prayer is going to be a genuine and distinctive Christian prayer
appropriate to Ascension Day, there must be logical strands
relating the lifting of hearts and minds to an ascension model,
and insuring that that ascension model is grounded in a disclosure
contect such as St Luke[21] intends to portray.

For a second example let us set the ascension model in another
context: the context of the king's throne or the victor's saluting
base. Such a context makes logically possible the most complex
kind of developed discourse about the ascension, such as we find
in chapter 4 in Ephesians. There, the ascension model is set in the
context of Psalm 68, a psalm associated with the victorious conqueror, the kind of psalm which always appeals to an Oliver
Cromwell or a Viscount Montgomery. Now in that psalm, verse
18, may be read: 'Thou art gone up, ascended on high, thou hast
led captivity captive, and received gifts from men.' Talk of the
ascension now interlocks with the story of a conqueror, a con-

[21] Acts 1. 4–11. Cf. Luke 24. 50–3.

queror king with his captive prisoners, who receives gifts from
the captured. And now we recall that the 'victory' of Jesus was
over death, and ironically enough the victorious Christ had already
received in full measure death's gift—itself. All this is, so to say,
absorbed by the text of chapter 4 in Ephesians, which concludes
the quotation with a significant change: 'he *gave* gifts to men'.
We do not account for the textual difference by supposing that
Paul's memory of the text failed him at this point, or that he
displayed a sort of inspired carelessness. Rather was he building
out the discourse as the spirit moved him. It is indeed relevant to
recall that there are old Jewish interpretations of the psalm which
remind us how Moses, who *ascended* into the firmament, gave the
words of the law and gifts to men. Or we might say that Paul
jumped to the theme of the next verse, Psalm 68.19: 'Blessed be
the Lord who daily beareth our burden: God is our salvation.'
So this victor, this conquering King, received our gifts which
were burdens, and gave genuine gifts to us instead: God's salvation. He received all we had earned—death; and gave us the
free gift, called alternatively 'grace' and 'eternal life in Christ
Jesus our Lord'. In this way, the model of ascension, using Psalm
68 for its development, supplemented maybe by other specimens
of cognate discourse, makes it possible for us to have an articulate
theology of the ascension which combines the two themes of
Christ the King and Christ the Saviour. Nay more; the resultant
discourse, like all reliable theologizing, now makes possible
some sort of empirical relevance, some sort of tie-up with facts.
It is not mere word-spinning. For the gifts he gave are vocational:
'He gave some to be apostles, some prophets, some evangelists,
some pastors and teachers.'[22] This is not the abstract catalogue
of gifts we have in the Epistle to the Romans,[23] where it is prophecy, ministry, and teaching. Here the primary emphasis is on
ourselves. So the final test of our talk about the ascension will
lie in the extent to which the discourse to which the model leads
can find empirical relevance in our life and behaviour. We are
reliably articulate about the ascension when our discourse points
through the model to the disclosure in one direction, and informs
our vocations in the other.

If I am asked how all this differs from a traditional view, when
it seems (as it does) to preserve so many of the traditional ways of

[22] Eph. 4. 11.   [23] Rom. 12. 6–7.

talking, I would answer as follows. What I have tried to do has been to plot the pattern of Christian discourse about the ascension so as to make clear, on the one hand, its empirical anchorage in a disclosure, and, on the other, the way in which we become reliably articulate. What should be evident is that talk about the ascension is no plain descriptive story. It is the development of a model in a way which, while it points to the significance and mystery of a disclosure situation, it also makes possible reasonable and empirically relevant discourse.

We shall, I think, always err if we develop our theology as though its assertions were descriptive and linked by tight deductions. Sheer frankness compels me to admit that this seems to be the character of the argument in 1 Thess. 4. 16–17. If Christ ascended, the argument goes, 'then the Lord himself shall descend from heaven . . . and the dead in Christ shall rise first, then we that are alive shall together with them be caught up in the clouds to meet the Lord in the air . . .'. What I am saying is how difficult it is for us to give to this argument such a pattern as makes it evocative of a disclosure, on the one hand, and empirically relevant, on the other. Here is someone being too articulate about the ascension.[24]

These lectures, as I said, are concerned to show how we can speak reliably about a mystery—how we can be theologically articulate, but not so articulate that we deny the very mystery which is basic to religion. In this lecture I have tried to show how the titles of Jesus are not to be understood as though their point was merely to increase our Lord's biographical data sheet. Even though this point may be given to some of the titles of Jesus, perhaps, e.g., 'Son of Joseph' or 'the Carpenter', nevertheless, I have argued, all the significant titles of Jesus will be those which are grounded in a disclosure, and enable us, in various ways, to be reliably articulate about the Gospel; to be articulate about God's disclosure in Christ in such a manner as always to relate it to the particularities of life and behaviour.

We then considered whether the church might add new titles

---

[24] We might develop the point like this. In the context of 1 Thess. 4. 16–17 someone might legitimately ask: 'What about my checked baggage?' at once revealing a routine-bound context for air travel, a denial of disclosures, and giving the discourse such empirical relevance as makes it cosmologically incredible.

to those already in use for Jesus, and I set out conditions on which I thought that new titles might be possible and profitable, a *sine qua non* for this being their unmistakable grounding in a disclosure and their embodiment of new articulations.

Last, I passed to a consideration of the ascension, recognizing that 'there is perhaps no point in the Church calendar at which the failure of communication is more obvious or more unfortunate'. What I have tried to do has been to show how we may become better aware of the logical game we are playing when we develop theological discourse by the model of the ascension: how the model arises in a moment of disclosure and enables us to be articulate in such a way that there arises a Christian narrative with practical implications, and in particular for our Christian vocations.

It may seem that I have only stressed the obvious, and in one sense I grant that what I have said is something whose conclusions everybody knew all along. But what I have tried to do as a frontiersman, constantly challenged to give a reason for the faith that is in me, is to give such an account of the language we habitually use as makes it appear to the unbeliever less of a jungle of crisscrossed verbiage than it is wont to do. What I have tried to do has been to plot some ways, however intricate, through this jungle—to try to show better how we have been talking when we have been talking theologically and to suggest points where it would have been better if we had stopped. And here for the moment, I do.

Paradox in Religion

I

In *Reasons and Faiths* Ninian Smart, after quoting a characteristic assertion from the *Iśa Upaniṣad*: 'It is both far and near; It is within all this and it is outside all this', remarks that such 'paradoxical pronouncements fulfil such a number of functions that by understanding the gist of them one can penetrate to the heart of the philosophy of religion'.[1] In *Christianity and Paradox* Dr Ronald Hepburn considering more practically theism, comments that 'paradoxical and near-paradoxical language is the *staple* of accounts of God's nature and is not confined to rhetorical extravaganzas'.[2] It seems then as if religious discourse not only revels in paradox but considers it illuminating. Here seem to be, if anywhere, what Professor John Wisdom would call revealing improprieties.[3]

But such reflections lead directly to the question with which I shall be concerned in this paper: can we do anything to distinguish illuminating and revealing improprieties from those which merely bewilder and confound us? It is a question which Hepburn himself raises early in his book: 'When is a contradiction not a *mere* contradiction, but a sublime Paradox, a mystery?' Though Hepburn has a number of constructive suggestions to make I think he would say that for the most part the religious discourse he examines displays vicious muddle rather than revealing improperties, so we are still left with the question on our hands. What Hepburn has done is to make the question all the more urgent and challenging. If certain paradoxes preserve and reveal something, what do they reveal, and how? Can we give any clues by which to recognize illuminating improprieties, revealing absurdities?[4] For our present purpose and without claiming that

---

[1] *Reasons and Faiths*, Ninian Smart. Kegan Paul, p. 20.

[2] *Christianity and Paradox*, Ronald W. Hepburn. Watts, p. 16.

[3] *Philosophy and Psycho-analysis*, John Wisdom. Blackwell, p. 112.

[4] Cp. Professor Gilbert Ryle who concludes his article on *Categories* in *Logic and Language* (2nd series), ed. A. G. N. Flew, Blackwell, p. 81, with the question: 'What are the tests of absurdity?'

our classification is either definitive or exhaustive but merely an attempt to bring some sort of order into a vast and complex topic, let us begin by distinguishing the following brands of paradox: First, there is what we might call *avoidable paradox* which spotlights some confusion or other, as for example when a blunder in argument leads to a plain and obvious self-contradiction. Since the muddle can often be cleared up by retracing the steps of our argument, and since (at best) it may have a useful negative point to make, we might speak of this brand of avoidable paradox as *retrospectively negative.*

On the other hand, there is paradox which, while it is avoidable, is only avoided when we are led forward to a new assertion which somehow arises out of the two original assertions. Since there thus arises some positive significance from the paradox, as and when it is resolved, we may say that it is *subsequently significant.* This is the case with an antimony (as with Kant) and with dialectic in general, but not, I think, with Hegelian dialectic in particular. For with Hegel, while any paradox of thesis and antithesis was resolvable in a synthesis, this immediately generated another paradox waiting to be resolved. So the Hegelian dialectic would be a better example of unavoidable paradox claiming to have some sort of rational structure.

This brings us to our second group: *unavoidable paradox.* The significance of such paradox (it would be claimed) arises from and is bound up with its permanence and unavoidability. But within this group there arises the possibility of an important sub-division. Such unavoidable paradox may have a discernible, if curious, structure in virtue of which it becomes revealing; alternatively, the paradox may permit of no such structure being discerned. The paradox will then be permanent without permitting of any logical examination or assessment and we might call it (*b*) *logically inaccessible,* to distinguish it from the former brand which we might call (*a*) *logically explorable.*

What I propose to do in this paper is to examine cases of paradox in religion which fall into each of these two categories and their two subdivisions.

II

Let us look first at what we have called avoidable paradox which is retrospectively negative, and begin with two examples from non-religious discourse.

1   An example which Ryle gives: the child finding it a paradox that 'the Equator can be crossed but not seen', for whatever can be crossed, like roads, bridges, hills, can generally be seen. Here paradox arises because of a failure to distinguish cartographical language and physical object language. But the paradox might also arise as a declaration that, having distinguished these two languages, we are at a loss as to how to relate them.

2   As a second example take the assertion: 'Since all roots inevitably benefit from treatment with ammonium nitrate, so then must the roots of quadratics.' But obviously the roots of quadratics cannot be treated with nitrate. Here is self-contradiction which arises from failing to recognize that here are two different uses of the token 'root'. Once we recognize this, it is clear that the paradox is sheer absurdity, and its negative point of little value.

Now religious discourse includes examples of paradox which may be regarded as of this negative and resolvable kind, and we will try to give parallel examples to the two we have just given.

1   As an example of religious paradox closely similar to the Equator case, let us recall an aphorism of William Temple's, 'I believe in the Holy Catholic Church and sincerely regret that it does not at present exist.'[5] Compare: 'I believe I can cross the Equator, but regret that it does not exist to be seen.' Here is paradox all right. But once again it has only a negative point to make, viz. that the word 'Church' used in a credal profession, and the word 'Church' used of a visible community, belong to two different logical areas. The problem of their relationship it leaves on our hands.

2   As with our second general example, let us now take a case of religious paradox which displays sheer confusion and utter muddle. I am bold to say that this seems to me to occur at a certain stage in the development of Trinitarian doctrine as H. A. Wolfson describes it.[6] He argues that in Judaism there was a pre-existent Wisdom and a pre-existent Messiah, though (he says) the two were never identified. We might have expected that to be a merit,

[5] *Life of William Temple*, F. A. Iremonger, p. 387, quoted by P. Hartill, *The Unity of God*, p. 139, and called (rightly) 'a paradoxical bit of rhetoric intended to focus attention on the sin of disunion'.
[6] *The Philosophy of the Church Fathers*, H. A. Wolfson, O.U.P.

for how could we ever *identify* the ideas of Wisdom and Messiah? We could point at a Messiah once he appeared, but could we ever point in the same way at Wisdom? A Messiah exists in time and might pre-exist before birth, but how can we talk in the same way about existent and pre-existent wisdom? However, nothing daunted, it was to Paul's credit (says Wolfson) to identify pre-existent Wisdom with the pre-existent Messiah and to use these terms interchangeably. Nor was that all. 'While there is no explicit identification in Paul of the Holy Spirit and the pre-existent Messiah, he undoubtedly identified them.' Further, in the Fourth Gospel, the pre-existent Messiah was identified with the *Logos* of Philo's philosophy. So we then had:

pre-existent Wisdom = pre-existent Messiah = Holy Spirit
(St Paul)
= pre-existent
Logos (Philo)

But from all this 'identification' arises the question: 'Is the Holy Spirit then pre-existent like *Logos*, or is it not?' which (since there was a one-stage and a two-stage account of this *Logos* pre-existence) develops into the question: 'Was there a Trinity before, as well as after, the Incarnation?' But how can God who is beyond change, undergo a radical constitutional upheaval? Here is paradox all right, and it arises (at any rate in part) from a failure to recognize that 'pre-existence' like 'root' in our general example, is being used interchangeably between vastly different logical areas. Utterly different uses of 'pre-existence' have been illegitimately 'identified'. It only needed 'pre-existent' to be then taken in all cases as straightforwardly descriptive (which presumably it might be in the case of a Messiah) and confusion was even worse confounded. Here is utterly unrevealing paradox generating bogus questions, which men were more anxious to answer than to examine. The overall result is the kind of increasingly profitless muddle which characterizes not a little doctrinal speculation.

III

Let us now pass to the second brand of paradox we distinguished above: paradoxes which are avoidable but, in contrast with these last examples, positively significant.

Starting once again with a non-religious illustration, let us recall the familar example of wave and particle theories in contemporary scientific method. To bring out the paradoxical character of this example, I think we have to formulate it as follows. Certain physical phenomena are best treated in terms of particle mechanics which presupposes that matter is discontinuous; at the same time, other physical phenomena are best treated in terms of wave mechanics which presupposes that matter is continuous. The world, therefore, is both continuous and discontinuous; a plain self-contradiction.

It might be said that this paradox belongs really to the first group, for 'matter' and the 'world' do not obviously belong to the same logical areas. But let us set that possibility aside and for the purpose of our present example notice only that the scientist working with this paradox does so with the intention that it must somehow and eventually be overcome in a more comprehensive and therefore more illuminating hypothesis. Whether or not this has been attained in the present instance by Bohm and others who talk about hidden parameters uniting the areas, I am not competent to say, but the possibility of their being right is enough to record for our purpose.

Granted that such paradox and procedure is not only justified but illuminating in science, what of possible theological parallels? Hepburn, who takes the example as a paradigm for understanding religious paradox, has no difficulty in showing that whether in assuming a parallel ontology, or some kind of similarity between a theological and scientific 'hypothesis', the scientific near-parallel at crucial points breaks down. But could we ever expect it to be otherwise? If the theological case were identical with the scientific, theology, like science, would be concerned with no more than observables. But—to raise already a major point to which I return presently—can there be any distinctively *religious* language which talks of nothing more than observables?

Even so, let us agree with Hepburn so far as to admit that *some* religious paradox has a *prima facie* affinity with the scientific case and I may take specifically an example from Christology. The doctrine of the *Communicatio Idiomatum*, sponsored by Cyril of Alexandria and receiving Conciliar authority in the Tome of Leo, argued that while the human and divine natures of Jesus Christ were separate, the attributes of the one could be predicated of the other because of their union in the one person of Christ. Here is paradox indeed. Natures supposedly wholly separate are found to be united. On one interpretation it would certainly be a vicious muddle, i.e., if it was supposed that a thing called a 'person' united two other things called 'natures' which were nevertheless utterly separate. Further, when the doctrine has been taken in this descriptive way, it has certainly led to what I would say is pointless controversy, viz., as between Luther and the orthodox. But if the doctrine means to assert that while words about 'human nature' and 'God' are logically diverse, yet they have to be mixed to talk about Jesus Christ, so that as used of Jesus, words like 'union' or 'Person', or Cyril's phrase 'hypostatic unity', are logical peculiars whose behaviour awaits elucidation—it may be right or wrong but it is not necessarily sheer muddle, and we may agree that some sort of encouragement for this task of elucidation can be derived from the scientific case. In this way the development of Christological doctrine can provide us with something close to the scientific parallel. But let us notice that it only does this by appealing in the end to crucial words and phrases which still await a logical placing. The original paradox may have been avoided, but only in a way which reveals more clearly than ever the characteristically preposterous core. In this way we are pushed on to the unavoidable paradox which is peculiarly religious.

It will be useful at this point to take an example from Nuer religion, for it leads us to the same sort of conclusion. In the religious discourse of the Nuer can be found assertions such as these: 'The twin is a bird'; 'The cucumber is an ox'. Professor Evans-Pritchard elucidates these assertions as follows:

When a cucumber is used as a sacrificial victim Nuer speak of it as an ox. In doing so they are asserting something rather more than that it takes the place of an ox. They do not, of course, say that cucumbers are oxen, and in speaking of a particular cucumber as an ox in a sacrificial situation they are only indicating that it may be thought of as an ox in that particular situation; and they act accordingly by performing the sacrificial rites as closely as possible to what happens when the victim is an ox. The resemblance is conceptual, not perceptual. The 'is' rests on qualitative analogy. And the expression is asymmetrical,

a cucumber is an ox, but an ox is not a cucumber. A rather
different example of this way of speaking is the Nuer assertion
that twins are one person and that they are birds.[7]

Professor Evans-Pritchard continues a little later:

It seems odd, if not absurd, to a European when he is told that
a twin is a bird as though it were an obvious fact, for Nuer are
not saying that a twin is like a bird, but that he is a bird. There
seems to be a complete contradiction in the statement. . . . But,
in fact, no contradiction is involved in the statement, which,
on the contrary, appears quite sensible, and even true, to one
who presents the idea to himself in the Nuer language and within
their system of religious thought. He does not then take their
statements about twins any more literally than they make and
understand themselves. They are not saying that a twin has a
beak, feathers, and so forth . . . when Nuer say that a twin is a
bird they are not speaking of either as it appears in the flesh . . .
they are speaking of the association birds have with Spirit
through their ability to enter the realm to which Spirit is likened
in metaphor and where Nuer think it chiefly is, or may be. The
formula does not express a dyadic relationship between twins
and birds but a triadic relationship between twins, birds, and
God. In respect to God, twins and birds have a similar character.

In such a case it is clear that what started as paradox concludes
as a group of more transparent assertions, viz., that in respect of
God or Spirit, twins, birds, cucumber, and oxen have a similar
symbolic function. The paradox only arises if, in Evans-Pritchard's
words, we mistake the rules governing the assertions and think
of the formulae as expressing a dyadic relationship rather than a
triadic relationship. But this does not mean that the example falls
into the negative class of avoidable paradox which we considered
above. For while it is true that the paradox has disappeared when
the correct structure of the formula has been recognized, it has
only disappeared on the introduction of another concept, viz.,
God or Spirit, whose logical behaviour remains unmapped. All
we can gather is that such a concept, while it somehow refers to

[7] *Nuer Religion*, E. E. Evans-Pritchard, p. 128.

observables such as beaks, twin births, cucumber skin, oxen, refers to more than observables as well.

The same conclusion might be drawn from a less obviously religious example: 'Hail to thee blithe spirit, bird thou never wert'. [8] Bird, obviously the skylark is. Shelley is therefore saying that here we have something which is both a bird and not a bird. Paradox indeed. Yet he might say it was justified in so far as what has a beak, feathers, and so forth, is a symbol of what is beak, feathers and more than any number of such items, i.e., spirit. But to reiterate our earlier point, the logical behaviour of 'Spirit' is still on our hands.

Let us conclude this section with a further note on the Nuer tribe which will lead us conveniently to our next group of paradoxical assertions. Much earlier in the book Evans-Pritchard has remarked that Nuer prayers

> as is the case among other peoples, are often repetitions, but rather in the form of parallelisms than of tautologies, for they are variations of meaning within the same general meaning. Different images are used to express the same general idea, each stressing a different aspect of it.

The important question which arises out of this remark is: Is the variegated and often conflicting discourse displayed by prayers only paradoxical and complex in so far as it contrives to bring together all kinds of ideas in curious concatenations,[9] thereby producing striking and unusual effects—the grotesque can often be the exciting and memorable—or does the discourse of prayer somehow contrive so to combine words and evoke images as to tell some new kind of story altogether, a story about what can never be cashed in terms of such words and images taken at their face value, a story about something which is not merely observable, a story for which the rules (if there are any) still need to be elucidated? This brings us to what is most characteristically religious paradox: paradox claiming to be of the unavoidable kind.

[8] *To a Skylark*, P. B. Shelley, ll. 1–2.
[9] Compare J. Newton's hymn (English Hymnal 405):
   Jesus! my Shepherd, Husband, Friend
   My Prophet, Priest and King
   My Lord, my Life, my Way, my End. . . .

IV

Let us begin with two typical examples of irreducible religious paradox arising as I shall try to make clear, from the attempt to describe what is both 'seen and unseen' in language primarily suited to observables:

1 'Religion is the vision of something which stands beyond, behind, and within, the passing flux of immediate things.'[10]
2 God is impassible yet loving, timeless yet purposive, both transcendent and immanent.

1   Let us notice that if we take this sentence at its face value it is plainly self-contradictory. What is 'beyond' cannot be 'within'. But the sentence has a religious point to make because it can be given (as I shall try to show) a different logical structure altogether, a structure which from the point of any descriptive language, is odd.

Let us begin with the 'passing flux' of what's seen: the replacement of one noise by another, one view by another, night following day. From this beginning the writer hopes to evoke a 'vision' said to be, preposterously enough, 'of the unseen'. To do this he offers us certain prepositions as operators or directives. '*Within*': try to subdivide and subdivide, ever to penetrate more and more closely into what's seen. '*Beyond, behind*': without leaving the 'passing flux' extend our view, add, develop, continuously. Now here it will be recognized, is a technique very similar to that which Bradley set forward for evoking what he called 'immediate experience'[11]—something which 'is not intelligible . . . in the sense of being explicable' but something which breaks in on us and satisfies us when no 'relational addition from without (or) relational distinction from within' produces anything but 'a sense of defect'.

Whitehead's assertion likewise must be understood by reference to a situation which is 'the passing flux' and more, a situation which breaks in on us (we must hope) as we practise the technique of subdivision and continuous expansion.

[10] *Science and the Modern World*, A. N. Whitehead, C.U.P., 1933, Chap. XII, p. 238.
[11] *Essays on Truth and Reality*, F. H. Bradley, O.U.P., Chap. VI, esp. pp. 188–9.

Further, the example supplies us, I suggest, with a general clue to the structure of *some* unavoidable religious paradox at any rate. Religious discourse in its most characteristic areas arises, we see, from the claim that there is something to be talked about which is not only spatio-temporal, but more than spatio-temporal as well.[12] Now supposing that we agree on this basic claim, what should we expect to be appropriate currency for such discourse? How should we expect to talk, in terms of observables, about what is observables and more, a 'more' never compassed by observables however far these are enumerated?

One answer—and I do not claim it is the only answer—will be that we may properly speak of a characteristically religious situation in terms of an infinite series of observables, and this suggestion may help to illuminate another sort of paradoxical utterance which follows immediately on the assertion from Whitehead quoted above. He continues: (Religion is) 'something which is real, and yet waiting to be realized . . . something whose possession is the final good, and yet is beyond all reach.' We may conveniently take with this, such Christian assertions as 'Salvation is both attained and yet not attained'; 'The kingdom of God has come and yet is to come'; 'Revelation is both final and progressive'. In all these cases there is on the one hand a characteristically religious situation which is the topic of the utterance, something called merely 'Religion' or more specifically 'salvation', 'The Kingdom of God', or 'revelation'. From this standpoint religion is 'real' and 'the final good', salvation is a 'state', the Kingdom of God is 'here and now', revelation is 'final'. But if we talk about such a situation we must talk of it in terms of a never-ending series of observables. So *our talk* will be of religion as 'waiting to be realized', 'beyond all reach', of salvation as a 'process', of the Kingdom of God as 'yet to come', or revelation as 'progressive'. But the paradox is not that there are, so to say, two different and incompatible kinds of religion, salvation, kingdom, revelation. The paradox merely calls our attention to the fact that *our* talk about what we are given in the characteristically religious

---

[12] Christian paradox is a special case which arises when an attempt is made to use the historical to talk about what is historical and more. While Christian assertions are in part 'about history', they do not stand or fall on historical criteria alone; nor is their historical reference always very determinate.

situation discourse in terms of observables will never be finite and complete. The situation will be talked about in terms of language and imagery whose span is in principle infinite.

It is with such a background that I have used, and I think justifiably used, on more than one occasion[13] mathematical parallels for religious paradox. For in mathematics, too, we meet unavoidable paradox. A series can 'have' an 'infinite sum' (or a 'sum to infinity') which at some point or other in a mathematical argument we 'see', without the series ever having a sum which is given by straight addition. It is sometimes said that a circle is a regular polygon with an infinite number of sides, even though no polygon, however many its sides, is a circle. This second paradox is specially illuminating because it gives us a technique for developing a sides story until we 'see' what a circle is. The mathematical case thus resembles the theological in so far as we have unavoidable paradox which (if the formalists will allow me to say so) is significant and illuminating in so far as it grounds characteristic phrases in a discernment and a disclosure, and gives them a logical structure of an unexpected kind.

A further point: on this background we may usefully take some theological phrases—I do not say all—as phrases generative of an infinite series, and it is this consideration which lies behind my suggestion of models and qualifiers as a guide to the structure of some—I do not say all—religious phrases. It is in terms of 'models and qualifiers' that we shall treat the second example of typical religious paradox.

2 *God is impassible yet loving, timeless yet purposive, transcendent and immanent*. If these phrases are taken at their face value, if they are given the logic which their grammar suggests, self-contradictions abound. How can what is impassible be loving, how can what is timeless display a purpose, do not immanence and transcendence mutually exclude one another? But suppose that the phrases are not to be taken at their face grammar. Then, while self-contradiction as such disappears, impropriety and unavoidable paradox inevitably remain. What can we do about it? Let me give even in outline, a possible treatment of this paradoxical assertion.

---

[13] See e.g. *Religious Language*, pp. 59, 69, and *Mind* LXV (NS), 258, April 1956, Note on *The Paradox of Omnipotence* (pp. 263–6).

God is impassible yet loving. Take first: *God is impassible.* Read 'impassable' as 'im-passible', and as such directing us to try to effect a disclosure by operating ('im'-like) on situations displaying 'passibility', i.e. in such a way as tries to overcome and deny that feature. In this way the theological word 'impassible' first presents us with a model situation, viz. a situation characterized by 'passibility', something which everyone religious or not, can understand. We then operate on this model with the qualifier 'im' in the hope that sooner or later a disclosure situation will be evoked. The idea is that starting with something which displays passibility we must endeavour to reach something which is stable, and recalling Bradley's example we may obviously try to do this by relational division from within, or relational addition from without. This technique must continue until (or so we hope) a disclosure situation is evoked.

When this happens the phrase 'impassible' has a second point—though a very negative one—to make, a point about language. It suggests that the word 'God', used to talk of what is disclosed, must have a logical placing away from all language suited to passible things.

What now of *God is loving*? Here we must notice at the outset, that the sentence as it stands, is already misleading, 'incomplete' in a sense not unlike that which Russell[14] introduced. So our first task is to substitute for the original sentence one of the following more complete versions: *God is infinitely loving; God is perfectly loving; God is all-loving.* What we have to do now to understand such an assertion is to construct a series of situations characterized by love (being in this way models) in such a way that there will (or so we hope) dawn on us a situation which includes and is more than them all. 'Perfect', 'infinitely', 'all' are qualifiers directing us to continue such a series along the right lines: to think away any imperfect, finite, limited feature of any and all terms in the series. In this way the qualifiers enable the construction to be developed to any length until the disclosure occurs.

Then, and secondly, the qualifier has again a point to make about the logical placing of 'God'. If, for instance, we have used the qualifier 'infinitely', the assertion that 'God is infinitely loving'

[14] *Principia Mathematica*, Introduction, Chap. III, p. 66.

makes the point that the word 'God' stands to language about
loving somewhat as the 'sum' of an infinite series stands to any
finite summation of its terms. We may remind ourselves indeed
that people have spoken of God as 'Infinite Love' which makes
the parallel with the infinite series exceedingly close. Alternatively,
if we have used a qualifier like 'perfect' or 'all', I suggest that
their claim would be that the word 'God' is a unique and ultimate
key-word dominating the whole of a theistic language scheme, an
'irreducible posit'[15] to which the theist appeals as his end-point of
explanation.

The same treatment might be given to 'time-less' on the one
hand, and to 'purposive' on the other. Both are examples of qualified models, though before the last can be developed it must
once again be completed by a qualifier—this time by 'eternally'.

Both elements of each pair of assertions in the original paradoxical utterance are thus harmonized by being tracked back to
the same kind of situation. Nor is there any self-contradiction
for we do not take the assertions at their face grammar. The logical
structure, for instance, of 'God has an eternal purpose' is on
our view as much like that of

$$\text{`}2 = \int_{r=1}^{r=\infty} \left(\frac{1}{2^{r-1}}\right)\text{'}$$

as it is like that of 'Aneurin Bevan has a long-term purpose'. But as
often in philosophy, to clear one problem is to make another more
prominent, and certainly, a major logical problem remains: how to
connect the word 'God' with verifiably descriptive words—something about which the theory of models and qualifiers makes only
outline suggestions; how to maintain both the logical uniqueness,
distinctiveness, and so on of 'God' and yet provide some account
of its union with descriptive words. And this, I may say (to complete this section), is the theme of the paradoxical assertion that
God is immanent and transcendent. Here is the crucial theological
paradox. But it is for the most part a proposition about the use
of words, viz.: how can the word 'God' be united with words like
'table', 'human beings', 'goodness', 'evil', 'beauty', and so on ('im-

---

[15] In a sense not unlike that used by W. v. O. Quine in *From a Logical
Point of View*, Harvard, p. 44.

manent') and yet be a word of unique logical status different in its logical behaviour from all other nouns? This latter is at one and the same time the claim of 'transcendence', and the point of the ontological argument.

So for the theist, at any rate, it looks as if any defence of the preposterous must finish up by facing this logical problem set by the word 'God', or 'Spirit', a problem which in its Christian version concerns also words and phrases like 'Person' and 'hypostatic unity'. The basic problem in assessing and defending unavoidable religious paradox is how words can be both united with yet distinguished from verifiably descriptive words—however many sorts of 'description' there be; what logical behaviour can we give to words which are to be united with verifiably descriptive words, without themselves being verifiably descriptive? Here is the basic problem and it arises from the claim of religion to talk of what is seen and more than what is seen, using as the basis of its currency language suited to observables.

V

It is at this point that there comes the great divide amongst those who are otherwise united in holding that paradox in religion is unavoidable. For some would say that no sort of reasonable account can be given of this unavoidable paradox; that theological phrases are logically inaccessible; that the problem we have just raised can never arise. Contrariwise, others would say that this unavoidable paradox is logically explorable, and they would try to make some suggestions as to the solution of the problem.

The difference between these viewpoints may be illustrated by reference to what has been called Tertullian's paradox: 'The Son of God died; it is by all means to be believed because it is absurd (*ineptum*). And he was buried and rose again; the fact is certain, because it is impossible (*impossible*).'[16] Some, recalling passages in Tertullian where he is critical of philosophers would interpret this to be a rejoicing in paradox which was logically inaccessible. Here (they would say) in the Incarnation was something quite opaque to all examinations of prying philosophers; something calling only for (I suppose blind) acceptance. Here is an anticipation

[16] *De Carne Christi*, Tertullian, Chap. 5.

of views which we find in Kierkegaard and most obviously in Karl Barth. But considering that the treatise is written against Marcion, and that its overall purpose is to reject what Tertullian himself called the 'docetic parody' which would have denied the 'reality' of Christ's earthly life, it can be argued that what is by contrast *ineptum* and *impossible* is the original unparodied story which must talk of Incarnation using words about observables like human flesh. And in so far as Tertullian used phrases which anticipated orthodox Christological doctrine, we may say that the paradox which he considered quite unavoidable he also considered logically explorable. Here is the second position with regard to unavoidable paradox. It is the position I would myself wish to defend and among other companions I think I would have at least Professor C. A. Campbell who argues both for a 'symbolic' theology and for non-theological clues to it.[17]

But let us look first at some of those who would say that the unavoidable paradox of religion is logically inaccessible. First, Kierkegaard. While all of us may welcome Kierkegaard's insistence that the basis of religion is in some curious empirical situation in which I am 'existentially' set, and while we might well agree that super-scientific descriptive metaphysics is not appropriate currency for what the religious man desires to talk about, yet in the end faith for Kierkegaard involves a 'leap' which he would say, is unbridgeable no matter how peculiar the structure of any proposed bridge. Or perhaps it is fairer to say that in his time nothing was available but metaphysical bridges of super-scientific design, and such bridges he uncompromisingly rejected. Now we may agree that faith involves some sort of 'going beyond'; we have ourselves spoken of 'more than what's seen' breaking in on us in a disclosure—a discernment to which the religious man responds with an appropriate commitment. But this is not so much a 'leap' into some new territory as that we find ourselves being carried

---

[17] *On Selfhood and Godhood*, C. A. Campbell, esp. Lecture XVII et seq. Here, too, I think, would come H. H. Farmer who, with Paul Roubiczek would argue in effect that while paradox is unavoidable in theology—for like all thinking it works by contraries—its oppositions are to be so plotted as to issue in a progressive transformation of our 'feelings'. Here would be paradox which, if successfully explored, would lead us to 'feel' what any assemblage of contrary concepts is bound paradoxically to express. Here, too, perhaps, should be placed Tillich:'Paradox has its logical place' (*Systematic Theology*, Vol. I, p. 64).

over into it, and then retrospectively have the job of mapping
the track by which we travelled, peculiar though it be. And since
Kierkegaard's time the possibility of very peculiar paths such as
he never contemplated has shown itself.

In our own day the most notable representative of this view
is undoubtedly Karl Barth who starts from the position that
God is not man. God is 'wholly other'. Man must not formulate
theologies which 'rob God of his deity'.[18] But then there is Jesus—
God *and* man—therefore any talk about Jesus will be paradoxical
indeed, for it will bridge the unbridgeable. Here, let us notice,
is a double degree of paradox. We have first the necessarily paradoxical character of any theology of the 'wholly other'. An incarnational theology however has to go even further—and here Barth
closely follows Kierkegaard. An incarnational theology must
somehow bring together in one discourse talk about this 'wholly
other' and about man. Barth's answer is to make such incarnational discourse unique and inaccessible, and to do this at the
cost of declaring that we never understand the 'real' meanings of
words when these are taken outside a Christian setting. There may
be something in such a claim. But how on Barth's severe dichotomy words outside Christian discourse have any meaning whatever is not clear. Granted that it is a blunder to rob God of his
deity, is it not also a blunder to rob God of his world, a world
which everybody, Christian or not, manages to talk about? If,
like Barth, we have paradox which is logically inaccessible, how
do we write intelligible books or begin to talk significantly about
religion to unbelievers? Perhaps (he would say) we don't. The
truth is that Barth can never do with logical links between Christian theology and ordinary discourse; but neither can he do without them; and the only conclusion is that in fact there must be
peculiar links whose logical behaviour awaits elucidation.

Meanwhile, from the philosopher's point of view Barth's mistake is at least two-fold:

1   Recognizing the uniqueness of the word 'God' whose logical
behaviour is indeed (as we are willing to grant) 'wholly other',
Barth translates this proposition about words into one of supposed

[18] *Church Dogmatics*, Karl Barth. Vol. II, Pt. I (authorized translation).
T. and T. Clark, p. 281.

facts which the words picture. How much of the paradox and the absurdity in which Barth revels arises from the consequent ontology which sponsors two worlds?

2   Barth further supposes that with a uniquely distinctive and compelling revelation—'self-authenticating' as he would call it (and let us allow that phrases like this may be apt labels for the exceptionally peculiar religious situation to which the Christian *quâ* Christian makes appeal)—there must necessarily go a unique and self-guaranteeing theology. Here we have an opposite blunder from (1); in this case we have the characteristic of a situation illegitimately transferred to language. In these ways then we would say that Barth has a mistaken view of the logical character of religious language and of its empirical anchorage, and we need not be put off any logical exploration of paradox by the old-fashioned epistemology which lies behind Barthian theology.

But there have been others less theologically minded who have taken a somewhat similar view of the logical inaccessibility of religious paradox. Mr Thomas McPherson has spoken of religion as the inexpressible,[19] arguing that the improprieties and paradoxes of religion can never be demonstratively linked with what religion talks about, and this is a point of view very similar to that of Mr Alasdair MacIntyre. For MacIntyre the religious man becomes religious by a total unquestioning acceptance of some authoritative demand. On this view 'belief cannot argue with unbelief: it can only preach to it'.[20] But *how* can it preach? *How* can its words manage to 'recount the content of its faith'?[21] Have we to say that these are bogus and unanswerable questions? The question is even more serious for MacIntyre because he rightly makes a point of emphasizing the extent to which theological language uses ordinary words, 'the large degree of resemblance between religious language and everyday speech'. Must we never attempt to map these resemblances, however peculiar their logical connections?

What light has this negative position to shed on the paradoxical character of religious assertions? All its advocates rightly claim that religion deals in unavoidable improprieties; that if religion

[19] *New Essays in Philosophical Theology*, ed. A. G. N. Flew and A. MacIntyre, S.C.M. VII
[20] *Metaphysical Beliefs*, ed. Alasdair MacIntyre, S.C.M., p. 211.
[21] Loc. cit., p. 211.

uses ordinary words it uses them in a very special sort of way; that religious discourse is not somehow high-powered scientific theory offering some kind of scientific explanation; that religion concerns us as persons in a vital total loyalty. But are they right in supposing that no account can be given of the logical structure of the phrases appropriate to this loyalty? There can, I suppose, be only one answer, and that is to try ourselves to do some logical exploration, and look for the results.

Here we may return to the starting point of this present discussion by reflecting that what this group does—apart from the many differences among its members—is to take such a word as 'God', and to make it so distinctive and ultimate as to exclude all connection with non-theological language. We are back with what we called the crucial problem in assessing unavoidable paradox in religion. So let us face the challenge put to us by such as Kierkegaard and Barth by returning to this crucial problem to see if there is any hope that the unavoidable paradox displayed by religious language can nevertheless be given some kind of recognizable logical structure. Can we do anything—albeit in outline—to suggest that logical exploration of unavoidable paradox may be worth while?

Let us start by taking one of the points which Kierkegaard and others emphasize, viz. that religious loyalty involves the whole of ourselves. In this way they direct our attention to the significance of the word 'I' for understanding religious discourse.[22] It is with some reflections on the importance of 'I' as a clue to religious paradox that I will end this paper.

Though normally we can ignore the point with impunity, there is in fact a lack of logical fit between my assertion 'I am doing x' (a state of affairs not restricted to 'objects', for how can 'I' to myself be wholly a matter of objects?) and 'He is doing x' said of me by another (wholly a matter of 'objects' or what we have called 'observables').[23] The difference—and it then gives rise to paradoxical assertions—is revealed in certain unusual cases. 'Did you

[22] Cp. *Subjectivity and Paradox*, J. Heywood Thomas. Blackwell. Esp. Chap. vi. C. A. Campbell loc. cit. makes the same kind of point from a quite different direction.
[23] Cp. *P.A.S. Suppl.* Vol. xxx. 'Self-Knowledge'. J. R. Jones and T. R. Miles, pp. 120–56, and *P.A.S.* 1958–9. vi. 'The Two Contexts of Mental Concepts'. J. R. Jones.

lecture yesterday'? we ask Dr X, and when in Descartes' phrase
he had let his mind go on holiday while he expounded for the
eighty-fifth time his favourite theory about the date of Galatians,
he replies with engaging frankness: 'I did and I didn't.' Paradox
indeed. We say of the athlete coursing round the track: 'He is
running magnificently today'; but the athlete says, 'Not a bit of
it—it's the new B.D.H. drug that is taking my legs round'. The
athlete runs yet he does not run. Alternatively, on some other
occasion the coach and the medical director may say: 'We cannot
understand how he keeps on running', 'He's running and yet he
can't be'. Whereupon the athlete comments: 'Oh yes, I am running—it's something like will-power!' And the coach comments
more significantly than he suspects, 'God alone knows what's
happening', for the paradox is near-theological. Or there are cases
of depersonalization when 'I' known to the world as Charlie
Bloggs dissociate myself wholly from Charlie Bloggs who is
laughing heartily over someone's misfortune. Charlie Bloggs is
both laughing and is not laughing. In these ways 'I'—somewhat
like 'God'—gives rise to unavoidable paradox in virtue of having
to be both associated with verifiable descriptions, yet distinguished
from any or all of them.

Secondly, we might notice that 'I' is only given its full—more
than 'objects'—use in a disclosure. If we ask: 'What does "I"
talk of?' we shall only know the answer when we come to ourselves,
when we are aware of ourselves in a disclosure situation,[24] when
according to Hume we 'feel a connection'[25] between all our
'distinct perceptions' which is something more than any and all
such distinct perceptions or observables—hence Hume's perplexity.
The logical behaviour of 'I' then, being grounded in a disclosure
and ultimately distinct from all descriptive language while nevertheless associated with it, is a good clue to that of 'God', and we
can expect the paradoxes of 'I' to help us somewhat in our logical
exploration of unavoidable religious paradox, to help us distinguish
the bogus from the defensible.

Incidentally, it may be helpful to summarize these suggestions
by reference to the theory of types:

[24] Cp. 'The Systematic Elusiveness of "I" ', p. 17.
[25] *A Treatise of Human Nature*, David Hume, Vol II, Appendix (p. 319,
Everyman edition).

1 Many ordinary absurdities—avoidable paradoxes, retro-spectively negative—are admittedly species of type-trespass.

2 The paradoxes most characteristic of religion would also be cases of type-trespass if the key-words of religious discourse such as 'God' were native to any one type-distinguished area, to any one language frame.[26] For it is characteristic of such key-words to be associated with any and all verifiable descriptions, i.e. to be frame-transferable by nature. This incidentally is the linguistic version of the doctrine of creation.

3 So if religious improprieties are to be revealing and not absurd, they must centre on categories which, while they have freedom of association with all type-distinguished categories, are not themselves native to any one language frame. The crucial question is: are there any categories which in this way fall outside a theory of types, and my suggestion has been that there is at least one word: 'I'.

4 'I' and its paradoxes may then provide a paradigm for reason-able paradox in religion, as solipsism is the primitive metaphy-sics.[27]

If this seems too vague and generalized a note on which to end, let me point to two practical conclusions which follow from our reflections:

(i) Any unavoidable religious paradox will be defensible only in so far as it can be so structured as to be evocative of a dis-closure situation comprising 'what is seen and more'. Failure to do this results in an irreligious theology.

(ii) Any unavoidable religious paradox will be the more de-fensible in so far as it can be explored in characteristically personal terms. Paradoxical theism centring on friendship will thus be more reliable than paradoxical theism centring on the law courts, on judges, generals or despots, and much more reliable than that which clusters around wholly impersonal models such as are used in mechanical and hydrodynamical theories of grace.

[26] Adopting this phrase from Ninian Smart's *Reasons and Faiths* (p. 10) and using it as he does, against the background of Dr Waismann's article on Language Strata (*Logic and Language*, 2nd Series, ed. A. G. N. Flew, Blackwell).

[27] Cp. Wittgenstein, *Tractatus Logico-Philosophicus*. 5.62.

E

VI

SUMMARY

There are presumably countless types of paradox, not least in religious discourse, and what I have tried to do has been to separate out and comment on a few specimens. Some of the paradox in religion may be sheer muddle, and we mentioned some patristic discussions of the Trinity as an example. Other paradox may plead in a negative sort of way, the oddness of certain religious phrases—Temple's aphorism was a case in point, though here we are left with words whose logical behaviour is still to be elucidated. The same is true about that kind of paradox in religion which we called positively significant, and of which we took the *Communicatio Idiomatum* as our example. What it leaves on our hands is the logical placing of key christological phrases.

When we came to what we called unavoidable paradox in religion we saw that its basic justification was that religious discourse must contrive to talk about 'what's seen and more' in terms of the language suited to observables, and I tried to show how some typically theistic assertions, paradoxical in character when regarded as directly descriptive, could be so structured as to be suitable currency for the religious situations they were meant to evoke and express. But this presented us with what I call the crucial problem of unavoidable religious paradox: How words which are not verifiably descriptive in any way can be linked with words that are.

Some would say that this question is bogus and that the unavoidably paradoxical character of theological language is logically inaccessible simply as a matter of fact, being revealing to the converted and unrevealing to those who are not. Sheep and goats must be most decisively separated. But part of the logically inaccessible paradox of theological language, at least for Barth, arose (we saw) because of an illegitimate supposition that theological words mirror and picture what they talk about.

On the other hand I suggested that some kind of logical exploration of unavoidable religious paradox was possible, and that we might be encouraged in such exploration by having as our paradigm the word 'I', the paradoxes associated with it, and the empirical anchorage it must be given. What I have tried to allow for is genuine mystery in the sense that 'what there is' is not restricted to observables, and to suggest that it is as apt currency for such mystery that there arises 'mysterious paradox', which is then neither a vicious muddle nor an inaccessible incantation, but paradox whose structure can be investigated and explored under the guidance of the logical behaviour of 'I'. 'I' is the best (perhaps the only) clue to all genuine mystery, all sublime paradox, and all revealing impropriety.

Talking of God:
Models, Ancient and Modern

In this paper[1] I hope to show how talk about God arises around, and derives from, what I shall call models. I shall then consider some of the problems raised by this view, and finally glance at some of its wider implications.

Let me start by recalling that at one time, and in the Old Testament in particular, people made free use of all kinds of pictures, images, metaphors, models[2] in their talk about God. No one has illustrated this more plainly than Eric Heaton in his book *His Servants the Prophets* where he remarks that, in the Old Testament, 'Yahweh's relationship to his people is represented under the figures of a father, mother, nurse, brother, husband, friend, warrior, shepherd, farmer, metal-worker, builder, potter, fuller, physician, judge, tradesman, King, fisherman, and scribe— to mention, almost at random, only a few of the activities of the community' (p. 71).

Let us remind ourselves of how and where these pictures, these models, occur in the Bible by taking up references which for the most part are those which Mr Heaton gives us.

---

[1] The paper incorporates, in a revised form, most of the paper given to the Modern Churchmen's Conference in August 1964 and subsequently printed in *The Modern Churchman*, Vol. VIII, No. 1 (New Series), October 1964; but it has been enlarged by the addition of a new section dealing with various difficulties raised by the views which are set out in what is now the earlier part of the paper.

[2] My preference is for the word 'model' because, by virtue of its wider use in contemporary philosophical discussion, it carries with it natural logical overtones and takes us at once into a logical context By contrast with 'model', 'image' seems to me to have too strong a psychological ancestry, and to beg or to by-pass too many epistemological and ontological questions. For the close relation between model and metaphor see my *Models and Mystery*, Chap. III. I choose 'model', then, because it is least likely to prejudice discussion and most likely to direct our attention to logical, epistemological, and ontological issues.

First, God is talked of in terms of phrases which spread from, and presuppose, a family model:

1 *Father*. There is the promise in Jer. 3.19, 'Ye shall call me "My father" and shall not turn away from following me.'

2 *Mother*. In Deut. 32.18 the Hebrews are accused of forgetting 'God that gave thee birth', or rather more explicitly in Isa. 66.13 God promises Jerusalem: 'As one whom his mother comforteth so will I comfort you.'

3 *Husband*. Not surprisingly in Hosea—the book which, as is well known, more than any other uses the model of personal relationship in its discourse about God—we find an express preference for the picture of God as husband instead of God as an overlord, a distinction which was as novel in a secular context as in reference to God: 'It shall be at that day, saith the Lord, that thou shalt call me Ishi [=My husband] and shalt call me no more Baali [=My Master]' (Hos. 2.16).

4 *Friend*. In Jer.3.4 'the companion of my youth' is used as an appropriate phrase for God, though the verse also speaks of God as 'My father'. Here God is spoken of at one and the same time as father and friend, a point to which I will return later.

But God is also pictured more widely in terms of men's work and crafts and professions; and again, for the most part with the help of Mr Heaton, we may recall many verses with phrases which point back to such pictures as these twelve I will now mention.

1 *The Shepherd*. God is a shepherd whose sheep are men: 'Ye are my sheep, the sheep of my pasture are many . . . saith the Lord God' (Ezek. 34.31).

2 *The farmer*. 'I will sift the house of Israel . . . like as corn is sifted in a sieve; yet shall not the least grain fall on the earth' (Amos 9.9).

3 *The dairymaid*. Job speaks of God as one who has 'poured me out as milk, and curdled me like cheese' (Job 10.10).

4 *The fuller—the laundress*. In Mal. 3.2 God is said to be 'like fuller's soap', a theme further developed in Isa. 4.4 which speaks of a time when God will have 'washed away the filth of the daughters of Zion'.

5 *The builder*. In Amos 7.7 we read that 'the Lord stood beside (*or* upon) a wall made by a plumbline, with a plumbline in his hand'.

6   *The potter.* 'Behold, as the clay in the potter's hand, so are ye in mine hand O house of Israel' (Jer. 18.6)—and the verse has echoes in Isaiah where as with the 'father and friend' of Jeremiah, we now have God as 'father and potter': 'O Lord, thou art our father: we are the clay, and thou our potter' (Isa. 64.8).

7   *The fisherman.* In Hab. 1.14, 15 men are 'as the fishes of the sea' and God 'taketh up all of them with his angle, he catcheth them in his net, and gathereth them in his drag: therefore he rejoiceth and is glad'.

8   *The tradesman.* The well-known opening verse of Isa. 55 comes readily to mind: 'Ho, everyone that thirsteth, come ye to the waters, and he that hath no money; come ye, buy, and eat: yea, come, buy wine and milk without money and without price.'

9   *The physician.* Jer. 30 says of Israel and Judah that their 'hurt is incurable', their 'wound grievous', that they have no 'healing medicines'. But in verse 17 we read that God will restore their health: 'I will restore health unto thee, and I will heal thee of thy wounds, saith the Lord.'

10   *The teacher and scribe.* The well-known verse from Jer. 31: 'I will put my law (my teaching) in their inward parts, and in their hearts will I write it'.

11   *The nurse.* 'I have nursed (nourished) and brought up children, and they have rebelled against me' (Isa. 1.2).

12   *The metal worker.* In Mal. 3.2.3 God is 'like a refiner's fire . . . and he shall sit as a refiner and purifier of silver'.

Finally, pictures from a national setting are also used in the Old Testament to enable man to be articulate about God. We have, for example, the models of the King, the warrior, and the judge:

1   *The King.* In Jer. 10.7: 'Who would not fear thee, O King of the nations . . . forasmuch as among all the wise men of the nations, and in all their royal estate there is none like unto thee', and verse 10 'The Lord is the true God . . . and an everlasting King'.

2   *The warrior.* We read in Isa. 63.1 how God comes 'marching in the greatness of his strength', and the theme is developed in the next few verses.

3   *The judge.* 'The Lord is our judge, the Lord is our lawgiver',

says Isa. 33.22, and the verse continues: 'The Lord is our King: he will save us'. The verse combines all the national models.

Here is theological language directly related, as Mr Heaton said, 'to the world of experience': here are religious situations linked with 'secular' situations; here is talk about God which has plain links with the discourse of ordinary life. Here is religious life and theological language linked with the life and talk of home and family and friends: linked with man's work and talk whether it be in the fields or in the city, whether it be the work and talk of the craftsman or that of a profession; linked with the life and talk of the nation. The same could also be said about the characterization of God as 'my rock, and my fortress . . . my strong rock . . . my shield, and the horn of my salvation my high tower' (Ps. 18.2). Here is language about God gaining its relevance by means of what I have called 'models'. Now, what is involved when models are used in this way? Let us answer this question by reference in turn to each of the three groups I have mentioned above.

First then, those models associated with home and friends. How do they come to be used in talk about God? Let us begin by recognizing that on occasion circumstances all 'go our way', as it is often said. On these occasions, the world displays predominantly favourable features, features which give rise to a sense of dependence, but dependence on what is reliable and secure. Such features are those, for example, which characterize the changing seasons in such a way that the farmer ploughs hopefully and harvests thankfully. Or it may happen that when we are faced with some major problem as to vocation, or emigration, or the suffering of an aged relative, or marriage, there occurs a complex set of circumstances, too complex and too diversified to be the result of any one man's design, which helps us to resolve the problem as well for those around us as for ourselves. Or it may be that we are walking in remote, mountainous country, and as night comes on we are filled with all kinds of uncertainties and anxieties. But then we refresh ourselves at a mountain stream, look up to the stars as symbols of stability, and find our path illuminated by the moon. A sense of kinship with nature strikes us; the Universe is reliable after all.

But, it might be asked, how do situations like this lead to homely phrases—what I have called models—being used in discourse about God? My answer begins by reminding ourselves that there are patterns of behaviour characteristically associated with a father, mother, husband, or friend which are reminiscent of the patterns of these natural circumstances—that there are, for example, features of a friend's behaviour—his reliability and trustworthiness—whose pattern resembles in an important way the pattern of seed-time and harvest. Moreover, in the personal case it is in and through such patterns that we see certain men and women—a husband, mother, father, friend—as more than what they plainly and obviously are, namely human organisms in specialized relationships. Around such patterns occurs what we may call a 'disclosure', as when we 'see' twelve lines on a blackboard as a box; as when a cluster of lines called more technically an 'envelope' discloses an ellipse to us; as when two images take on another dimension and become a scene with 'depth', looking (as we say) 'very real' in a 3–D viewer. When such a disclosure occurs around a human pattern we speak of knowing people as they 'really are', of there being 'deep' affection between us, of loving them 'for themselves'. You may recall the 'pop' song: 'I love you for a hundred thousand reasons'—these reasons no doubt ranging from purely verifiable features and behaviour—hair, eyes, shape, tone of voice—to more distinctively personal reasons—trustfulness against the evidence—until as the climax: 'But most of all I love you 'cos you're you'—someone whose uniqueness and transcendence is disclosed in, and through these patterns of behaviour. 'Husband', 'mother', 'father', 'friend'—these are words which while they are undoubtedly associated with certain characteristic behaviour patterns have a transcendent reference as well —and are grounded in disclosures.

Building on these reflections, my next suggestion is that the human case acts as a catalyst for the cosmic case, to generate a cosmic disclosure. The cosmic pattern chimes in with the human pattern; the human pattern has already led to a finite disclosure— of persons—and their matching then evokes a cosmic disclosure around natural events such as seed-time and harvest. It is as and when a cosmic disclosure is thereby evoked that we are able to speak of God—what the cosmic disclosure discloses—in terms of the models with which the finite situations have supplied us. It is on these occasions that we speak of a 'sense of kinship' with the

Universe, of a 'friendly' valley—so friendly that, as Ps. 65 would express it, 'the valley laughs and sings with us'.[3]

To turn now to the second group of phrases—those which originate in models taken from man's work and crafts. Once again there must have been, at least in the case of Israel, a correspondence of patterns. There must, for example, be some pattern discernible in the behaviour of sheep which was repeated in the social behaviour of the Israelites. Alternatively, the events of the nation must be such that words like 'straining' and 'sifting' become appropriate, so that it becomes possible to speak of the nation going through a severe period of testing, or through trying times, or being wounded or hurt. In all this no religious phrases are begged. Even the most secular man might speak of Germany smarting from the grievous wounds of Versailles, or France being incurably hurt by the war of 1870–1. Or we might speak of the life of a nation being strained or soured, of its public representatives being no longer upright, of our lives being moulded by current events or caught in the net of circumstances.

The phrases might be used, and no doubt often are used, without any religious overtones whatever. That indeed, so far, is my point, namely that these phrases relate to patterns of events recognizable by all, believers or not. What further conditions are wanted for theological language to arise? If genuine theological language is to arise, the characteristic behaviour of what the Income Tax Schedules call a 'trade, profession, or vocation', i.e. shepherd, farmer, dairymaid, fuller, builder, potter, metal-worker, fisherman, tradesman, physician, teacher must, as in our own case, disclose an activity which gives to the overt 'professional' behaviour a distinctively personal and transcendent backing. We ourselves may then be used as catalysts to evoke a cosmic disclosure around the national pattern.

So once again—and this time when national events display patterns which, having their counterparts in human activity, become at the next move occasions of a cosmic disclosure—a corresponding pattern in the universe may lead to a cosmic disclosure, reveal God, and make possible the use of an appropriate model.

---

[3] I have of course tried to set out the exercise in its logical order; but it may well be that in appropriate circumstances we immediately talk of the world being 'friendly' and 'co-operative'.

The third case—the case of those models which originate in the context of national or international politics—King, warrior, judge —is different again. Here the model carries within itself the possibility of limitless development, and so the possibility arises of evoking a cosmic disclosure by developing a pattern whose range is unlimited.[4] Let me illustrate from the case of King. Each King, as the old Bidding Prayer phrases it, is over all persons and in all causes as well ecclesiastical as temporal within his dominions supreme. So why in principle impose any limit on the concept—any restriction of power in space and time? Then, as the King-pattern is developed, at some point or other a cosmic disclosure may occur, when (as we would say) the God of all power and might, the King of the whole earth will be disclosed. The model of warrior likewise embodies in itself the possibility of limitless inclusion, through victory, until the same kind of build-up of a power pattern leads to a cosmic disclosure. Or the Judge —easily universalized by the concept of justice he embodies—points to yet another limitless pattern which can generate a cosmic disclosure, and so become another model for God.

Now it is in terms of these models that we become theologically articulate, that we talk about God. Sometimes this discourse is well developed as it is already in some of the verses we quoted; on other occasions it is hardly developed at all though the *prima facie* possibility of considerable development is always implicit. Let us recall some examples.

The model of a father gives rise to talk about 'backsliding children' who if they but turn and are faithful will inherit a pleasant land and enjoy a distinguished heritage (Jer. 3.18, 19); talk of a husband leads to talk of a betrothal 'in righteousness, and in judgement, and in lovingkindness, and in mercies' and in 'faithfulness' (Hos. 2.19, 20). The shepherd is one of the most developed models, as we may see in Ezek. 34, for example, verses 12, 13, 14, 'As a shepherd seeketh out his flock in the day that he is amongst his sheep that are scattered abroad, so will I seek out my sheep . . . and I will feed them upon the mountains of Israel by the watercourses . . . I will feed them with good pasture . . . there shall they lie down in a good fold.' Again the potter leads the religious man to say as of God that 'when the vessel that he made of the clay was marred in the hand of the potter,

[4] See, for example, my *Religious Language*, esp. Chap. II.

he made it again another vessel' (Jer. 18.4). We have seen already from Jer. 30 how the physician, like the shepherd, model is prolific in its articulation possibilities, and the same could be said about King, or warrior, or judge. For example, God is the King who reigns for ever, gives his people the blessings of peace (Ps. 10.16; 39.11)—and (Dan. 4.34, 39) his dominion is everlasting, he doeth according to his will . . . among the inhabitants of the earth. The theme of God as judge characterizes many psalms, for example, 7. 8–11; 58.11; 135.14, to take three almost at random. God as the powerful warrior is epitomized in Ps. 68. 'Let God arise, and let his enemies be scattered', a psalm which has led many a soldier from Cromwell to Montgomery to be theologically articulate— perhaps indeed too articulate, though that is to anticipate diffi- culties to which I shall now very soon turn.

In these ways, then, in terms of a model set in a cosmic dis- closure, we talk about God, and our theology contrives to be relevant. But such articulation is no free-for-all; it develops under checks and balances. There are cautions to be exercised, and problems to be faced, and to these various difficulties we now turn.

In the first place, it is clear that while undoubtedly, and as we have seen, some models are much more fertile than others, giving rise much more quickly to much more discourse, every model is sooner or later inadequate. Models like father, shepherd, physician, King may be much more fertile than builder or tradesman, but even discourse about fathers, shepherds, physicians, and Kings must sooner or later be incongruous. No one is so captivated by the physician model that he is emboldened to ask whether God will benefit from the new deal to be given to consultants by the Ministry of Health. Some models may take us a long way in theological talking, but eventually even they must grind to a halt. While therefore a model gives us relevance, and there will be a high or a low degree of relevance depending on the fertility of the model, we must be alert to the solecisms it will sooner or later produce.

There will be at least two cautions which we shall always observe. First we shall not remain content with any one model. Already we have seen how God was spoken of as King and judge; as father and friend; as father and potter. So the language that is most reliable will be that discourse which is licensed by, and consistent with, the widest possible range of models. We can already see in broad outline the character of this multi-model discourse. It will speak of God as caring for, providing for, as guiding, testing, healing, and cleansing, as possessing a moral authority and calling forth a total devotion and response; and something of this same discourse might well be derived from impersonal models, for example, rock, fortress, shield. Because a model like Protector or Guide by being more fertile for providing discourse is more 'dominant' than models such as Shepherd and Potter, God will be more reliably spoken of as Protector and Guide than as Shepherd or even as both Shepherd and Potter. But we shall need to see the limitations of even these strands of discourse, and if we look for discourse which harmonizes these dominant strands in such a way as to exclude the limitations of each, we may well arrive at discourse about love or perhaps activity; when we shall conclude that God is spoken of most reliably as 'Love' or perhaps as just 'the living God'. The important point to recognize is that such characterizations of God as these are utterly valueless and positively misleading unless they are suitably contextualized in a multi-model discourse. It is a point which Professor Flew overlooked—or worse, parodied—in his criticisms of talk about God's love in the Falsification controversy,[5] and it is a point which few of his critics explicitly recognized. So the first caution to be observed in talking about God is: use as many models as possible, and from these develop the most consistent discourse possible. Never suppose the supply of models has been exhausted.

The second caution we shall need to observe is this. If we are to talk reliably about God we must be alert to the need to fit our discourse at all points to patterns of events in the world around us. The discourse is, as we have seen, derived from models, by no matter how complex a route, and there will always be the possibility—nay more, the necessity—of relating our discourse to events of the world around us. We must always give our language the kind of empirical fit which is exemplified in our earlier illustrations of seed-time and harvest, the moor-land walk, national events, or a monarchical constitution. Talk about God will not be related to the world around us as a scientific hypothesis is related to it. But meaning and relevance is no prerogative of scientific assertions.

[5] See, for example, *New Essays in Philosophical Theology*, ed. A. G. N. Flew and A. MacIntyre (S.C.M. Press), p. 99.

These reflections and cautions have already raised a number of points to whose fuller discussion I now turn.

One problem on which we have already touched may be developed as follows: if we speak of God in terms of models such as King and friend and potter and shield, can we express preferences between these models and give reasons for our preferences? Can we speak of one model, for example, King, being better than another, for example, shield; of this model, for example, King, being less good than that of, say, Father; or of some particular model, for example, criminal, being quite inadequate? These questions lead us naturally to another problem. To use the concept of model, it might be said, presupposes some independence access to what is modelled, presupposes an original with which the model may be compared. Must not this whole talk of models therefore presuppose some knowledge of God which is quite independent of models and symbols and against which the success (or failure) of a particular symbol or model can be measured? Indeed, without such an independent access to God, can we ever avoid a sheer relativism? It might be granted by the critic that models may be useful as sermon illustration, and, in words reminiscent of Locke, may commend theology to those who 'have not leisure for learning and logic'. Said Locke: 'When the hand is used to the plough and the spade, the head is seldom elevated to sublime notions, or exercised in mysterious reasonings. 'Tis well if men of that rank (to say nothing of the other sex) can comprehend plain propositions, and a short reasoning about things familiar to their minds, and nearly allied to their daily experience.'[6] Are models, then, along these lines no more than visual aids for those who cannot rise to the transparent view provided by theological concepts? Models may be of psychological and even sociological importance, but (it is alleged) they are of no epistemological or ontological significance. Indeed (it is said) they either beg or by-pass epistemological or ontological questions.[7]

[6] *The Reasonableness of Christianity*, ed I. T. Ramsey, para. 252, p. 76.

[7] The reader will already notice by recalling note 2 on p. 120 above, that part of this objection arises from confusing a model with an image, from thinking of all models as 'picturing models', as not only in a popular sense 'pictures' but related to their originals as photographs are to that which they picture. For a further discussion, see below, p. 131, and my *Models and Mystery*.

We have here particular versions of two problems which are quite central to contemporary discussions of religious language, the problems respectively of preference and of references. The *reference* problem may be formulated as follows: how, with this account of models and disclosures, can we be sure we are talking about God, and not merely about ourselves or, as it is sometimes expressed, about our own 'experience'? The problem of *preferences* is: if, as is the case, we have a vast variety of models for God, on what grounds do we grade models, and express a reasonable preference for one model rather than another? We will consider each of these two problems in turn.

THE PROBLEM OF REFERENCE

Let us first recall that on my view, belief in God arises from what I have called cosmic disclosures, situations where the universe 'comes alive', where a 'dead', 'dull', 'flat' existence takes on 'depth' or another 'dimension'. Such situations can occur on countless occasions of the most varied kind—by a fireside, or on a country walk; on a wind-swept moor, or in the crowds at Charing Cross; while reading the Bible, or attending Mass— there is no situation which cannot in principle give rise to a cosmic disclosure, and some we have examined in greater detail above. Now because of the cosmic character of such a disclosure, because of its all-embracing range, because in it the whole universe confronts us,[8] I think we are entitled to speak of there being a single individuation expressing itself in each and all of these disclosures. In other words, from any and every cosmic disclosure we can claim to believe in one x (where x for the moment remains to be elucidated) precisely because we talk of there being 'one world'.

Now, as will be evident from what has been already said, not even a cosmic disclosure brings with it a privileged interpretation, any more than does any other situation or 'experience' (if the word 'experience' be allowed). Indeed the principle of choice between different explications is a question I shall face presently when we look at the problem of preferences. Nevertheless, I would claim that it is quite clear that cosmic disclosures are ontologically

[8] Witness such expressions appropriate to cosmic disclosures as 'Here I stand, I can no other' (a Luther *contra mundum*), or 'You're the *whole world* to me'.

privileged in so far as they disclose that which confronts us as a basic 'given', that which is set over against ourselves in every situation of this kind, that which individuates the universe.

It is, I hope, evident that on this view when we appeal to 'cosmic disclosures' we are not just talking about ourselves, nor merely of our own 'experience', we are not just appealing to our own private way of looking at the world. If that were so, then the appeal to cosmic disclosures would be a scarcely-veiled form of atheism, which is what Professor Ninian Smart supposes to be the case.[9] On the contrary, a cosmic disclosure reveals something of whose existence we are aware precisely because we are aware of *being* confronted. Indeed, we speak of a disclosure precisely when we acknowledge such a confrontation, something declaring itself to us, something relatively active when we are relatively passive. In a cosmic disclosure the whole universe is individuated and particularized in this way.

I realize, of course, as I hinted above, that I have not yet given any reasons for speaking of what a cosmic disclosure discloses of *God*; I have given no reasons for talking of the objective reference of a cosmic disclosure in terms of God. But those reasons cannot be given without considering the problem of preferences to which I now turn.

THE PROBLEM OF PREFERENCES

The cosmic disclosures from which, on my view, belief in God arises are all characterized by some model. This will, I trust, be clear from what I have already said above. But speaking more generally, we may distinguish at least two possibilities. The model may, by development in various ways, have generated the cosmic disclosure. All our earlier examples illustrate that first possibility. But, taking a broader view, we may remark that some cosmic disclosures 'just happen'. This is the case of what used to be called 'religious experience'—when a model would be self-selected —being some kind of focal point—with regard to each particular situation of this type. In other words, a cosmic disclosure will in the one way or in the other supply a model as that which alone enables us to be articulate about what has disclosed itself to us.

[9] See, for example, *Theology* LXVIII, No. 535, January 1965, pp. 33–5, with which might be taken *Theology* LXVIII, No. 536, February 1965, pp. 109–11, and *Theology* LXVIII, No. 541, July 1965, pp. 351–2.

A cosmic disclosure will supply a model either because it has been generated by the use of the model,[10] or because the situation itself highlights a particular feature within it. Models are in this way and to this degree, but only in this way and to this degree, self-authenticating. If there is no model, there is no sensible articulation, and no test possible of the claim to have had a cosmic disclosure. Some mystical experiences seem to be in this curious epistemological position, and to be in this way ontologically problematical as well as verbally baffling.

It is at this point that I will take up an earlier footnote[11] and confess that while my use of the word 'model' has obvious affinities with a popular use of the word which (as I remarked in the footnote) lies behind the second objection which gave rise to this discussion, nevertheless my use of the word 'model' is a somewhat technical one. A theological model is a way of understanding what has been objectively disclosed in a cosmic disclosure; like all models it is never a perfect replica; but it is further and most importantly unlike ordinary 'picturing models' (for example, the boy's model train) in that its objective reference is never given independently of the model. It is indeed what I have called a 'disclosure model', a type of model not without its parallels in science and elsewhere. If the reader wishes for a more adequate discussion of the general question of the status of a theological model, I would respectfully refer him to my *Models and Mystery* where the topic receives a somewhat fuller treatment. For our present purpose, my point is merely that it is most important not to be misled by features of modelling which do not carry over into the theological cases. We must not assimilate theological models to models which picture their originals. But, it will now be asked, what then in a cosmic disclosure are the models of? How can we claim them to be models of God?

At this point let us recall what was said on the problem of reference. Since there is only *one* reference for *all* disclosure illustrations, it is this which, in ways better or worse, *every* model contrives to talk about. For this purpose, any particular model supplied by a particular cosmic disclosure will have to be incorporated with every other possible model, and this means that its articulation possibilities will have to be earned as it rubs its

---

[10] See the three groups of examples above.
[11] Footnote 7 on p. 129 above.

shoulders with other models. A model will thus establish itself in two ways:

1   By justifying itself as far as it can alongside other models. Each model enables us to talk in a certain way of what a cosmic disclosure discloses—this we have seen by reference, for example, to the models of father, husband, shepherd, potter, physician, and King. As we have remarked above, we develop discourse from each model only with a constant eye on other models; at various points these other models will supply stop cards to inhibit further discourse in that particular direction. Talk about God thus develops by a mingling of discourse from different models. Now, the more a model can exist successfully in competition with other models, the more justifiably does it provide discourse about what the cosmic disclosure discloses. One model, for example, Protector, is better than another, for example, Laundress, if its discourse is more widely ranging. A model like person is better than, say, shepherd or potter because it can say all that these other models can say and more besides; in this way it can absorb the discourse from two or more models. Summarizing we might say that this first set of criteria which enables us to express preferences between models is explicitly related to their relative dominance in the discourse.

2   But there are other criteria of preference between models, and these arise from the way the multi-model discourse 'fits' the universe. There is obviously the logical possibility that there could be theological discourse arising from a dominant model which in that way was definitive, which nevertheless failed on this second test. The model of love will certainly have to meet the challenge of evil and suffering in the universe and in this way to grapple with the 'problem of evil';[12] but even more importantly there will have to be specific situations which can be legitimately 'interpreted by love' if the model of love has any initial justification at all. There must be a pattern of empirical circumstances which fit 'loving' discourse when used of God. Such a fit is pragmatic in the widest sense; but it is not given by experimental verification in a strict scientific sense. This was the point I tried to make and illustrate in the three groups of examples above. The kind of empirical fit which provides a second set of

[12] That of course was Professor Flew's point in the discussion to which we have referred above.

criteria for preferences between models is much more like the kind of fit which detectives look for between certain new clues and a 'theory' of the crime with which they are provisionally working.

But this brings us back to our crucial question. Suppose we have developed discourse as comprehensively, consistently, coherently as possible, making the most economical and coherent development of as many models as possible, and granting that this discourse talks of that 'other' which the cosmic disclosure has disclosed to us, can we legitimately say that this is discourse about *God*? Under what conditions do we rightly speak of models being models for God?

Let me answer that question by taking first an illustration I have used elsewhere. Suppose we draw a series of regular polygons with an ever-increasing number of sides, and further draw them such that their vertices are always equidistant from a fixed point. What shall we produce? The plain, down-to-earth man will say: 'A lot of polygons'—and he is obviously and undoubtedly correct. But is that the whole story? For my present purpose I hope not. At some point or other, something else, I suggest, may strike us, something else—besides the polygons—is 'seen'; something else is 'disclosed'. We *might* say 'a circle'. But suppose we had never heard about circles and yet that the disclosure had occurred. Suppose that in these circumstances we then used the symbol x to talk of what was then disclosed, of that to which polygon talk led when it was developed in this way. If now we wanted to speak of x—to contextualize x—talk of polygons would be a good approximation; indeed, it would be the only *reasonable* approximation—because polygon talk has led us to this which had been disclosed. It would, for example, be unreasonable to talk of x in terms of democracy. Further, the larger its number of sides, the better approximation to x would a polygon be. So that if someone said: 'I'd love an x-like swimming pool', we should know that, *reasonably*, he would be more satisfied with a pool of 1008 sides than with one of three sides. In this way, we should talk of what is disclosed by means of approximations we have traversed *en route*, and there would be the possibility of reasonable preferences. Finally, if after all this someone discovered one day a treatise on circles, it might soon become evident that there were close similarities between circle-discourse and x-discourse, and on that basis there might be a reasonable recommendation to read '*x*' as 'circle'.

Now in the same way, we might choose to call what a cosmic disclosure discloses as '*x*' and we have already seen that there could be good grounds for belief in 'one *x*'. Further, we should then talk about *x* in terms of any model which the various routes to a cosmic disclosure had provided; and we should talk the more reasonably about *x* in terms of this or any model, the longer it had been cautiously developed under checks and balances, which amounts to saying the greater the number of models which had been incorporated into our discourse. Any one model would enable us to be articulate about *x*, in some way or another, but if we wanted to talk as adequately as possible about *x* we should build out the most consistent, comprehensive, coherent, and simple discourse from as many models as possible. Now, if we did this, my contention is that we should see a language emerging which fitted closer and closer to the language which a believer uses about God, and because of this increasing fit, the further we had gone, the more reasonably should we then conclude 'For *x*, read God', and the more reasonably should we talk of the models being models of God, and of the cosmic disclosure disclosing God.

It is in such ways as these that I should grapple with the various epistemological and ontological problems which are raised by an appeal to disclosures; that I should defend my claim that cosmic disclosures have an inalienable objective reference and my claim that the word 'God' can be legitimately used to specify this reference. Further, it is along these lines that I should argue that when the word 'God' is so used, we speak of God in terms of discourse derived from models, between which an expression of preferences is possible; and that the word 'God' thus derives its meaning in use as and when it is contextualized in multi-model discourse, which is subject both to logical criteria and the criterion of 'empirical fit'.

This, in outline, is the way in which I would justify my claim that the models occurring in cosmic disclosures are models of the one God, who reveals himself in any and every cosmic disclosure.

What now have these reflections taught us as we seek to explicate theological language today?

1   Theological language, and talk about God in particular, often passes men by because it brings with it no cosmic disclosures. Its models have been drained of their disclosure possibilities by the

vast sociological, psychological, and cultural changes which separate us from the Biblical, and not least the Old Testament, world. Kings and judges are contextualized in an oppressive, insensitive Establishment; warriors vary between bawling sergeant majors and brass-hatted dunderheads; trades, and even professions, are irritating frustrations from which a man escapes as frequently as possible and with as much money as possible in order to 'live'. In our present society, human relations within a family are perhaps the only group of traditional models which continues to offer any hope for relevant theological language.

In order to instil talk about God with new relevance, we must seek to discover where in the world and where in man's life and work, disclosures are most likely to occur. A relevant theology must learn new occasions for moments of vision.

Perhaps scientific discourse may not be unhelpful. In particular, if (as we have suggested) activity is a central theological concept, it may be that we shall discover new models amongst whatever represents the scientific concept of energy. More particularly, the Principle of the Conservation of Energy may be a means of pointing to a cosmic disclosure by mounting a series of energy considerations. Again, we may recall Ralph Waldo Trine's implicit use of the phenomenon of resonance in the title of his well-known book *In Tune with the Infinite*.

On a still wider canvas, may we hope that sleek sports cars will replace strong towers; or personnel manager replace the good shepherd? If these or any similar suggestions seem fantastic, it is either because sleek sports cars and personnel managers evoke no disclosures whatever or, if they do, which may be more likely, it is because we cannot discern reminiscent patterns in the universe which can thereafter lead to cosmic disclosures.

Our Victorian great-grandfathers did not hesitate to write theological discourses entitled 'Railways to heaven'. But for them railways were opening up a world which was itself evolving with a wonderful novelty and with apparently limitless possibilities: a cosmic disclosure justified railways as a theological model. But there is little about British Rail to generate cosmic disclosures. If we look for transport parallel in our own day, let it be granted that for some—and I believe Professor Coulson is amongst them—Heath Row, like kings and judges of old, can be set in an ever-widening cosmic perspective which surveys aircraft, airlines, languages, nationalities . . . until a cosmic disclosure is evolved. If that is so, there is no reason why some should not speak of God in the Control Tower bringing men to the arrival gate where they would be. If that language jars, let us be sure to ask ourselves why it does.

Meanwhile, the philosopher of religion finds unexpected significance in the girl who screamed at the Beatles because (she said) they seemed so much bigger than herself and for whom, quite consistently, Liverpool was heaven. Here, in so far as there was a sense of finitude, was a cosmic disclosure: Beatle-language was virtually theological language. If we wish to coin a relevant theology it is our duty to learn, not to scoff.

But I have roamed enough in an area where prejudices flourish, where men can be blinkered and insensitive, and where words are contextually hazardous; and those are only some of the difficulties which confront us as we try to make our theology meaningful.

2 Whether our models are old or new they must be developed with circumspection. It is significant that Mr Heaton in the very sentence where he praises the Old Testament writers for their relevance—acknowledges that 'it was occasionally a crude tradition' (p. 73). Sometimes, models were developed in the Old Testament without adequate circumspection. We must learn our lesson. Models have to be developed with an eye both to other models, and to what we want to say about the universe in terms of the history and science and sociology and moral insights of the times.

A reliable theology will need to be in constant dialogue and conversation with other disciplines, as much to listen as to speak.

3 Further, all models in theology must be accompanied by *qualifiers*, those words in theological language which preserve the mystery and transcendence of God, for example, 'perfect', 'infinite', 'all', 'only', and so forth. Mr Heaton, after granting that on occasion Old Testament theology issues in crudities, remarks that nevertheless 'the prophets knew how to discriminate and were acutely aware of the seven limitations of all human language for conveying the full richness of their knowledge of Yahweh', and when they discriminated it was to exclude 'everything which suggested that [God] was capricious and [like the deities of Canaan] unworthy of man at his best'. It is the purpose of qualifiers to remind us of the need for this discrimination. So, in relation to

2, qualifiers might well help us to be cautious about developing a model. But in helping us to discriminate and to be cautious they have another and more characteristic purpose as well.

This purpose is to point us unmistakably to the cosmic disclosures in which all talk about God must be grounded. Take, for instance, the qualifier 'infinitely' in 'God is infinitely loving'. It may be thought to be merely a formal courtesy phrase or even a disingenuous addition to by-pass intellectual difficulties.[13] It might be supposed that 'God is loving' says all that it is important to preserve—something which is clear and relevant. But 'God is loving' is just as inadequate and as incomplete a theological assertion as 'God is infinite'—though both are relevant. The first generates discourse which (as we have seen) enables theology to be intelligible and to fit the world, and the second points us to the transcendence and mystery of a cosmic disclosure.

It is true that by themselves qualifiers *describe* nothing, and for that reason may be thought to be utterly irrelevant theological jargon. But they are in fact words or phrases whose relevance is to be found in the cosmic disclosure to which, when they have models to qualify, they point. Prayers and hymns of adoration are largely catenae of qualifiers and it entirely accords with these philosophical reflections that for their relevance they depend on a meditation which, in suppplying the models, relates the prayers and hymns to the life of the world.

4 We are thus brought naturally to my fourth point. Theologians have far too often supposed, and mistakenly, that the most generalized doctrines were most free from all contamination (as it would have been judged) with metaphor, or as I would say, models. But none of us must ever despise the models whence our theological discourse is hewn, for without these we have no way to the cosmic disclosure and no way back to relevance. Without its models, theology will always run the risk of being no more than word-spinning. There is a theological sophistication which, as Mr Heaton remarks, is 'pitiful self-deception'. He continues: 'Metaphor—*mere* metaphor—is all we have to help us understand God, no matter how discreetly we try to disguise the fact by thinning out a selection of images into pseudo-philosophical "doctrines". The "fatherhood" of God, the "Kingship" of God,

---

[13] Cf. again A. G. N. Flew and the Falsification controversy, *New Essays in Philosophical Theology* (S.C.M. Press), pp. 98–9.

the "love" of God, the "wrath" of God and the rest remain
metaphorical because they were and still are attached at some
point to human experience. They would be incomprehensible (and
therefore useless) if they were not.' Only when we remember
that will our preaching 'become at once more personal, more
imaginative and more intelligible'. He concludes: 'At the moment
it really does seem that we are all desperately afraid of leaving
the well-trodden path of theological jargon and of claiming that
measure of imaginative freedom which all the great preachers
from Amos to St Paul assumed—not as a right, but as a pastoral
necessity.'

5 Presented with some theological phrase, then, of whose
meaning (if meaning it has) we are doubtful or even inclined to
deny, my recipe for understanding it is:

(*a*) Do not be content to take the phrase in isolation, but search
for its appropriate context, verbal and non-verbal.
(*b*) At this point try to pick out the model(s) from which the
context is derived; these should help us to discover that 'basis
in fact' for the theological assertion—its bearing on the world
around us.
(*c*) At the same time no model will ever be a picturing model;
if that occurred the language might seem to be relevant but it
could not be *theological*. See, then, how any particular model has
been qualified to generate that cosmic disclosure in which I am
bound to think that the ultimate ground of all theological
assertions will be found.

Theology must always have some fit with the world around
us—that is true and a point which it is important to emphasize.
Further, this 'fit' arises in virtue of the language to which the
different models collectively give rise. But those models originate
in a cosmic disclosure, and here is the basis for all talk about God.

This I would say is even true of doctrines such as those of the
future life, of creation, and of angels. Which means that in all
theological assertions the logical stress is always on God. In this
sense there is something that we may call a logical imbalance
about theological assertions, and this is what the qualifiers help
to exhibit. Theological assertions are not flat or uniform as we
might say 'The cat is on the mat' is flat and uniform. If we speak
of God catching men in his net, and gathering them in his drag,

do not let us have such an interest in fishing that we revel in developing discourse of the net and drag, and forget that it is not necessarily theology at all. If this seems an incredible mistake, think of those who have lavished time and thought on the details of the Last Assize or the temperature of hell in a way which denied the very character of the God of whom they were talking.

Talk about God, and theological assertions in general, then, point us in two directions: in the one direction to that cosmic disclosure where God reveals himself; and in the other direction to some particular models into whose discourse they fit, discourse which relates to patterns in the world around us. Talk about God must combine understanding and mystery; it must relate to models and disclosures. Meanwhile, the believer is committed to an endless exploration of countless models, in this way constantly improving his understanding of the one God who confronts him in any and every cosmic disclosure.

PART
3
The Logic of Faith

Religion and Science:
A Philosopher's Approach[1]

In recent days there has been a variety of attempts by very diverse people, and not always for the same reasons, to stress not so much, or even at all, the conflict between religion and science as their radical difference and independence. Professor John Wisdom, for example, began a notable essay on *Gods*[2] by saying: 'The existence of God is not an experimental issue in the way it was'—looking back, rightly or wrongly, to the time when Elijah proved his case before the prophets of Baal. Professor A. G. N. Flew broadened the point by arguing, again rightly or wrongly, that while the believer in God can allow nothing to count against his belief, everyone knows that scientific generalizations on the other hand can always be falsified and will be set aside if events so demand.[3] But it is not only unbelieving philosophers who insist on differences of this kind between science and religion. In his book *Mystery and Philosophy* the late Michael Foster emphasized the way in which he thought that scientific method came dangerously near to being irreligious. 'The aim of modern science is man's mastery over nature' (he says) and nothing is more typical of these masterful intentions than 'the experimental method' which 'is a method of commanding nature to answer man's questions'. It is a 'putting of nature to the question'. But if theology put God to the question and tested its theories by results, it would be, Mr Foster would say, 'to tempt the Lord God in the way prohibited', i.e. in the temptation narratives. These various quotations make two points:

1 That modern science encourages man to develop his own mastery and subjects nature to an inquisition, and

2 That scientific method has to be set entirely aside when we turn to religion and theology. Indeed, to investigate God by

---

[1] Based on a lecture given at Sion College, London, 30 November 1959.
[2] *Proc. Aris. Soc.*, 1944–5, pp. 185–206.
[3] See e.g. *New Essays in Philosophical Theology*, Chap VI.

the methods which natural science uses, would be to yield to a temptation of the devil, which the religious man must renounce. There is a methodological incompatibility between religion and science.

Now let me make it clear from the outset that it is not the purpose of this paper to assert the logical identity of scientific and religious discourse. That view belongs to a past age. Differences, and important differences, of methodology there certainly are. Yet I wish to show how the two approaches, *despite* their differences, are not incompatible. On the contrary, they have their meeting places. Nay, more, they may be and must be united.

Further, at the outset, let me emphasize that for the most part this paper will be concerned with scientific *method*. Science is not the name for some logically homogeneous group of assertions. It is rather a *method* in the development of which several kinds of logically distinguishable assertions are made, some, though not all of which, have theological associations of the kind we must explore. Let us turn to scientific method and look at some of its logical features with a view to answering the question: how far is the approach, the attitude, the methods, of the scientist compatible with a religious attitude? For this is the question which spotlights for the philosopher the crucial point of present-day discussion about science and religion. The debate is not about conclusions, but about methodology.

For our purpose we shall distinguish five features in scientific method; five stages as the scientist proceeds from his simplest generalization to the most complex hypothesis:

1 THE START

Science starts with ordinary common-sense assertions about what can be seen, heard, touched, tasted, or smelt. For example, the following assertions would be among those of interest to the scientist: 'There is a stone falling'; 'See the planet moving'; 'The water is boiling'; 'These vegetables are decomposing'; 'Those rabbits are reproducing'.

2 SIMPLE GENERALIZATIONS

The scientist's next move is to formulate invariants within such ostensible diversity. To illustrate this second stage of scientific method let us take the simplest kind of scientific situation: Tom,

Dick, and Harry, who are all boiling water. The scientist links these situations not merely because the phrase 'boiling water' would be used by each of them—for this is a very vague phrase with a very open texture—but because a thread of mercury in a glass tube—a thermometer—measures in each calorimeter or beaker more or less what is called 100° Centigrade. Here, very roughly described, is the background to the simplest kind of scientific generalization: 'Water boils at 100°'. Here is a phrase— '100° Centigrade'—which, as an invariant, not only brings precision and clarity into the assertions of Tom, Dick, and Harry, but unites all the Toms, Dicks, and Harrys boiling water in the kingdom. Yet already we must make two points which are often forgotten by those who make too superficial generalizations about scientific method. The first point is that even this simple generalization is not bound rigidly to the facts. It is suggested by them, yes. But in the end it is an option, which goes beyond them. How many thermometers measure accurately 100° Centigrade? Or would continue to register this temperature if peered at through lenses, and so on? The simple generalization is (as I have said) very closely associated with the facts, but it is reached in a disclosure which occurs when we survey the different thermometers, where upon a certain figure '100° C' suggests itself, forces itself on our attention. The generalization depends on the 'facts', but does not, in any science worthy of the name, merely report them in close detail.

The second point of importance is to recognize the important part which the appeal to 'experimental error' can play. Here is a trump card which will safeguard most simple generalizations which are grounded in disclosures occurring around a group of closely similar spatio-temporal events. It can for so long, and in so many ways, feather-bed useful and simple generalizations which the scientist wishes to keep.

3 DEVELOPMENT OF SIMPLE GENERALIZATIONS

But let us not be unfair. Refuge will not always be taken in experimental error. Provided we are only boiling water in the cellar or in the attic, as well as in the kitchen, all will be well. But suppose we go to the top of Ben Nevis. We shall say that water 'is boiling', but our thermometer will not read 100° C at the top of Ben Nevis.

It will read somewhat less (say) 99·8° C. For some time we may talk about experimental error, but when a vast company of climbers, armed with thermometers, has boiled water at the top of Ben Nevis, and when all of their thermometers have significantly measured less than 100° C, the earlier generalization will be modified. It would not so much be shown to be wrong, for the situations to which it gave precision and unity before, would still be given precision and unity by it. It would still, over a certain area, be a reputable invariant. But its inadequacy has now been indicated. The simple invariant needs to be further extended, and we now say 'Water boils at 100° C at normal pressure'. Or (still more accurately and typically) 'Water boils at a temperature t when the pressure is p' and where for some function of t and p, $f(t, p)$ $= 0$. Further, when p is 'normal', $t = 100°$ C. With this more complicated phrase everyone's kettle is now covered, whether in laboratory, kitchen, attic, or cellar, or even on Ben Nevis. We have now produced a much more resistant generalization, a much better invariant arising in a disclosure which encloses many more spatio-temporal data than did its predecessors.

Further, we could now deduce that down a Lancashire coal mine, or a French limestone cavern, water will boil at a temperature greater than 100° C. Notice that we can *deduce* such an assertion from our generalization, and further, that this assertion can be subsequently *verified*. Here is a crucial element in scientific method—verifiable deductions, and it is an element which (as we shall see) theology cannot and must not provide.

4 LARGE-SCALE HYPOTHESES

But the scientist's interest will not stop here. The better the scientist the more comprehensive, extensive, and powerful must be his invariant. To illustrate the high generalizations at which the scientist aims, let us take a very mixed group of common-sense assertions such as the following, and for our purpose it does not matter whether they are true or false:

'An apple is falling to the ground.'

'A planet is moving to an ellipse.'

'That bullet will score a bull's-eye.'

'A Britannia locomotive with twelve carriages will slip on certain inclines.'

'The road must have a better camber at that corner if buses are not to turn over.'

'High water at Greenwich yesterday was 10 p.m.'

'A partial eclipse of the sun, visible in England, occurred in November 1959.'

Now what the physicist does when searching for newer and more far-reaching theories is to bring together such diverse situations as these assertions describe, hoping that some common feature or other will strike him, will (in other words) evoke a disclosure. It is in this way that scientific 'insight' is associated with what we have called invariants, features (hitherto unnoticed) which the diverse situations have in common; and the more diverse the situations that an invariant unites when it becomes the occasion of a disclosure, the more original and distinguished the scientist. For example, in the case of the apple falling and the planet moving these two situations, hitherto regarded as wholly disparate (as disparate indeed as earth and heaven) may suddenly 'connect'—as they once did presumably for Newton. 'A moment of vision' occurred around a common feature: in this case, 'force producing movement'.

At this point we need to make an important complication to the story. When the events are sufficiently similar (as in the case of boiling water) and the common feature is sufficiently simple (as in the case of thermometers registering 100° C), the scientist may well imagine that no currency beyond the mathematical symbols (here: '100° C') is required to do justice to what is disclosed.

But when invariants are associated with vastly diverse situations two possibilities arise:

(i) As in the simpler case, so in this, mathematical symbols may still be invaluable as currency for the invariant.

(ii) At the same time the disclosure which embraces so much spatio-temporal diversity, may well also suggest some word of a metaphysical brand, especially if a similar disclosure embracing a similar diversity has been in the past the basis for such a metaphysical word. For instance, a certain invariant arising in a disclosure which embraces great diversity (such diversity as is indicated, for instance, by the assertions at the start in this section) may be expressed in terms of the symbols for a mathematical point (x, y, z). But since this invariant arises in the same sort of context in which metaphysicians have spoken of 'particle' or 'atom'—

when a disclosure likewise embraces various 'things' of maximum diversity—the invariant may be given a metaphysical interpretation as well. We may thus call the invariant (mathematically) (x, y, z), or (metaphysically) 'a particle'.

Now in the old days the mathematical symbols and the metaphysical concept were virtually equated. Here were the days when mathematics was thought to describe 'reality', which was neither more nor less than mathematics talked about. But today the question arises: Is 'mass', for example, merely short-hand for something measurable, a mere label for the symbol 'M', or does it tell us of some metaphysical secret of the universe vouchsafed in a disclosure? Or again, in the case of 'force': here is a word which may be taken as merely labelling what can be symbolized mathematically as 'rate of charge of momentum', $d/dt(MV)$; or it may be a concept from metaphysics, when it is assimilated to 'power' and 'activity'.

Those same two possibilities can arise not only about mass and force, but, for Newton, they also arise about absolute space and absolute time. They also arise around an atom for Dalton, natural selection for Darwin, periodicity for a theory of the elements, the electron when used as a basis for an electronic theory of valency or of co-ordination compounds, and so on; and with continuous creation for Hoyle. All these words might work metaphysically or not. Let us look a little more closely at this ambiguity which such key words display.

Let it be granted that, so far as physics and chemistry go, we might take words like 'force' or 'absolute space' in Newton's hypothesis, or 'periodicity' in the case of the elements, as no more than convenient co-ordinating words or classificatory devices which have neither meaning nor function other than the heuristic use they are thus given. On this view dominating ideas rounding off a scientific theory of high generality would be just jingles whose use is assimilated to the appropriate mathematical symbolism, or spatio-temporal pattern of scientific interest. With such a status they would resemble very closely Kant's ideas of reason as used 'regulatively', and it is interesting to remember that Kant himself compared this regulative use of an idea of reason with the physicists' use of the concept of 'images', under whose unifying power various haphazard generalizations became a theory of reflection, from which could be deduced countless easy deductions which are subsequently verified.[4] But are the key-ideas of large-scale scientific theories no more than jingles?

Certainly most scientists in theory, and all scientists in practice, have behaved as though the key-words of a scientific theory were more than jingles. Newton's hypothesis, as we have seen, was linked with a 'metaphysical' background (however uneasy or otherwise the relationship between them both in his own mind). Dalton's Atomic theory had its ancestry in the more or less vague atomic 'meta'-'physics' of Democritus, Boyle, and Newton. Even though the periodic table may seem to be exceptional and a plain case of nothing but a classificatory idea, I think it is quite clear that someone like Mendeleyeff, who elaborated it for the first time, thought he had somehow been taken nearer to what he would have called the 'Truth': a full insight into the universe.

At any rate it is certainly the case that as scientific hypotheses increase in scope and importance, embracing a whole variety of generalizations, scientific method sponsors increasingly scientific invariants or absolutes which happen to have an ambiguous status. Now one possibility of science being different from, yet united with, theology, depends precisely on the possibility of these key-words, which arise in relation to disclosure situations, being capable of more than a mathematical interpretation. Does science itself rule out that possibility? Or, on the contrary, does it even hint at it? This question leads us at once to two important if rather difficult topics.

(a) The first topic is known as *operationalism*, which for our present purpose can be seen as a method of giving these scientific absolutes a wholly scientific placing. Certainly we must allow that at least since Einstein, many scientific concepts, some of which in earlier days seemed highly metaphysical, e.g. absolute space, have been given an 'operational' definition, referring more or less directly to what can be measured and calculated. So absolute space is given a relativistic setting. Here are concepts which Bridgman calls 'instrumental',[5] and which Dingle[6] would suggest can be derived from an analysis of what measurement involves. So far it

[4] *Critique of Pure Reason*. Appendix to the Transcendental Didactic. 'The Regulative Employment of the Ideas of Pure Reason', N. Kemp Smith (abridged translation), p. 301.

[5] *Nature*, 166, 1950, p. 91. See also the discussion by M. B. Hesse, *Science and the Human Imagination*, Chap. VII.

[6] *The British Journal for the Philosophy of Science*, I, 1950.

F

looks as if scientific procedure could get rid of all hangovers from earlier metaphysics.

But it is significant that when one sort of metaphysics has thus been expelled by this empirical rigour, the need for other concepts with a curious logical status has immediately shown itself. We have needed other correlating concepts—key-ideas, dominating analogies—not altogether unlike what Bridgman calls 'paper and pencil' concepts not unlike the correlating concepts to which Dingle would give a pictorial use, where such pictures are associated with flights of the imagination, and (let us remember) talk of imagination is never very far from talk about disclosures.

So, as scientific hypotheses increase in scope and become wider generalizations, it is true that operationalism often purifies these hypotheses from crude metaphysical speculations which have hung around from the beginning as man's vision is extended, as he seeks a theory of the universe. But, as the second type of concept suggests, it is a mistake to suppose that in consequence hypotheses at some time might dispense with 'queer ideas' altogether. Certainly the ideas may get fewer, but if anything, they get queerer. The further operationalism goes, the more the need for correlating unifying concepts. So we do not seem able to avoid the conclusion that scientific method, when it reaches this fourth stage, demands metaphysics. One sort of metaphysics is expelled, only to make room for another. Nor is this surprising. For if our account is correct it suggests that the key-words derive from, and witness to, the scientist being more than a detached observer; that they may arise from that kind of transaction with—even rapport with—the universe we have called a disclosure.

Operational concepts are thus founded in what the scientist does, and the theory of operationalism brings the observer centrally and actively into the scientific situation. This means that our earlier question—about the double interpretation of key-words—is now transformed and becomes: Can an account ever be given *by* the scientist himself, *of* the scientist himself, in wholly scientific, i.e. 'object', terms? Here is a question which is surely to be given a negative answer: otherwise, we would objectify the subject.[7] So room is left for metaphysical key-words.

---

[7] For a further discussion see: *Proc. Aris. Soc.*, Suppl., Vol. XXXIII, 1959. I. T. Ramsey, 'Paradox in Religion', esp. pp. 214–15, and I. T. Ramsey, *Freedom and Immorality*, esp. Chaps. I and II.

(b)   The same conclusion is reached by considering the development in physics known as *information theory*, which would analyse scientific knowledge in terms of the acquisition of information. We have seen already, from our independent approach, that scientific conclusions always witness to the language tool being used to extract them. Information theory likewise emphasizes that scientific answers are always relative to the particular scientific questions that are being asked at a given time, and to the features of situations being thus examined.[8]

But the further claim is now made that typical scientific concepts like entropy, and generalizations such as the uncertainty principle, are nothing more than indicators which register and exhibit the kind of questions being asked. In other words they reveal nothing more than the character—the logical structure—of the scientific language being used. Once again scientific method with empirical rigour, may be brushing away subsistent entities by the dozen. At the same time, however, the scientist is becoming essentially involved in his science. Scientific procedure becomes more and more akin to a question-answer game with its language resembling the logic of a dialogue. Key-words now relate to large-scale options made by the scientist in his interchange with the universe and scientific theory expresses a scientist's attempt at conversation with the universe. There is no suggestion that the scientist is a Grand Inquisitor.

It looks then, as if science cannot exclude metaphysical words. Though it may try to lay less and less weight on them within scientific method, scientific method itself involves the scientist as an active subject who cannot himself be objectified and restricted to observables. Scientific method then points to a metaphysical supplement. But does it ever positively *need* these words? Does scientific method ever call explicitly for metaphysics? So we come to 5.

5   THE CONVERSION OF HYPOTHESES: THE DEMAND FOR A TOTAL MAP

It is now time to see what happens when a hypothesis, no matter how previously convincing or comprehensive, is modified or converted and (as we shall see) this will in the end afford us an

---

[8] Once again we can see why scientific hypotheses, if any use at all, are never wholly outmoded.

answer to the question we have just raised. In the conversion of hypothesis certain key-words, around which cluster on the one hand mathematical equations and techniques, and which on the other hand are associated with disclosures, these key-words are replaced by others allowing of more powerful generalizations. One of the best known examples is the progressive modification of the phlogiston theory of combustion and its ultimate replacement by the oxygen theory. Another example is the Newtonian hypothesis which with all its glorious generalizations and dominating concepts, had in the end to give place to others. Experimental data in heat, light, and electro-magnetics led respectively to the concept of entropy, the theory of relativity, and to the quantum theory, for none of which a straightforward Newtonian treatment could be given. Thus arose Einstein with the idea of relative space; and nearer our own time, Eddington with his cosmical number and so on.

Notice that a scientific hypothesis may be modified or there may be a conversion, but a scientific hypothesis is never given a knock-down falsification. There is no comparison with a betting game, no scientific hypothesis is ever 'dead right' or 'dead wrong'. It is merely that one scientific absolute from a certain point of view produces a more powerful synthesis than another. But the usefulness of the old absolute remains. A scientific hypothesis, if it is ever any use at all, will always continue to have that use.

When people speak, as they once did, of a scientific hypothesis being completely falsified the idea was that fact and language were both homogeneous. So H_1 was said to be a good approximation for an area of facts A_1. But when, for some reason or another, A_1 became A^2, an area which included A_1 and something else, whereupon another hypothesis, H^2, was demanded it was said either that H_1 was somehow or other 'in' H^2, or that H^2 was a hypothesis which had once been supposed valid, was now false. But what we have come to see is that there is only the most remote logical kinship between H_1 and H^2. Here are two distinct logical areas. But the point was only seen when scientific method demanded and profitably used both the hypotheses H_1 and H^2 at the same time.

Not long ago the scientist was puzzled by this demand and possibility, and to recall a hackneyed example we may mention the two theories of light—the corpuscular theory and the wave theory—both of which were demanded for scientific inquiry. Here were phenomena demanding on the one hand treatment in such mathematics as suggested wave pictures, continuous wave motions; on the other hand treatment was also demanded in terms of mathematics whose pictures were discontinuous corpuscles or particles. At first, with the old picture of scientific method and hypothesis in mind, scientists tried somehow to make the two hypotheses one. But by this time the attempt has been seen for what it is—a wild goose chase, and scientists must be content to use, at one and the same time, languages of different logical structure about similar situations. Here, briefly and crudely expressed, is the theory of complementarity.[9] The picture of scientific language, far from being homogeneous as was at one time supposed, has rather to be pictured as a hierarchy of logically diversified languages.

Nor let us suppose that this outlook is all that modern. Let us notice a footnote which is to be found in a quite elementary book published some twenty-five years ago: F. B. Finter's *Introduction to Physical Chemistry*. He says, in connection with the atomic theory (p. 15), 'Even if we attempt to "explain" chemical reactions in terms of electrons instead of atoms, the validity and the use of the atomic hypothesis remains unchanged. We are only superimposing an additional "electronic hypothesis, in an attempt to get still nearer the truth".' Finter spoke of Dalton's atomic theory, but the same could be said for the Newtonian hypothesis and, I would dare to say, the phlogiston theory.

Where now is this leading us? For the moment it seems as though we are left with what is often now called the fragmentation of science. Ask 'why' question in one way and we get a question-answer game played in the language H_1; ask 'why' questions in another way and we get a question-answer game played in the language H^2.

Yet we must recall that scientific method never gives up its fifth

---

[9] The example may stand even though claims have been made that in this case fragmentation has been overcome. This claim I would counter on logical grounds, but in any case fragmentation in general remains simply because no scientific theory of any real use is ever 'falsified'. Nor do more comprehensive scientific theories say *everything* which was said by the more restricted theories they often replaced. Cf. the preceding paragraphs and the next two paragraphs.

feature, its hope of sponsoring some one overall scheme, one total language map, for the whole universe. But how is this going to be reached from a multiplicity of logically variegated languages? Has the old idea of science to be abandoned? Can scientific method never again give us one theory of the universe? Are we committed to a scientific Tower of Babel? That is the problem which contemporary science by its increasing fragmentation sets us. We shall see presently that it is precisely at this point that science can profitably and properly call again on those metaphysical words which for the first four stages of its method it had rather cold-shouldered. But before continuing our argument, let us summarize our position so far in four points to see how far and where this scientific methodology is compatible with religious attitude.

1   The scientist, as we have seen, does not keep all that close to 'the facts'. What he needs besides and more than the facts, is insight, intuition, some sort of disclosure. To that degree the scientist is not particularly 'humble' before 'the facts'. At the same time, he has generalizations from which deductions can be made which can be verifiably tested. Now here is a divergence between the hypotheses of science and religion, if religion be allowed hypotheses at all. The scientist has options which are always just a little far-fetched, but they can find currency in, e.g. mathematics, which permits of deductions, verifiable or falsifiable as the case may be.

2   Yet the scientist does not put the universe to the test; he tests rather his generalizations, the invariants which have been disclosed to him, which have been grasped by his insight, an insight correlative with a disclosure. The scientist does not put the universe to the question. He rather puts his question—about his provisional invariants—to the universe and lets the universe decide for him. All he puts to the question are his theories. He sponsors some invariant and follows it through till the universe gives him an answer, tells him whether his faith has been well-founded, or not; whether his insight has or has not been reliable, whether or not he is a false prophet. Here is something potentially religious.

3   Further, the scientist is always willing to revise his beliefs to sponsor alternative absolutes. In this sense he is humble, and again potentially religious.

4   At the same time the scientist searches for an overall scheme and to this extent his whole aim might be said to be to control

everything by scientific techniques.[10] Here, it might be said, and here especially, is Michael Foster's strong point. But can the languages of science give us a completely exhaustive map? The brief answer is, logically, no. For what exceeds the language of science are the very disclosures which scientific method itself demands, and which become the more prominent, and their logical status the clearer, as scientific method proceeds.

On what conditions, then, shall we ever possess one adequate language-map of the universe—a map embracing not only the diverse languages of science, but also the supplement which those languages seem to need? The question has brought us back to the point where we paused in the discussion, and it is time to take up the matter again. Fragmentation, we noticed, is logically inescapable if we are to be mere scientists. As a scientist, a man is doomed to disappointment if his aim is an overall scheme. Each generalization, each theory, has its significance which is never wholly taken over by another. The scientist has a diversity of options. But now the vital question recurs: Can we, and on what conditions can we, recapture the old ideal of science as providing us with one language map of the universe? Where can words be found to unite the diverse languages of science? Where can science find its hopes justified? What does conversation and dialogue with the universe imply?

Here at the end I venture to outline a possible answer. I would like to argue that it is at this point that science and religion become supplementary in a way which helps both, yet humbles both.

There is no space to do more than give a mere outline. But let us approach that outline with such reflections as these.

If a word (or words) is to unite the diverse languages of science, it must occur in phrases which are entailed by all kinds of scientific

[10] Some might think that the technologist was of all scientists the most 'dangerous' to religion, the one whose methods and practices reflect nothing but a striving for mastery, and that Michael Foster might well have had the technologist in mind rather than the pure scientific thinker. Now it is true that the technologist will have little time for disclosures. Rule of thumb methods, the slide-rule and so on, represent best his habits and practices. At the same time, his scientific progress raises moral problems of the highest magnitude: and it may be that here he finds his disclosures—moral disclosures—which can supply him with the 'compensation' he needs. In short, the salvation of technology may well have to be found in the moral issues to which it stirs the technologist.

assertions. Yet it must not itself be native to any one of the logically diverse languages of science, or fragmentation will remain. But because the key-word is *not* native to the language of science, it now follows that key-assertions will never entail verifiable deductions. How can this be? Have we any paradigm for such words or phrases?

Let us begin by taking the assertion 'I exist'. This certainly is entailed by all kinds of scientific assertions. 'He has a heart beating', 'He has a blood count of X', 'He has a digestive system characterized by all that the bio-chemistry of fats, proteins, carbohydrates, and enzymes can teach us', 'He has such and such reflex actions', 'He has such and such brain potentials': 'I exist', is entailed by all these, when said of me. But 'I exist' entails none of these. We cannot necessarily *deduce* from 'I exist' any of these *particular* assertions. Yet the affirmation of my existence is that which gives all these varied assertions their concrete reference; is that which unites them all.

Now what I suggest is that the word 'God' must be seen as a logical kinsman of 'I' in having, at least in these two respects, a similar logical behaviour. 'God exists' entails no particular verifiable assertions. Theology can provide no verifiable deductions. But this does not mean that it has no empirical relevance. On the contrary, like 'I exist', 'God exists' is a phrase which is in fact entailed by and so linked with verifiable language, while entailing none of it. The latter point used to be expressed in old-fashioned language by people who said 'The world is not necessary to God'. As to the earlier point, namely: that scientific assertions entail 'God exists' as some entail 'I exist': this used to be expressed as 'God is necessary to the world'. Further, the basis for 'God exists' is an affirmation which arises around the universe in a moment of disclosure, in a moment of worship, indeed in prayer. It is thus like the basis for 'I exist'.[11] Here, in worship, scientific assertions are integrated with, yet distinguished from, the theological assertion of God's existence.

Let us go back for a moment to Professor Wisdom and Elijah. Not even here had we an experimental issue. The fire did not test a hypothesis. No assertion about fire coming down can be deduced from 'God exists' or from anything Elijah said. When the fire

[11] Cf. I. T. Ramsey, loc. cit and *Religious Language*, esp. pp. 61–5; also *Phil. Quarterly*, July 1955, pp. 193–204.

came down it did something very different from providing the verifiable criteria for a hypothesis, something very different which Wisdom (and, it may be said, others) does not sufficiently distinguish. It answered a prayer. Indeed we may, with due deference, suggest that in many ways the story would have been religiously more enlightening if the fire had not come down. For it would have shown us better how the religious man can keep his affirmation but modify and develop his theology. As it was, the verifiable success might have tempted Elijah or his opponents to think that God could always be tested, would always provide verifiable criteria and then God would have become a scientific concept. Here I entirely agree with the protests that Mr Foster makes.

Yet if religion and science are not identical, I want to emphasize that they are complementary. Religion can give to science that affirmation of the universe which it needs. It can give to science the basis of fact presupposed by operationalism and information theory; it can supply a suitable key-word to organize the logical diversification of large-scale scientific theory. Religion can give all this to the scientist. But the scientist must then, *in the end*, give up his verifiable hopes. For this key-word 'God' has not a scientific logic so that 'God exists' entails no verifiable conclusions; beside 'I', its kinsmen are rather those 'metaphysical' words which science has from time to time sponsored, and which (as we saw) were currency for disclosures, even though the scientist for most of his working day might find a mathematical understanding of the disclosure quite adequate.

Science can satisfy religion in its venture after fuller and fuller relevance, after more and more adequate discursive expression. But theology must then share in the tentative character of science, and be prepared to lose any verbal and verifiable guarantees for which it might once have yearned. We can regain the old ideal, alike of science and metaphysical theology, for one map, only when that map loses in the end its purely scientific character; only when it sponsors some metaphysical words of which 'mass', 'force', 'evolution' were once favourites, though I have outlined a means of substituting 'God' for them all. I have suggested that the scientist can only secure his wildest dreams when he becomes religious. At the same time the theologian can only secure his wildest dreams when he becomes scientific.

Science and religion may find a synthesis in their methods. But the cost to each is great. The theologian must admit a tentative theology; the scientist must admit key-words which cannot (and it is a logical *cannot*) be given straight scientific verification. Yet theologian and scientist meet where all meet—in the affirmation of the universe which is wonder and worship at what the universe discloses.

Facts and Disclosures*

It is tempting for me to begin with, and I recognize that readers may well ask at the outset for, a definition of 'disclosure'. But, as is no doubt episcopally very appropriate, I shall not altogether fall a victim to this temptation. For the sake of clarity, however, I would point out from the start that, negatively at any rate, I do not use disclosure in what might be called the newspaper sense of disclosure, i.e., a sense which carries with it overtones of information disclosed. I use 'disclosure' not in relation to information, but to refer to situations about which various metaphorical phrases are commonly used. Such phrases, for example, are those which speak of situations 'coming alive', 'taking on depth', situations in which 'the penny drops', where we 'see' but not with eyes of flesh, where something 'strikes us', where 'eye meets eye', and where 'hearts miss a beat'. Such situations may be of a dramatic and spectacular kind to which a metaphor like 'the ice breaks' is plainly appropriate, or they may be of the kind where we gradually come to 'see' so that we speak more appropriately of 'the light dawning'. They occur, to take other instances, when we see the 'point' of a puzzle drawing, or when we see that a particular sequence e.g., $\frac{1}{2}, \frac{2}{3}, \frac{3}{4}, \frac{4}{5}, \frac{5}{6}, \frac{6}{7}$, has an upper bound of one. It is with such situations in mind that I speak of disclosures.

Now I often use the word 'disclosure' to talk of the kind of situations in which all religious language is directly or derivatively grounded, and these disclosures are often supposed by my critics to be just some peculiar kind of 'experience', thought to be 'subjective'. As a result, it has been supposed that like some other present-day philosophers of religion I, too, deprive religious statements of any objective reference and *a fortiori* of any transcendent claim. But sometimes I have suspected that in such controversy objectivity was supposed to characterize only such things as tables, pennies, trees. All these, it will be claimed, are plainly objective facts. Are they?

* Meeting of the Aristotelian Society at 5/7, Tavistock Place, London WC1, on Monday, 24 January 1972, at 7.30 p.m.

Again, when philosophers find theological discussions intricate and unsatisfying, they often thrust in questions such as: 'Is it or is it not *a fact* that Jesus rose from the dead?' 'We are prepared to say, for the sake of argument, that Jesus "as a matter of fact" lived and was crucified; but is it *a fact* that he ascended?'

A favourite question not so many years ago was: 'Is the existence of God a matter of fact?' Some, like Professor Hick, talk of religious facts as though they are some special brand of fact, which inhabit the religious world. For instance, in *Faith and the Philosophers* (p. 239), Professor Hick writes: 'The ordinary religious believer has always supposed that such a statement as "God loves mankind" is a true declaration concerning an ultimate order of fact, which sustains and governs all the more proximate types of fact. . . . A conviction as to the reality of God is, Christian faith will insist, either a response to fact, rendered appropriate and rational by its conformity with fact, or it is delusory and is rendered inappropriate and irrational by its divergence from fact.' Lastly, in the days of anti-metaphysical warfare the leading question used to be about the sort of fact which would justify metaphysics. What do we make of all this appeal to 'fact'?

What I hope to do in this chapter is to clarify what I mean by disclosures by facing some of these problems which arise around talk about facts. In other words, I hope to clarify the relation of facts to disclosures, and to suggest that the concept of disclosure is both necessary and useful to bring coherence into talk about facts, as well as being a concept in terms of which we can understand better what is at issue in many traditional problems of philosophy.

I begin with a quotation from J. L. Austin's *Sense and Sensibilia*. Austin begins with a question we can make our own: 'Where then are "empirical facts" to be found?' He replies: 'Ayer's answer is quite clear—they are *facts about sense-data*, or as he also puts it "about the nature of the sensible appearances", "the phenomena"; this is where we really encounter "the empirical evidence". There are in his view—his *real* view—no other "empirical facts" at all. *The* hard fact is that there are sense-data; these entities really exist and are what they are; what other entities we may care to *speak as if* there were is a pure matter of verbal convenience, but "the facts to which these expressions are intended to refer" will always be the same, facts about sense-data.' Austin grants that 'the official interpretation of these and many other such remarks is that, strictly speaking, they are concerned with the logical relations obtaining between two different *languages*, the "sense-datum language" and "material-object language", and are not to be taken literally as concerned with the *existence of anything*'. But, as Austin argues, behind this question of logical relationships is the presupposition that 'in fact sense-data make up the whole of "our resources" ' (p. 107). These sense-data and 'observable facts' as 'facts about sense-data' are supposed to be the basis for all certainty. It is this same claim for an incorrigible base in sense-data which is made when philosophers have talked about 'immediacy'. The point can be made as Austin makes it in his comments on Warnock's treatment of Berkeley where he is elucidating what Berkeley means by 'immediately perceive'. Says Warnock: 'I say, for instance, that I see a book. Let it be admitted that this is a perfectly correct thing to say. But there is still in this situation something (not the book) which is *immediately* seen. For, whether or not any further investigations would confirm the claim that I see a book, whatever I know or believe about what I see, and whatever I might see, touch, or smell if I came closer, there is *now* in my visual field a certain coloured shape, or pattern of colours. This is what I *immediately* see . . . This is more "fundamental" than the book itself, in the sense that, although I might immediately see this pattern of colours and yet no book be there, I could not see the book nor indeed *anything at all* unless such coloured shapes occurred in my visual field.' Why 'immediately' see? The answer is because it is thought that here is a 'basic', 'minimal' form of assertion involving no inferences. Hence, 'immediate' is a word which seems to be used to express such a close and direct relation with 'facts' that assertions arising in such a situation of immediacy cannot be mistaken. Austin's comment is: 'His statements of "immediate perception", so far from being that from which we *advance* to more ordinary statements, are actually arrived at, and are so arrived at in his own account, by *retreating from* more ordinary statements, by progressive hedging. (There's a tiger— there *seems* to be a tiger—it seems *to me* that there's a tiger—it seems to me *now* that there's a tiger—it seems to me now *as if there were* a tiger.) It seems extraordinarily perverse to represent as that on which ordinary statements are based a form of words which, *starting from* and moreover incorporating an ordinary statement, qualifies and hedges it in various ways. You've got to get something on your plate before you can start messing it around' (pp. 141–2).

What Austin protests against is a dichotomy between material objects and things of some other kind. 'It seems that what I am to be said to see "immediately" must be what is "in my visual field". But this latter phrase is not explained at all; isn't the book in my visual field? And if the right answer to the question what is in my visual field is to be, as Warnock assumes, "a coloured shape", why should one further assume that this is "something, *not the book*"? It would surely be quite natural and proper to say, "That patch of red there *is* the book" (cp. "That white dot is my house"). By ignoring the fact that coloured shapes, patches of colour, etc., can quite often and correctly be said to *be* the things that we see, Warnock is just quietly slipping in here that dichotomy between "material objects" and entities of some other kind which is so crucially damaging. Furthermore, he has himself admitted in several earlier passages that patches of colour, etc. can be and are said to be seen in a perfectly ordinary, familiar sense; so why do we now have to say that they are *immediately* seen, as if they called for some special treatment?' (p. 136).

Before coming to an appraisal of Austin, let us look at the philosopher from whom this way of talking took its origin, i.e. Russell, where we find the same appeal to some basic datum, a datum which is given immediately and all this in contrast to what is vague and corrigible. Let us recall the classic passage in *The Problems of Philosophy* (p. 17). What we are immediately aware of, says Russell, are sense-data, 'Let us give the name of "sense-data" to the things that are immediately known in sensation: such things as colours, sounds, smells, hardnesses, roughnesses, and so on.' They contrast, he says, with 'the real table if there is one'. This 'is not *immediately* known to us at all, but must be an inference from what is immediately known'.

He develops the point a little on page 30: 'It is our particular thoughts and feelings that have primitive certainty. And this applies to dreams and hallucinations as well as to normal perceptions: when we dream or see a ghost, we certainly do have the sensations we think we have, but for various reasons it is held that no physical object corresponds to these sensations. Thus the certainty of our knowledge of our own experiences does not have to be limited in any way to allow for exceptional cases. Here, therefore, we have, for what it is worth, a solid basis from which to begin our pursuit of knowledge.' The well-known distinction between knowledge by acquaintance and knowledge by description comes some pages later: 'We shall say that we have *acquaintance* with anything of which we are directly aware, without the intermediary of any process of inference or any knowledge of truths. Thus in the presence of my table I am acquainted with the sense-data that make up the appearance of my table—its colour, shape, hardness, smoothness, *etc.*; all these are things of which I am immediately conscious when I am seeing and touching my table' (p. 73). In contrast to this immediate awareness of sense-data: 'There is no state of mind in which we are directly aware of the table; all our knowledge of the table is really knowledge of *truths*, and the actual thing which is the table is not, strictly speaking, known to us at all.'

My first point will be that what is given immediately, what is given without inference, is disclosure-given. But it is not a sense-datum; it is rather objectivity, something other than ourselves, an objective reference. This, and this alone, can be claimed as certain, basic, immediate, without inference and so on. What Russell does in *The Problems of Philosophy*, Chapter I, is to tell a story directed to a disclosure. The story begins with himself sitting in a room and then he invites us to 'concentrate attention on the table' (p. 11). He then talks about its colour, its texture, its shape, what it feels like to the touch, employing on the table—as he himself implies later—a Cartesian method of systematic doubt so as to discover what in the end exists with certainty. Though the pattern of the argument is anything but clear in Russell, it seems as if in the end he is saying: 'But there is obviously something known with certainty, something immediately given, and whatever is immediately given let us call sense-data'. What I am suggesting is that his story, while casting doubt left and right, points us in this way to what is given immediately. What this is dawns on us when, at some point or other in the story, a disclosure occurs. But what is given at that point of disclosure is not a sense-datum, it is simply an awareness of something other than ourselves. What Russell has done in effect is to give us that supplement to Descartes' argument that Descartes himself should have reached. For when his methodological doubt converged on a disclosure, it was not only a disclosure of subjectivity but of a subjectivity matched by objectivity. The main difference was that while he had to hand a word—'I'—which he could use with more or less plausibility about what was self-disclosed, there was no given phrase or interpretative scheme by which to talk about what had been objectively disclosed. The word 'sense-datum' was tailor-made by Russell to talk of what was in this way infallibly and objectively given.

Russell comes very near to making this parallel with Descartes when he discusses Bismarck on page 85 of *The Problems of Philosophy*. He is willing to assume that there can be 'direct acquaintance' with oneself. The extraordinary thing is that he does not seem to realize that we can talk quite sensibly about those who were 'acquainted with Bismarck' and that we ourselves, had we been alive at the time, might have been so 'acquainted' with Bismarck. He assumes that this kind of acquaintance would have to be in terms of descriptive phrases such as 'The first Chancellor of the German Empire'. While it is perfectly true that no one could have that same direct acquaintance with Bismarck as Bismarck had of himself; nevertheless, besides having knowledge of Bismarck by description, we might well have had knowledge of Bismarck by acquaintance, and this would have been when around some appearances of Bismarck with or without descriptive assertions there was a disclosure of what might have been called 'the real Bismarck', Bismarck's 'real self', a disclosure of Bismarck which was matched by a self-disclosure on our part.

The point I am making about sense-data was being implied, I believe, by Austin in the passage I quoted from the end of *Sense and Sensibilia* (pp. 141–2). I would suggest that what Warnock and others do is to begin with ordinary statements and to develop talk which leads to a disclosure. What Austin calls 'retreating from . . . ordinary statements' or 'progressive hedging' I would see as a reputable philosophical route so as to arrive at a disclosure. We might well start with 'There is a tiger' and by Austin's route we would arrive at 'It seems to me now as if there were a tiger'. What I am saying is that the point of this exercise is to disclose objectivity while leaving the tigerish description problematical. What Austin shows us indeed is that in vain we seek for infallible language as an expression of objective reference. Material-object language will not suffice or we would never have illusions; sense-datum language will not suffice not only because there is no sense-datum language—Russell's 'simple terms' are as bogus as anything could be—but because no one has ever made it clear what is meant by a sense-datum. Not surprisingly, I would say, for, not being content with an objective reference whose expression was problematical, those who have worshipped sense-data have not only sponsored a common-sense dogmatism styled in the idiom of perception language, they have wanted the language to correspond with certainty to indubitable units of the universe. All we need do to reach the position of some theologians is to read for 'sense-data', 'God'.

What happens when philosophers sponsor sense-datum language is that some assertions are taken as basic incorrigible accounts of the objectivity which is given in a disclosure. In this way, the objectivity, the objective reference, and the relevant assertions are confounded. The significance of talk about sense-data is that it is rather talk grounded in the disclosure of a reference. Sense-data were supposed both to give a secure objective reference and also to guarantee the certainty of assertions explicating this objective reference. But the certainty of the reference only arises in a disclosure and is never transferable to the assertions themselves.

When we say, recollecting Austin's remark, 'The dot in the distance is my house', we are saying that the objective reference of both 'dot' and 'my house' is the same. While I agree with Austin that this objective reference is not what Ayer—and I would say Russell also—claims, I am still not clear what he himself wishes to say. For my part, I would say that this objective reference is what strikes when, having heard a good deal about someone's house and then in a concrete situation seeing the dot, a disclosure occurs. I do not think Austin sees this referential point. But he rightly sees negatively that the intuition and the immediacy cannot relate to the assertions themselves or to 'things' like sense-data. The reference of empirical facts, i.e. what empirical facts are facts about, what are sometimes called 'objective' facts, is to be found when disclosures occur around physical-object talk developed in a certain kind of way, but the 'objectivity' is never given incorrigibly in terms of descriptive language.

Let me endeavour to put the same kind of point in terms of Russell's distinction between knowledge by acquaintance and knowledge by description. What I am suggesting is that both of these arise at one and the same time out of the same situation.

There is an 'immediate' direct incorrigible feature, and this is the objective reference which is disclosure-given. There is also the interpretation, the descriptions, the talk, and there is something which is less or more reliable. It may be more vague or more precise, but it will never have, indeed logically it could not have, features that belong only to disclosures and never to assertions.

So when we appeal to 'the facts' in any argument or discussion I suggest that our appeal is twofold:

(a) We are in part appealing to a situation where an objective reference, objectivity, individuation, is given immediately, i.e. in a disclosure or intuition, and

(b) in such a situation we declare ourselves prepared to take as 'basic' an assertion *b* so that we say 'As a matter of fact *b*' where *b* relates in one way or another to the visible, actual, audible phenomena which characterize the situation.

To talk of *x*'s being an empirical fact is to talk of the objectivity disclosed around *x*, the kind of objectivity which is disclosure-given.

If now we turn to J. L. Austin's *Philisophical Papers*, and to the chapter *Unfair to Facts* we shall find Austin discussing the position of Strawson in relation to the distinction between 'facts' and 'things'. Says Austin (p. 103), 'Strawson points out, truly enough, that "while we certainly say a statement corresponds to (fits, is borne out by, agrees with) the facts, as a variant on saying that it is true, we *never* say that it corresponds to the thing, person, etc., it is about" '. Austin admits that 'Here is a case, certainly, in which "things", "events", etc., are used differently from "facts" '. And certainly there are important differences between these words. But firstly, there are important similarities also.

'For example, although we perhaps rarely, and perhaps only in strained senses, say that a "thing" (e.g. the German Navy) is a fact, and perhaps never say that a person is a fact, still, things and persons are far from being all that the ordinary man, and even Strawson, would admit to be genuinely things-in-the-world whatever exactly they may mean. Phenomena, events, situations, states of affairs are commonly supposed to be genuinely-in-the-world, and even Strawson admits events are so. Yet surely of all of these we can say that they *are facts*. The collapse of the Germans is an event and is a fact—was an event and was a fact.

'Strawson, however, seems to suppose that anything of which we say ". . . is a fact" is, automatically, *not* something in the world. Thus:

'What "makes the statement" that the cat has mange "true" is not the cat, but the *condition* of the cat, i.e. the fact that the cat has mange. The only plausible candidate for the position of what (in the world) makes the statement true is the fact it states; but the fact it states is not something in the world.

'I cannot swallow this because it seems to me quite plain:

1 That the condition of the cat is a fact;
2 That the condition of the cat is something-in-the-world— if I understand that expression at all.

'How can Strawson have come to say that the condition of the cat is *not* something in the world?'

The whole point turns, of course, on the ambiguity of 'being in-the-world' or being 'something-in-the-world'. Plainly, the Cheshire cat's grin is 'in-the-world', but not in the same sense as the cat is 'in-the-world'. I suggest that why Strawson wishes to say that the condition of the cat is *not* something in the world turns on the view he takes as to what 'things' *are* 'in the world'. Though we say, or once might have said, 'The German navy is "in the world" ' we don't normally say, for example, 'The German navy is a fact', but we do say, for example, 'It's a fact that the German navy is efficient, powerful, collapsed and so on'. I suspect that the difference arises between Austin and Strawson because Strawson is, for better or worse, rather clearer than is Austin about his ontology and where objective reference arises. In other words, for Strawson (if I interpret him right, and if I do, I agree with him) we must distinguish existence and reference, or reference and objective reference. Austin wants to call a 'fact' whatever is 'there', and certainly such an existential claim is an important part of the logic of facts, but it does not relieve us of the other question of objective reference, as Austin seems to think it does.

I think we can say that for both Austin and Strawson talk about a fact presupposes an area of discourse equal in size to or greater than a certain minimum amount. To put it differently 'It is a fact that the German navy . . .' needs a supplement relating to some state of affairs if it is to make sense. Such a state of affairs is, says Strawson, a 'fact' but it is not in the world as the German navy is (was) in the world. We might say that the existence of the German navy is a fact, e.g. to be reckoned with, but we do not say that the German navy is a fact. Yet we could certainly say that the existence of the German navy was a fact. Which only goes to show that talk about fact certainly involves an experienced claim, of one kind or another, i.e. either an existential (reference) claim for, e.g., the German navy, or an existential claim for the 'facts and features' of the world.

For Strawson, a thing in the world—an entity—implies ontological independence so that the cat's condition is a pseudo-entity. But of course the cat's condition is 'a state of affairs', a 'set of circumstances' and so on. The bother is—and it is a complication of which Austin makes use—talk about facts is sometimes a way of making precisely the second kind of existential claim. So Austin can say, 'It seems to me . . . that to say that something is a fact is at least in part precisely to say that it is something in the world: much more that than—though perhaps also to a minor extent also—to classify it as being some special kind of something-in-the-world' (p. 106). On this problem of the relation between facts, states of affairs and things, we may distinguish Austin and Strawson as follows. For Austin, or so it would seem, all existents are facts and all things in the world are facts, and so he moves easily, and I agree with Strawson perhaps too easily, between things on the one hand and facts, states of affairs, situations, features, sets of circumstances, and so on, on the other. Strawson says (*Proceedings of the Aristotelian Society, Supplementary Volume* XXIV, p. 135): 'The whole charm of talking of situations, states of affairs or facts as included in, or parts of, the world, consists in thinking of them as things, and groups of things' and 'the temptation to talk of situations, etc., in the idiom appropriate to talking of things and events is, once this first step is taken, overwhelming'. As Strawson expresses his point in a relevant footnote, in deliberate opposition to the earlier Wittgenstein: 'The world is a totality of things, not of facts'. He remarks that to 'talk of facts, situations and states of affairs, as "included in" or "parts" of the world is, obviously, metaphorical'. In other words, Strawson is much more clear and explicit about his ontology than is Austin. But does he relate satisfactorily states of affairs, matters of fact and things? For Strawson, objective reference is given and only given by way of things (and, as we shall see later, by way of persons), and things are quite different from what happens to be the case, states of affairs and so on. Strawson would have to grant, or so it would seem, an existential status to facts in the sense that talking about facts is talking about what is the case. But he would wish to have 'things' in the world of some quite different ontological status. The distinction is between 'existents' and 'thinghood', or in more traditional terms between events and substances. There *are* states of affairs, e.g. a cat's mange; but there *are* also cats, in a different sense of 'are'. It is these 'things' that sentences are about, these 'things' give sentences their objective reference and must be distinguished from 'facts' which the sentences 'state'. For Strawson, such 'things' are independent particulars known in a realist, common-sense kind of way as objects contrasted with facts. Strawson is right to see that Austin ignores the question of objective reference; but is Strawson right in finding objective reference in such a realist common-sense way by appealing *ad hoc* to 'things' as independent particulars?

On this matter of facts and things, I would mediate between Austin and Strawson in the following way. I am with Strawson in seeing that Austin needs to give an account of objective reference over and above what he speaks of as the existential claim made by talk about the facts. Facts and features are in the world, and of the world, but not in the world as are things. But I believe that Strawson still needs to give his concept of 'thing' further analysis. In what cirumstances does objective reference arise? It seems to me that it arises when we have a context of sufficient area to generate a disclosure and this would be the case when we have specified enough states of affairs, circumstances or features that lead to a disclosure of what Strawson would call a 'thing', a thing which exists as the objective reference of these features.

In short, the concept of disclosure can mediate between Austin and Strawson. It is needed to give Strawson the objective reference he wishes his 'things' to have; it affords a necessary development of what Austin says. We begin to see why there must be some kind of minimum context when talk about facts is going to give us an objective reference, and why there arises what seemed to be an exceptional case but is not. When we say: 'It is a fact that the German navy exists', this is no exception at all. For the logic of talk about fact here is to make a claim for objective reference, and not to talk of a feature of the world.

May I develop these remarks just briefly in a metaphysical direction and hint at some theological possibilities? Let us call an 'existent' everything that is in any way discriminated, particularized, in any situation. Now it has been my argument that at some point or other when we talk in one way or another about a number of such existents there may occur a disclosure of 'objectivity'. It is this which causes Strawson to talk of persons and things as basic units of individuation, when around the behaviour patterns of what are called bodies, and around the physical history of what are called material objects, an objective reference is disclosed.

Now partly because I know myself in a self-disclosure, and partly because there is a *rapport*, a matching, in certain situations of friendship, or even hate, where I 'come alive' as others 'come alive', we can agree with Strawson in taking persons as irreducible.

This point can be developed a little further in relation to Hume. Let us turn to his well-known confession in the Appendix to *A Treatise of Human Nature*: 'When we talk of *self* or *subsistence*, we must have an idea,' Hume argues, 'annexed to these terms, otherwise they are altogether unintelligible.' But, says Hume, 'Every idea is derived from preceding impressions; and we have no impression of self or substance, as something simple and individual.' The conclusion is therefore clear: 'We have, therefore, no idea of them in that sense.' What then are we to say? Hume's well-known answer is that 'We only *feel* a connexion or determination of the thought to pass from one object to another . . . thought alone feels personal identity, when reflecting on the train of past perceptions that compose a mind, the ideas of them are felt to be connected together, and naturally introduce each other.' In other words, as we reflect on this train of 'distinctive perceptions' a feeling, a sense, of personal identity breaks in on us. As we survey this train of particular perceptions, there is a self-disclosure. I think we are entitled in such cases to speak of finite centres of objectivity, 'finite' because the disclosure arises around a circumscribed area of facts and features in and through which my own finite individuality is disclosed.

But what is the case with things? Impressed with stories of illusions; with the variation in sensible qualities owing to light of different colour and intensity; impressed with the variety of stories that can be told scientifically so that the 'givenness' of the familiar facts and features of, for example, this chair disappear, I see no reason to take any similar plurality of objective reference in the case of things. Things have a particularity in so far as a disclosure occurs around a circumscribed area; but what is disclosed around a particular set of facts and features is in Locke's famous phrase a 'something' which cannot itself be further specified. Here is an objective reference, having no easy *rapport* with myself as in the case of persons; it cannot of itself be further specified except in terms of the facts and features which are evident to us. Beyond that, it is something 'I know not what'. This interpretation indeed illuminates, I think, the phrase from Locke which has, I believe, been traditionally repeated without a careful enough examination. Locke did not doubt there was a 'something'; but he was quite clear that it was a 'something' about which he could not talk as if it were, in his sense, an 'idea' or set of ideas. It is pertinent to recall here an example he gives in his correspondence with Stillingfleet.

In a letter to Stillingfleet, Bishop of Worcester, dated 4 May 1698, Locke contrasts himself with 'those who lay all foundation of certainty in clear and distinct ideas', and he complains that the Bishop of Worcester joins him with 'these gentlemen'. These gentlemen of course include that philosophical *bête noir* John Toland who in 1696—some six years after Locke's *Essay*—had published his *Christianity not Mysterious*. Undoubtedly, Toland allowed no kind of certainty to arise except that which was founded in clear and distinct ideas. Locke, however, wishes to grant that certainty can arise where ideas are 'not in all their parts perfectly clear and distinct'.[1] This brings Locke to his own example of what he means by obscure and confused ideas.

> Suppose you should in the twilight, or in a thick mist, see two things standing upright, near the size and shape of an ordinary man; but in so dim a light, or at such a distance, that they appeared very much alike, and you could not perceive them to be what they really were, the one a Statue, the other a Man; would not these two be obscure and confused Ideas? And yet could not your Lordship be certain of the truth of this proposition concerning either of them, that it was something, or did exist; and that by perceiving the Agreement of that Idea (as obscure and confused as it was) with that of existence, as expressed in that proposition.

[1] Second Reply to the Bishop of Worcester, Oates, 4 May 1698.

Let us in fact develop Locke's example a little. Suppose there is mist in the park; we see 'two things standing upright', and of them both we use the word 'statue'. This would certainly be, on Locke's view, a case of obscure and confused ideas, for leaving out the difference which keeps the statue or man distinct, we would be applying one word 'statue' to them both. Suppose now the mist slowly lifts and the light slowly improves, there will no doubt be times when we wish to use the word 'man' of both, then the word 'statue' of both again, and so on. For a long time, in other words, we shall be the victim of obscure and confused ideas in not knowing what words to apply to the situation. But at the end, when the mist has cleared or we are sufficiently near to them both, we can apply the word 'statue' and 'man' respectively and have reliable labels. Yet while all this is true, Locke's point is that there would be one assertion that could be made about both things with certainty from the start, viz. that in each case 'something exists'. Whatever idea we had of either object, we could discern an agreement between that idea and the idea given by the word 'existence'. At all times while the mist was clearing we could be sure that something existed. We could say all the time with intuitive certainty 'I knew it was something'. Once there had been a disclosure of objectivity we would then have intuitive certainty about something or other. So far, the case is interesting enough, but soon it becomes extremely significant, for Locke continues with what on a traditional interpretation of Locke would be a rather astonishing giveaway.[2] 'This, my Lord, is just the case of Substance, upon which you raised this argument concerning obscure and confused ideas; which this instance shows may have propositions made about them, of whose truth we may be certain.' So with intuitive certainty can often go ideas whose name is problematical; with intuitive certainty, what is now problematical language. It would seem that for Locke the word 'substance' relates precisely to this intuitive certainty of 'something'—what I am aware of when I cannot be wrong in seeing or hearing, tasting or smelling, touching 'something', though I can be wrong, and I may often be wrong, in labelling this 'something'. For the 'ideas' by which I discern it might well not be classified appropriately or graded satisfactorily.

I think that the same kind of point can be made about universals—they, too, are best understood in terms of particular instances

[2] Second Reply to the Bishop of Worcester, loc. cit.

which lead to a disclosure whose objective reference is in its articulation problematical. We may usefully recall Russell's discussion of the matter in *The Problems of Philosophy*: 'It is obvious, to begin with,' he says, 'that we are acquainted with such universals as white, red, black, sweet, sour, loud, hard, etc., i.e. with qualities which are exemplified in sense-data. When we see a white patch, we are acquainted, in the first instance, with the particular patch; but by seeing many white patches, we easily learn to abstract the whiteness which they all have in common, and in learning to do this we are learning to be acquainted with whiteness. A similar process will make us acquainted with any other universal of the same sort. Universals of this sort may be called "sensible qualities" ' (pp. 158–9). In other words, it is as and when we see instances of a particular sensible quality that there may break in on us, sooner or later, a disclosure, and we give the name universal to this of which we are then aware. But this always translates back into particular instances of that which we speak of as the universal, for example, colour. Universal words are no more, though no less, than words which bear witness to a disclosure reached in a certain way, viz. by surveying a series of particular qualities. Categories like substance and universals are best seen as labels for different routes into a disclosure of that which is other than myself.

My conclusion then is that the objective reference given in a disclosure to which, for example, stories about things, or universals have led, cannot be further characterized except as the One disclosed in and through the Many, or a 'reality' disclosed through 'appearances'. But for some it has been labelled Absolute, and for others God, though these words only gain a meaning in use in so far as they hold together the different strands of discourse which provide the stories leading to a disclosure of the one individuation, the one objective referent, what Locke called 'something'.

There are perhaps two points to make before drawing this discussion to an end with a few concluding remarks. In some ways, the two points can be seen as complementary answers to the same question as to the reliability of disclosures. First, it might be asked how illusions fit into this treatment. I would say that in some illusions, there is no disclosure at all—just a plain mistake in supposing that the hot tarmac road on a sunny day had a covering of water. In other cases of illusion, and especially in dreams, there certainly may be a disclosure. In that case, there would certainly be an objective reference. The problem of dreams and illusions is then how to interpret reliably the 'something' which is disclosed in this way. For any phrases or concepts which are readily at hand will, for all kinds of reasons, have to be rejected. Indeed, it needs something as complicated as a scientific theory in the case of illusions, or something as complex as the account given by Freud or Jung (to say nothing of Joseph or Daniel) to spell out reliably what is disclosed in a dream.

This links, secondly, with the well-known difficulty about disclosures. Can we be mistaken about them? When a disclosure has occurred, we certainly cannot be mistaken about the objective reference, the objectivity which has been disclosed. We cannot be mistaken about that 'something' which is other than ourselves. But we can certainly be mistaken about the articulation of this which is objectively given. Indeed, I have been at pains to point out that there are no guaranteed articulations. In that sense, we can never be absolutely right about what a disclosure discloses if by that phrase we mean, not the objectively disclosed, but the way in which we talk of it, something admittedly closer to what we spoke of as the newspaper sense of the word 'disclosure'.

I would now like to point briefly to the wider significance of this concept of disclosure:

(i) In this context, the problem of induction is the problem of justifying a claim based on a disclosure which goes 'beyond the facts'. On this view, the problem of induction is structurally the same as the problem of justifying a metaphysical claim. If e.g. we consider a series of temporal terms—moments—in temporal relations, then that which is disclosed when such sequence leads to a disclosure will be that of which words like 'eternity' speak, an 'eternity' beyond time, which 'completes time'; an eternity given in an 'immediacy' which a phrase like 'totum simul' claims.

(ii) The antithesis between 'fact' and 'value', the well known distinction which Hume introduces at the beginning of Section III of the *Treatise*, between 'is' and 'ought' would, on the approach I have been elaborating, be one between 'facts' and 'disclosures'. Value arises in this way around the facts and is disclosure-given, and in common with other disclosure categories is specially concerned not only with that which confronts us objectively in a disclosure, but with the matching self-disclosure as well.

(iii) Again, in the well-worn distinction between 'fact' and 'interpretation', it would follow from the point of view I have been elaborating that in any situation the objectivity, the objective reference can be spelt out in terms of diverse interpretations all of which organize certain facts and features of the world and none of which are sacrosanct. Only sense-datum theorists and certain theological dogmatists have supposed that some were. This puts into another light the old maxim: 'Facts are sacred; comment is free.' It would rather seem, on the view I have been putting forward, that 'the facts' in the sense of facts and features of the world are there ready to be organized and so are 'free' in so far as they never bring with them a guaranteed interpretative scheme of that which is objectively given. In such a case we may say, facts are free; comment is sacred; for that comment must spell out as reliably and responsibly as possible what it is an endeavour to portray. Facts and features are only supposed to be sacred when they have the status of sense-data and when they are thus worshipped there is nothing free about either facts or the language which talks of them. It is only 'fact' in the sense of objective reference disclosed around the 'facts' as organized in an interpretative scheme that is sacred—being that to which talk of persons and God points.

(iv) When a basic claim is made for 'facts' where 'fact' is related to a point of agreement in some dispute, then we must recognize that even when agreement is reached on the 'facts' the objective reference is still something different altogether, something given immediately and intuitively in a disclosure whose characterizations may be infinitely corrigible but where, as we suppose to be so in this case, we may sometimes reach relatively stable and agreed interpretations and contexts. Perhaps we begin to see what used to be called 'negative facts'. These would be talk about words and the world entirely without reference. In Frege's distinction we would talk with sense but no meaning.

(v) I cannot, of course, pretend to answer in any detail all the questions I raised at the start. But I hope that I have said enough to show that if religious language is grounded in disclosures, being an endeavour to talk about what disclosures disclose, what there is more than the facts and features of the world, it undoubtedly has an objective reference. Hence, we can talk of 'facts' in relation to religious discourse when such talk registers a claim for objectivity; and what is objectively disclosed, being more than the appearances in and through which it is disclosed, has a chance of being rightly called 'metaphysical'. Further, if the Christian claim is true, talk of crucifixion, resurrection and ascension will involve facts and features of the world, what are sometimes called 'matters of fact'. But Christianity only adequately talks of these occasions as and when their stories disclose an objective reference as well, whose spelling out would have to be in theological as well as in plainly empirical terms.

On the view I have been setting forward, the distinction drawn by Professor Hick between 'an ultimate order of fact' and 'more proximate types of fact' would be the distinction between the given metaphysical, objective reference which all material objects—and even human bodies considered as material objects—can disclose, which is disclosed or self-disclosed in persons, and facts where the word relates to matters of fact, the facts and features of the world around us. In short, the relation between the two orders of fact is the relation between disclosures of objectivity and the facts and features of the world around us.

The Logical Character of
Resurrection-belief

'Many men today are encouraged to regard religion as a cheat because they suspect their preceptors of failing to face the results of scientific discovery and biblical criticism . . . and even of not telling the whole truth as they see it.' So says H. J. Paton in his Gifford Lectures, *The Modern Predicament*. No doubt something of what Paton has in mind might be developed by saying that there seems often a discrepancy, a gap, between preaching and teaching, between sermons and theology: a gap of which theological students, young curates and directors of post-ordination training are (amongst others) painfully aware. The gap yawns wide at all the historical commemorations of the Church's year; it is perhaps most threatening of all at Easter. The apostles (we are told) 'with great power gave their witness of the resurrection of the Lord Jesus'.[1] By contrast, Paton would say, contemporary witness is superficial if not disingenuous.

Did the resurrection occur? The burden of Easter sermons is that it did; and all Christians to be Christians must believe that it did.

But there is then the other side which leads to Paton's dissatisfaction, and which creates, he would say, part of the 'modern predicament'. . . .

What of biblical criticism—not to say scientific discovery? Do we as Christians believe that Jesus walked through closed doors?[2] Do we believe that he appeared after death with 'flesh and bones' and ate fish?[3] Of course, there may be and are variant readings, and verses of doubtful authenticity by which to meet this point or that . . . but, what is then left of the resurrection? Is it enough to say with one commentator after another: 'The difficulty of harmonizing the different accounts of the resurrection is great', yet 'dishonesty would have made the evidence more harmonious' so that the discrepancies 'show rather the comparative independence

[1] Acts 4.33.   [2] Cp. John 20.19.   [3] Luke 24.39, 43.

of the writers' and all the more 'confirm their united testimony to the main fact on which they all agree'—the empty tomb. At any rate a critical attitude towards the New Testament has meant that the 'resurrection' has been taken to describe an ever-narrowing class of events, leaving for some only the empty tomb. But then comes the question: How long will it be before even this remnant is discredited? Meanwhile, if the Scripture holds all these difficulties, is our religion already a cheat? Can we preach the resurrection against such a background of theological reservations and difficulties? Can we legitimately profess belief in the resurrection while having reservations about the closed doors and the fish? Must our witness of the resurrection be intellectually compromised? Must our sermons be isolated from our theology?

We shall meet questions such as these only by answering first the question: What *is* Christian belief in the resurrection? and it is with that question that this article will for the most part be concerned. So many of our present difficulties arise because belief that the resurrection occurred is often taken to be logically isomorphous with belief that certain facts like 'eating fish' occurred. But is that logical assimilation justified?

Two hundred years ago the answer to this question would have been easy: 'Yes'; but let us realize from the outset that it is this easy answer which leads straight to the difficulties we have been enumerating. The resurrection was, we read, 'a thing to be judg'd of by men's senses', it was a 'Matter of Fact and an object of sense'.[4] The worst that disbelievers like Thomas Woolston could do was to argue that the resurrection was an *imposture*; to counter such assertions it was enough that believers like Thomas Sherlock should describe a mock *Tryal of the Witnesses of the Resurrection of Jesus* so as to establish that the apostles were 'not guilty' of giving false evidence. The resurrection was something which could be evidenced—that was common ground: the apostles were witnesses to a 'Matter of Fact and an object of sense'. The view has survived, of course, to our own day. Some ten years ago I chanced to have rooms in a Victorian vicarage, over the wash-basin of which was the saying of a certain nineteenth-century bishop—I think none other than Westcott. The saying was to the effect that

[4] Thomas Sherlock, The Tryal of the Witnesses of the Resurrection of Jesus (1729) (*Religious Thought in the Eighteenth Century*, J. M. Creed and J. S. Boys Smith, 1934, pp. 72, 73).

he was '*more certain of the Resurrection than of any other fact*'. As I stood shivering at that wash-basin with cold water coming out of the hot tap, ice on the windows, razor cuts on my face, I wondered: here were stark realities—facts if any were—blood, cold water, ice . . . certain as anything could be . . . 'matters of fact and objects of sense'. . . . But has the resurrection *that* kind of certainty?

What I propose to do in this article is, first, to show by reference to the resurrection narrative that belief in the resurrection is *something more* than belief in a matter of fact; thereafter to mention one or two implications of this view; and last of all to return to Paton's criticism. Let us begin then by turning to the resurrection narratives to see there what belief in the resurrection involves, and let us look first at the Emmaus story.

Here were the two disciples puzzled, sad, disappointed—and they 'communed and questioned together'. As they shared this fellowship of questioning, this discussion, this exchange of points, this engagement, 'Jesus himself'—the risen Lord—'drew near and went with them'. They saw the risen Jesus, as we might see any other companion on a walk, but, we read, 'their eyes were holden that they should not know him'. We need not read into that verse any divine teleology; at the same time let us notice that it was not their reasoning, rather was it their eyes, their vision, that was restrained, restricted, held in check, held back, so that in fact they did not know him. Their lack was not a correct interpretation or adequate categorical scheme, but rather a full discernment, a deeper vision—the penny hadn't dropped, the ice hadn't broken. However, within their fellowship of questioning, further points are developed, and by Jesus himself: 'Behoved it not the Christ to suffer these things and to enter into his glory? And beginning from Moses and from all the prophets, he interpreted to them in all the Scriptures, the things concerning himself.' We are told afterwards that at this point their hearts 'burned within them', but I suggest that we take the word καίω as rather implying that at this point their hearts had just been *ignited, lit*, as a torch. . . . And it was a torch that only flared, only gave full illumination . . . when? The full disclosure was made, they *knew* the risen Christ in the fellowship of a village supper-table; in the intimacy of a home. Stranger . . . Teach . . . Interpreter . . . Friend . . . and then . . . the Risen Christ. . . . But at this point, the point

of full disclosure, '*he became invisible*'. To know the risen Christ
was an empirical fact—something which was incontrovertibly the
case, but *not* as an 'object of sense'. . . . Here was a situation
epistemologically odd, as odd indeed as the word ἄφαντος. In the
Bible it occurs only once besides here, and then of angels becoming
invisible: and in Classical Greek I understand the word has only
a poetical use—which for us means that the word has an ancestry
which is nothing if not logically odd. In short, the risen Christ
became 'invisible', but he was still there and known—but 'there'
oddly, and 'known' oddly—odd from the point of view of 'objects
of sense'. It was not like coming to know that this stranger in plus
fours dining at the club is in fact Archbishop Makarios in disguise,
cause for gratification and smoking-room excitement. Rather was
there here a recognition distinctly odd. It was one which restored
to the disciples vitality and commitment they had lost; they were
not merely gratified: they were empowered. They 'rose up that
very hour' and went to Jerusalem as *witnesses of the resurrection*, a
fact they knew now in its fullness, and they knew it in this fullness,
notice, when he 'vanished out of their sight', though not out of
their loyalty. . . . There had been a fellowship of questioning, an
exchange of points illuminated by Bible study, but all these were
preliminaries to something else, to that full disclosure which came
in a situation more than 'objects of sense', and which came in such
a way that we speak of it as a disclosure given by the initiative of
God. Not only had the Scriptures been 'opened', but their eyes
had been 'opened', and if the word be taken in its wider context,
both had been 'opened', as a womb, to be creative of new life, new
duties, a richer existence.

But, you might say, does this not come dangerously near to
making resurrection belief entirely independent of 'objects of
sense'—and if we had nothing but the Emmaus story that challenge
might be serious. So we pass now to what, on the face of it, is the
other extreme—St Thomas. We *need* Thomas. Here is the plain,
down-to-earth empiricist. 'Except I shall see in his hands the
print of the nails, and put my finger into the print of the nails
[tactual as well as visual verification is needed] I will not believe.'
There is then the invitation—'see my hands', 'reach hither thy
finger'. . . and Thomas who has *seen*, *believes*. Is his resurrection-
belief, then, belief in a matter of fact, objects of sight and touch?
If St Thomas had said, 'I admit it's Jesus after all', or 'I'm assured;

I'm prepared to witness in a court of law, at a "Tryal of Witnesses", that it is the same body', that might have been our conclusion. But when St Thomas is assured, his language goes beyond perceptual or legal language. He confesses: 'My Lord and my God'. Here is a commitment which goes beyond what is seen; a witnessing which is more than trials and law courts take account of. Thomas sees . . . but not only perceptual objects. He believes in the resurrection as an 'object of sense' and more.

But you may puzzle—an 'object of sense' and more? How can that be? We might anticipate the answer by recalling that resurrection assurance came in the friendly intimacy of a homely meal . . . but for the fullest answer let us go to our third and last example: Mary Magdalene. For Mary, Jesus was not some great teacher or national figure—he was someone who had changed her life. She wasn't perplexed by the political or theological implications of it all like the disciples on the road to Emmaus, nor did she formulate empirical doubts like St Thomas—what mattered was that she had lost a friend, and all she could do was to go to where there was still a reminder of him—the tomb where his body lay. How powerful a symbol of friendship the human body can be! Then, not even satisfaction at the tomb . . . no body . . . no relevant 'matter of fact', nor 'object of sense'. Then, as much as the two disciples or Thomas, she starts asking questions, seeking explanations. 'They', perhaps the Jews, perhaps the gardener, must have taken away the Lord's body . . . and it is in this mood of explanation-seeking that she says to someone she takes to be the gardener: 'Tell me where you've put him; I'll take the body and care for it.' Here is a situation, here is thinking, so much concerned with 'objects of sense', such as bodies, as to merit no more than the descriptive phrase 'the gardener'. . . . Do you remember how in the *Patris*, in his native country, when Jesus was rejected by those who a little while before had been astonished by his preaching and marvelled at his mighty works; do you remember how, with the rejection, came descriptive phrases 'the carpenter', 'the son of Mary', 'brother of James'? So, likewise, 'the gardener' . . . when there is no disclosure.

Then, the situation 'comes alive', takes on 'depth', loses its impersonal 'official' character . . . the risen Christ discloses himself and on an intimate greeting is appropriate currency: 'Mary'. . . . The resurrection cannot be netted in the language of definite

G

descriptions. The logical difference between 'Mary' and 'the gardener' tells how much *more* the resurrection *is* than an 'object of sense'. Here then is our special point arising from the story of Mary Magdalene: the resurrection is a situation which is a matter of fact *and more*, an 'object of sense' *and more*, precisely as the most intimate personal interchange is all that, too. Further, just as to human love we respond with a full devotion—so Mary's response is not 'Teacher'—how limited a portrayal that word gives—but rather 'My Master, Lord, chief, prince' . . . almost the same language as St Thomas . . . words which are currency for a *full* loyalty, to tell *now* of the same *full* commitment she had known before in Jesus. *Here is resurrection-belief, a total response to something which touches us personally.* Perhaps after all in gracing a wash-basin mirror in the Victorian vicarage the bishop's assertion was more significant than we realized. Freezing water, shaving soap, blood—these may be facts, i.e. 'objects of sense'—but of none of them was I so certain as (looking into the mirror) of another 'fact' an 'object of sense' and more, 'myself'—that 'I'm I', a conviction which in so far as it goes beyond perceptual 'matters of fact' affords something of a parallel with our assurance of the risen Christ. Further, in so far as the bishop's extreme language was trying to emphasize the *all-embracing* significance of resurrection-belief, the *total* commitment the resurrection evokes, we might say that his chief fault was to express a most important point in the most misleading language possible; which is what so often we Christians have done. The Christian witness cannot be expressed in logically straightforward language without doing itself injustice and digging its own grave; and we ought to say 'boo' to the geese of various kinds which could tempt us to try. But to come back. We must indeed distinguish in relation to the resurrection:

(*a*) First the 'matters of fact' which are 'objects of sense' and about which empirical questions can be asked; which legal witnesses talk of, on which historical discussion can be centred, for which verification can be sought.

(*b*) Then, the situation which is such 'matters of fact' *and more*—a situation which is empirically odd, and one to which we have a clue in some personal situations. To know what 'resurrection' means, demands such a fuller discernment. If in this life only we have hoped in Christ; if Christ is for us exhausted in perceptual terms; if the risen Christ is no more than a matter of fact which is an 'object of sense', then we are of all men most pitiable.

(c) Finally, such a fuller discernment which embraces 'objects of sense' and more, evokes and is fulfilled in a response, a commitment, in virtue of which we become, by our response, Christian witnesses of the resurrection'—'obedient to our heavenly vision'.

Just a few points now by way of illustration and conclusion: and the first to show how easy it has been for Christians, as well as their opponents, to mistake the logic of what they were saying, and they fail to do justice to the logical complexity of their contentions.

We have urged that the resurrection narratives do not so much record 'facts', tell of 'objects of sense'; as evoke situations, situations of discernment-response for which we have parallels in the devotion we give to those whose love we return. Now that discernment which is centred on Jesus is called by us Christians 'eternal life in Christ Jesus', and it is against such a background as this that we must understand such ostensibly simple phrases, e.g. as that Jesus Christ 'opened unto us the gate of everlasting life'.

But if all that is the case, then not only does 'resurrection' exceed all 'objects of sense', but 'immortality' and 'eternal life' are no logical kinsman, and (*pace* Dr C. D. Broad) Christ is no term in an argument for immortality from analogy, but rather a focus for resurrection-vision and devotion.

So we can see how logically skew and cross-purposed are such objections as are commonly raised: if Jesus opens the gate of everlasting life to Christians, do only Christians survive? Can Christians argue that we are immortal because Jesus is immortal, when what is so obvious is that Jesus is utterly different from us? How easy to get off on the wrong logical foot—and for Christians it can be as easy as for their opponents. Did not A. A. Sykes, in 1740, declare that the resurrection was an 'argument for immortality from eyesight', displaying the proposition that we are immortal in such large empirical letters that even the least philosophical could read and understand. Resurrection for Sykes, was a plain 'object of sense'; 'immortality' was a kinsman of 'eternal life'.

Eschewing such over-simplification as leads only to puzzles and needless difficulties, we have stressed the logical peculiarity of the resurrection. Was there an empty tomb? Did Jesus eat fish? Did the resurrection occur? All these seem plain isomorphous questions, questions of the same form about 'matters of fact'. But recall $\frac{2}{3}$, $\frac{3}{4}$, $\frac{0}{0}$. All *seem* to belong to the same logical family, but what of the last? An ugly duckling indeed. Similarly, we have pleaded the logical peculiarity of resurrection: that the situation on which the Christian faith is based is nothing if not odd: another ugly duckling! What 'resurrection' stands for includes but transcends 'empty tomb' and 'eating fish', as much as 'loving' includes but transends 'meeting', as 'devotion' is more than 'efficient support', as 'I' tells of more than public behaviour exhausts.

What now of Paton's criticism? Are we cheating in our witness? Does there not still remain a gap, a logical gap between, on the one side, the phrases in terms of which the Christian faith is *preached*, and one the other side, that clear unambiguous language which stands for 'objects of sense'? Is there not a gap between the swans and the ducks? Certainly there is a gap; indeed, the whole concern of this article has been to expose the gap for what it is. But we would only be cheats if we could do nothing, or would do nothing, about bridging the gap. We should, for example, be cheating if once we had distinguished between the 'resurrection' with its peculiar logical status, and 'matters of fact' about which ordinary questions of evidence can be asked, we said that the 'matter of fact' assertions did not matter. At its most naïve this cheat would be a prejudice against theology such as was expressed in the old revivalist ditty: 'The Religion of Paul and Silas is good enough for me.' At its more sophisticated, it could show itself in a desire to take the Scriptural narratives so symbolically that it does not matter whether the stories are fiction, fable, or fancy.

But in emphasizing the distinctive character of the Christian belief in the resurrection, it has been no part of my purpose to deny its essential reference to 'objects of sense' as well. Indeed, on the contrary, I have tried to give a hint about how the two points can be combined, about how the logical gap can be bridged. The hint comes from recognizing what has likewise to be both distinguished and related in situations of human love and devotion. For here, too, there are 'objects of sense' and more. Characteristically personal behaviour is more than 'what's seen'; or, if it is not, religious people are cheats indeed. We shall be helped to meet

Paton's criticism if we concentrate on this personal model, and in particular if we develop the theme that while of course all personal loyalty is anchored in some facts of an empirical kind, personal devotion never builds on empirical fact with a nicely calculated less or more. In this way 'personal devotion' can be a logical paradigm by which to understand 'resurrection witness'.

History and the Gospels: Some Philosophical Reflections

I hope I may usefully begin by formulating two severely contrasting views of the relation of the Christian faith to history, which have been held by Christians.

1   There have been those who have said that all that mattered was the facts, so that the only controversy was whether the facts occurred or not; the only point of dispute was, e.g. did water in fact change into wine, were the bread and fishes multiplied, or were the gospel writers liars? To be a Christian was to believe that the narratives were authentic, that the facts they described occurred: to disbelieve their occurrence was apostasy. This is a view sponsored or implied by many orthodox Christians in the eighteenth century and in more recent days by many of those who sought after the Jesus of history. For example, when Thomas Woolston in *Six Discourses on the Miracles of our Saviour* (1727–9) had argued that the figurative, mystical interpretation of the miracles which he found in some of the Fathers should be adopted, so as to exclude questions of their historical truth, he was answered by Thomas Sherlock in *The Tryal of the Witnesses of the Resurrection of Jesus* (1729) of which Leslie Stephen says that it contains 'the concentrated essence of eighteenth-century apologetic'. It is in fact a defence of the apostles against an accusation of lying. At a mock trial, the judge says to the foreman: 'Are the Apostles guilty of giving false evidence in the case of the Resurrection of Jesus, or not guilty?' The foreman answers: 'Not guilty.' Jesus rose from the dead with flesh and bones, ate broiled fish and so on; whoever believes that is indubitably Christian, whoever denies it is an unbeliever. To be a Christian is to believe that the facts described in the gospels occurred.

2   But in our own day we have had such as Alasdair MacIntyre saying: 'What I want to suggest is that everything of importance to religious faith is outside the reach of historical investigation.'[1]

[1] *Metaphysical Beliefs*, London, 1957, p. 206.

Or again: 'To the reference to an act of God, historical enquiry is irrelevant.'[2] Admittedly, the resurrection, for example, is 'a belief about history' but it is not a belief, he says, which rests on 'historical grounds'.[3] MacIntyre's view is that its grounds are elsewhere—in what we take as *authoritative*. Then, having taken something as authoritative, no questions about history can make any difference to the belief, which is independent of all historical considerations. But the cost of giving this safe independency to Christian belief is to segregate and seal off the Christian faith and to make it in every way 'unreasonable'; to make it intellectually and morally irrelevant—lacking connection with the ordinary world of men's talking and acting. It is not surprising that Mac-Intyre has recently become sceptical of the faith he once professed in this fashion.

Where is the truth here? Undoubtedly Sherlock takes too narrow and simple a view of the logic of religious assertions; nor is the antithesis one between truth and falsity; between the historical and the 'figurative'. MacIntyre, on the other hand, takes too isolationist a view of the distinctive logic of Christian assertions. He defends the Christian faith only at the cost of making it *sui generis*. If we ask: on what grounds do we accept the authority which enables us to disregard historical grounds? MacIntyre's answer would be: on no grounds at all—'to ask for reasons for . . . religious belief is not to have understood what religious belief is'.[4]

In contrast to MacIntyre, I would urge that Christians must be able to give *some* logical pattern by which to link together assertions about 'historical events', and assertions about their commitments, about their response to what they take to be authoritative. To leave religious assertions logically segregated from historical assertions would certainly be disingenuous. How then are we to connect religious and historical assertions? Have we any clues to illuminate this connection? Are we able to provide from anywhere patterns of what is reliable reasoning in this case; of how the transition can be defended; of how a religious assertion is logically linked with a historical assertion? The ultimate problem is that Christian faith cannot be content to do without 'history'; neither can it be content with 'history' alone. Can we do anything to illuminate this complex relationship between history and the Christian faith? Can we do anything to unravel the tangle

[2] Ibid., p. 207.   [3] Ibid., p. 207.   [4] Ibid., p. 207.

of questions which surrounds this topic? Can we mediate between Sherlock and MacIntyre?

Meanwhile, a philosopher like Professor L. A. Reid, not at all unsympathetic to Christian claims, comments in a recent book:

> One is questioning whether there is not in much Christianity a too exclusive emphasis upon *historical* assertion (which is after all contingent and sometimes, in theologically important instances, markedly 'weak') as central to faith, as though it *were* the essence of religion itself, instead of containing or *revealing* the timeless essence.[5]

'How far' (he has asked earlier) 'should disputable particular historical statements be made an intrinsic (or essential) part of the affirmation of religious belief?'

In a notable article written with characteristic robustness, penetration and honesty, the late Dr Norman Sykes gave us his own reflections on the problem and I hope I may be forgiven for quoting from him at some length.[6] Sykes starts with a reference to Gibbon and Bury:

> 'I have read somewhere', observed Sir Maurice Powicke in his Riddell Lectures (1937), 'that Gibbon did one great service to mankind: he freed history from religion.'[7] In attempting to put asunder what Judaism and Christianity at all events had regarded as divinely joined together, Gibbon was in accord with the temper of the *Aufklärung* which aspired on the one hand to discredit revealed religion, and on the other to rid history for ever of the incubus of supernatural events and intervention and therewith of the notion of a providential ordering of its course . . . It is necessary to emphasize this primary objective of the emancipation of history from religion, for so long as it continued to dominate historical circles, one of the first principles of Christianity was eradicated. 'Historians', commented J. B. Bury, 'have for the most part desisted from invoking the naïve conception of a "god in history" to explain historical movements. A historian may be a theist; but, so far as his work is

[5] *Ways of Knowledge and Experience*, London, 1961, p. 167.
[6] *Journal of Theological Studies*, 50, 1949, pp. 24–5; 27–8; 29–30; 32–3; 36–7.
[7] F. M. Powicke, *History, Freedom and Religion*, Oxford, 1938, p. 43.

concerned, this particular belief is otiose. Otherwise indeed . . . history could not be a science; for with a *deus ex machina* who can be brought on the stage to solve difficulties, scientific treatment is a farce.'[8] With this affirmation there emerges the second motive in the severance of history from religion, namely the desire to establish the place of history among the strictly scientific disciplines. The writers of the age of reason and their successors of the nineteenth and twentieth centuries were moved less by a desire to proclaim the sovereignty and autonomy of history within its proper sphere of investigation than by the wish to ally it with the spreading movement of natural science. Historically considered, this was a natural consequence of the rise of natural science during the late seventeenth and early eighteenth centuries; for this movement had elevated natural religion at the expense of revelation through history. With the vast extension of the scope of scientific discovery in the nineteenth century, this tendency was accentuated; and amongst historians the *dernier cri* became the shibboleth that history is a science, no less and no more. This conception received its classical expression in this country in the inaugural lecture at Cambridge in 1903 of J. B. Bury.

Sykes continues:

It is the more remarkable therefore to observe how completely within a generation this conception of history as 'a science, no less and no more' has vanished from the contemporary historical landscape. In the very place where Bury had preached the new evangel with such fervour and iteration, his disciple Professor Harold Temperley in his inaugural lecture in 1930 could affirm that 'in my own memory the idea that history is a science has perished'[9]. . . The reasons for the breakdown of this conception of history are so plain and emphatic that we may wonder why it enjoyed so great a vogue. . . . History . . . is concerned with events which are particular, concrete and non-recurring; and the general laws which are invaluable to the sciences are, as

[8] J. B. Bury, *Selected Essays* (ed. by Harold Temperley), Cambridge, 1930, p. 33.
[9] H. W. V. Temperley, *Research and Modern History*, Cambridge, 1930, p. 18.

Tennant has said, 'tools for other purposes than that which history has in view'.[10]

If then historical study is concerned with unique and particular events and with the acts of individuals, it becomes at once patient of a mutual reconciliation with religion, and the divorce effected by Gibbon may be repealed. For in a myriad examples in the course of Christian history it is not only the influence of individual personalities upon the course of events which must be admitted but also, and of much greater significance, the origin and inspiration of that influence, not in economic or social factors, but in a spiritual source, namely the grace of God acting in and through human personalities, self-surrendered to his will. The conversations of St Paul, St Augustine, St Francis of Assisi, Ignatius Loyola, and John Wesley (to name but a tiny fraction of the host which could be summoned to testify) constitute, as Dr Figgis insisted, 'the supreme refutations of the impersonal view of history'.[11] Moreover, in their spiritual experience the action of God upon individual actors in the drama of human history, and therewith on the events of that history also, is one of the factors which the historian may not dismiss from the compass of his study. Save at the cost of making nonsense of his record, the historical student may neither ignore the religious strand in human affairs nor dismiss the interpretation of its meaning given by Christianity as the work of God who πολυμερῶς κἀι πολυτρόπως spake in time past unto the fathers by the prophets.

Sykes now turns to the implications of all this for his topic and ours:

... in obedience to the scientific conception of history, a generation of biblical critics devoted themselves to the attempt to discover the 'Jesus of history' by disentangling the facts of the public ministry and teaching of Jesus from the theological interpretations imposed upon them by the apologetic necessities of the apostolic age, and by separating the residual 'religion of Jesus' from its encasement in the 'religion about Jesus'. Their watchword was stated in the affirmation of my own revered teacher in New Testament studies, B. H. Streeter, that 'history is the effort to find out what actually happened, not to force

[10] F. R. Tennant, *The Philosophy of the Sciences*, Cambridge, 1932, p. 93.
[11] J. N. Figgis, *Christianity and History*, London, 1905, p. 62.

upon the evidence an *a priori* point of view.'[12] Building, therefore, upon the foundation of the conclusions of students of the
synoptic problem about the literary relationships of the syoptic
gospels to each other and to the Fourth Gospel, this school of
criticism concentrated attention on St Mark in preference to
the supposed expansion of his simple historical tradition in the
other synoptists, and particularly in preference to the Fourth
Gospel. For it was believed and hoped that the critical study
of St Mark would unveil the facts of the life and ministry of
Jesus without the refractory element of theological interpretation, and that 'here at any rate we have historic fact without
interpretation'.[13] Even when further study raised doubt on
these matters by diminishing the sharpness of the distinction
made between the Synoptists on the one hand and the Fourth
Gospel on the other, and by demonstrating that in St Mark
theological interpretation was 'already present in large measure',
the idea persisted that the Jesus of history, if discoverable,
would consist of fact without interpretation. . . .

But (says Sykes) 'if the validity of Collingwood's argument be
accepted the historian is not concerned to ask for fact without
interpretation'.

Further, as Sykes finally points out, not even Bury was unsympathetic to a wider view of history, and could write:

Our apprehension of history and our reason for studying it must
be ultimately determined by the view we entertain of the *moles
et machina mundi* as a whole. Naturalism will imply a wholly
different view from idealism. In considering the place of history
in the kingdom of knowledge, it is thus impossible to avoid
referring to the questions with which the so-called philosophy
of history is concerned . . . Perhaps it may be said that such
interpretation is quite a separate branch of speculation, distinct
from history itself, and not necessarily the concern of an
historical student. That is a view which should be dismissed,
for it reduces history to a collection of annals. Facts must be
collected and connected, before they can be interpreted; but I

[12] B. H. Streeter, *The Four Gospels*, London, 1924, p. 543.
[13] R. H. Lightfoot, *History and Interpretation in the Gospels*, London,
1935, p. 15. Sykes adds a further quotation in the footnote: 'Interpretation
was not looked for in St Mark's gospel as it stands; it was regarded as a
history rather than as a Gospel' (p. 16).

cannot imagine the slightest theoretical importance in a collection of facts or sequences of facts, unless they mean something in terms of reason, unless we can hope to determine their
vital connection in the whole system of reality.[14]

Sykes remarks:

> Having thus affirmed the legitimacy and necessity of construct-
> ing a philosophy of history, Bury claimed this as the specific task
> of the student of history:
> In order to lay bare the spiritual process which history
> represents, we must go to history itself without any *a priori*
> assumptions or predetermined systems. All that philosophy
> can do is to assure us that historical experience is a disclosure
> of the inner nature of spiritual reality. This disclosure is
> furnished by history and history alone.[15]

Sykes concludes:

> It may be that philosophers, mindful of Lessing's dictum that
> accidental truths of history can never become the proof of
> necessary truths of reason, will refuse Bury's invitation to over-
> leap the broad and ugly ditch dividing history from philosophy.
> But the Christian theologian at any rate need not hesitate, for
> that ditch has already been spanned for him by the unvarying
> tradition of Christianity to attach the highest significance to
> those *gesta Dei per Christum* in history, which are at once events
> of the historical process and the basis of theological doctrine.

Three points immediately concern us in these passages from
Dr Sykes' article, and by discussing them we shall later take up
a fourth. First, Sykes reminds us of the day when history was
cherished as a science, neither more nor less, partly (he says)
because it helped historians to jump on the scientific bandwagon,
but partly too, because it seemed to emancipate history from concepts of providence and supernatural intervention, which had for
long made it jejeune. But, as Sykes tells us—and this is the second
point—this concept of history as a science is now rejected by
historians, chiefly because the distinctive character of science and
its methods has not been more clearly seen. History differs from

[14] J. B. Bury, *Selected Essays*, pp. 46–7.
[15] J. B. Bury, loc cit., p. 51.

science in having for its topic the unique acts of individuals, and these individuals include people like St Paul and Wesley, influenced by the grace of God. Thirdly, because individuals think, history is to be seen as a study of man's reflective concern about the world and people around him. Here is what the historian tries to portray. This means that we shall only see the point of historical writing when we look on it as writing designed to talk about and to put over the reflective activities of men, their 'influences' in, on and about the world. On this view history, to make its point, must be a matter of 'fact and interpretation'. It was this feature of historical writing that the 'Jesus of history' school completely overlooked, so that they could better be described as the 'Jesus of scientific history' school.

But this particular discussion of 'fact and interpretation', and the alliance with Collingwood which it inevitably involves, tends I think to take us away from the main issue, and here I agree with what Dr T. A. Roberts says in a concluding paragraph of his frank, critical and courageous book *History and Christian Apologetic*. Referring to the article by Sykes, he says:

> Dean Sykes has maintained that there was a misconception at the heart of the work of the Jesus of History School, namely its preoccupation with the search for historical fact divorced from interpretation, when in reality no such facts exist. This radically mistakes the real problem. The misconception of the Jesus of History School was the belief, betrayed by their methods and conclusion, that the documents of the Faith are a legitimate field for the full and unfettered exercise of the methods of historical investigation. Consequently they failed to realize that this must effectively deny the possibility of divine intervention on the plane of history in any concrete and manifest form.[16]

The point of course is mentioned in Sykes' article, though Dr Roberts is quite right in claiming that its real import is perhaps overlooked. We might well express it like this: scientific history in principle is bound to rule out all supernatural evidence, and it is with this view of history that we may say with Dr T. A. Roberts:

> Historical study must dismiss the account of the raising of

[16] *History and Christian Apologetic*, London, 1960, p. 173.

Lazarus as something extremely improbable, implausible, and legendary, or as an account of a type common in the age when St John wrote his Gospel.

But what perhaps Dr Sykes does not make clear is that a Collingwoodian view of history does not necessarily provide for such events as the raising of Lazarus either, whereas the Christian view demands them. Here indeed is the real rub about miracles, and it is undoubtedly the miracle stories which have given an edge to this controversy. Scientific history excludes miracles: Collingwoodian history does little to take them in: Christianity seems bound to have them. If the gospel narratives had been the story of a remarkably inspired good and wise man they would have been throughout credible; insights into the character of historical writing would certainly have helped us more fully to understand the narratives—but we would never have become Christians. For this, miracles (and prophecy fulfilments) were a necessity; but (for our clear thinking) they are an unfortunate necessity. To be clear about miracles is to be clear about everything; in the concept of miracle every problem of apologetic is included. Indeed, perhaps Dr Sykes' article does not make his concluding general point as clear as it deserves to be, and needs to be made—and here is the fourth point I promised eventually to reach. Historians themselves have now realized that they need some sort of help from philosophy, that there must be a philosophy of history at least in the sense that philosophy must allow for the kind of topic—at a minimum man's actions in the world—of which the historian claims to treat. *But* the crucial question here of course for the Christian is: Is there an acceptable brand of philosophy which allows for the topic which the Christian theologian wishes to talk of? The point is that different approaches presuppose different topics for 'history'. For the scientific historian, history is concerned with certain groups of spatio-temporal events relating to man's overt behaviour. For the historian who talks about 'fact and interpretation' history is concerned with persons who 'think' and 'will', and he might allow that such persons are more than the overt behaviour they display, are in this sense 'transcendent', and worthy topics of religious discourse. But even this is not sufficient for the Christian. For the Christian is concerned with a situation which has reference not only to spatio-temporal events and transcendent persons, but also and most distinctively, to God. The basic metaphysical reference is clear in such a remark as we find about the raising of Lazarus in Dr T. A. Roberts' book, immediately following on the quotation we gave above.

> But for Faith, which believes in the Christ, the raising of Lazarus is something which happened through the power and authority of him who came to reconcile the world to God.

Here is a situation—a display of God's power in the raising of Lazarus—for whose discussion the currencies of science, Colling-woodian history and metaphysics will all presumably be needed.

It is at this point that Bultmann becomes important. In relation to the problem of history and the gospels, Bultmann's importance is to see that we shall not answer it without involving ourselves in philosophical considerations, without invoking some kind of philosophy.[17] If I may put my conclusion at the start, my ultimate criticism of Bultmann is that he then associated with the Christian faith that philosophy which of all others is likely in this connection to be of least help. For it is that philosophy of all others whose reasonable explication is, and in principle, most problematical. But that is to to anticipate.

Let me begin by remarking that just as discussions of history and the gospels have often been confused by giving too great a prominence to talk about 'fact and interpretation', and then over-looking and neglecting the philosophical point involved, so the true significance of Bultmann in this connection has often been missed. I thus agree entirely with Canon G. F. Woods when he points out in his *Theological Explanation* that discussions of Bultmann have often been clouded by considering Bultmann in relation to historical scepticism about the gospels. Canon Woods is quite right in seeing Bultmann rather as one who, aware of the limitations of historical method, points to a situation distinc-tively personal as the sort of topic which Christian writings—

---

[17] The same kind of important general point is implied by Dr J. M. Robinson in his book, *A New Quest of the Historical Jesus*, London, 1959, from which Professor Nineham quotes on p. 261 of his *Journal of Theo-logical Studies* article referred to below: 'The material preserved in the gospels is the kind of material which fits best the needs of research based upon the modern view of history *and the self*' (loc. cit., p. 69: italics mine).

neither purely scientific nor purely historical—have been trying
to explicate. As Canon Woods remarks:[18]

> ... the realisation of the need to demythologise arose not because
> the biblical historians lacked some important evidence but
> because their method was neither able nor designed to disclose
> the full meaning of the Christian gospel. Bultmann advocates
> a policy of demythologising the proclamation of the Gospel not
> because he is a historian who finds his evidence deficient but
> because he is a historian who understands some of the limitations
> of the historical method when employed to display the true
> meaning of the Gospel . . . He has certainly shown the inability
> of empirical studies to disclose the full meaning of the New
> Testament preaching. Both scientific and historical studies have
> their place in theological enquiry, but neither is able without
> assistance to offer any ultimate explanation of the world.

Canon Woods then discerns in Bultmann a preference for explanation in terms of persons. He continues:

> Within this field, he [Bultmann] chooses those [explanations]
> which are satisfying to our moral insight. This may be the posi-
> tive motive which has moved him to denounce mythology. But
> I find no clear exposition of the *reasons* which should lead us to
> prefer personal and moral analogies. Our proper preference
> for them cannot be explained on the basis of any type of
> existential analysis of human nature which denies the signifi-
> cance of reason and conscience. If Existentialism gives no more
> than a neutral account of what we are, it is still not plain why
> we should prefer to use in Christian theology the analogies
> which are both personal and moral.

Yet, Canon Woods concludes:

> I believe that Bultmann's call to demythologise the New Testa-
> ment preaching is beginning to show increasing affinities with
> the claim that all ultimate explanation is in personal terms and
> that in the Christian faith we have the ultimate explanation
> which we naturally seek.

We are now in a position to revert to the questions I raised at
the beginning: Can we provide from anywhere patterns of reliable

[18] loc. cit., pp. 208–10.

reasoning to show how a religious assertion is linked with a historical assertion, how the Christian faith cannot be content to do without history, nor can it be content with history alone?

We can see what Bultmann's answer would be. Take whatever minimal historical events can be agreed in the case of any gospel narrative—be it the feeding of the five thousand or the raising of Lazarus, or anything else. To know 'what happened', to know what the gospel writer was trying to put over, place the minimal events within an 'existential situation' such as Heidegger and others have taught us to recognize. So far as Bultmann is here hinting at the kind of situation in which Christian language is grounded, he is both important and correct. My basic criticism (and here I follow Canon Woods) is that by taking Heideggerian existentialism as his παιδαγωγός—the tutor or chaperone to bring in the Christ—he has in principle denied himself the possibility of establishing a reasonable link between the historical and the 'existential'. He has done nothing to help us distinguish between a better and a worse argument in this field. It is in fact very significant, and not at all unexpected, that Bultmann can have both conservative and sceptical disciples.

We have now, however, been brought to the central point of my paper, and before going further I would like to underline it. it is this. We shall never illuminate—let alone solve—the problems which cluster around history and the gospels unless and until there is some kind of agreement (1) about the kind of event, occurrence, situation—let us not call it 'fact' for that is bound to mislead us—to which the Christian appeals as 'having happened'; some philosophical account of what it is we are talking about when we say of the healing of the paralytic, of the feeding of the five thousand, of the raising of Lazarus, of the Cross, of the resurrection, of the post-resurrection appearances, '*it*' happened; (2) about the lines on which we test and measure the reasonableness of belief in such events, occurrences and situations. Both these are questions for the philosopher, and I will now try to take them up.

All I propose to do is to approach from another direction and with certain different emphases the kind of point which Canon Woods makes in his book. Like Bultmann I appeal to situations 'existentialist' in so far as they are 'personal', but I am more hopeful of their transparency to the light of reason.

Suppose it could be argued that the disclosure which occurs when the Christian discerns the grace of God in Christ and responds to it with the commitment of the Apostle Thomas, can it be aptly modelled in terms of the characteristically personal disclosure which can be called 'love', or in terms of the trust we are prepared to place in some man? The kind of situations I have in mind can be sketched without much difficulty. Take first the case of what would be called 'falling in love'. It is well known that this response and commitment can occur around a very minimal area of facts—a smile, a look of the eyes, some small incident which, from one point of view, could be said to be quite trivial. What happens in such circumstances is (I would suggest) that around these spatio-temporal trivialities a disclosure suddenly occurs, when the 'light dawns', and when there is a commitment in response to what is discerned. Or, to take the second example, suppose we are considering the possibility of asking someone to undertake a delicate, dangerous, and highly confidential mission. Two or three possible agents come to mind. As we survey such facts about each person as are known to us, there may suddenly occur, about one of them, a sense that *this* is the man. There will have been a disclosure in response to which we have made our decision, our commitment.

Suppose we now ask of these two cases—but is that a genuine 'falling in love' or not? Is that man 'really' trustworthy? What can we say about the pattern of reliable discourse which meets these questions? It will concern itself, I suggest, with at least five points:

(*a*) There must be *some* pro-factors which we recognize as the grounds of making the presupposition of love or trustworthiness at all, and all the better for the reasonableness of our discourse if these factors are ones which we have already associated with talk about love and trustworthiness hitherto.

(*b*) There must be the *possibility* that this presupposition of love or trustworthiness harmonizes with a vast area of X's behaviour towards me.

(*c*) On the other hand, while there may be some contra-factors, the existence of these will not, by itself, invalidate our presupposition.

(*d*) Even so, there must certainly be the logical possibility of rejecting our presupposition if too many contra-factors come to light. Further, this logical possibility will remain even though the exact point when the presupposition will be rejected cannot be specified beforehand. Incidentally, in this connection it seems to me that, in what contemporary philosophers call the falsification controversy, religious people have been far too inclined to grant their opponents' interpretations of such phrases as 'I will trust God though He slay me', as though religious belief could never entertain the possibility of critical contra-factors.

(*e*) Here, a curious point. It may well be that as our perspective is broadened, what we supposed to be a pro-factor at the start, indeed that in which our judgement of love or trustworthiness originated, may turn out to be mistaken or itself ambiguous. But that, by itself, will not weaken our judgement of love or trustworthiness if, by that time, our wider perspective is sufficiently stable to incorporate it.

Here, then, are some generalizations about our judgements of love and trustworthiness; here is an outline pattern of discourse by which we might justify the assertion that someone exhibits genuine love, or that someone is trustworthy and exhibits dependable behaviour. It is with this background, with this idea of reliable argument, that we may now profitably approach theological claims based on historical events.

On such a background, if we are presented with the question 'Did the resurrection occur?' we must trace out a similar kind of five-fold pattern:

(*a*) We must first ask: To what initial pro-factors do we appeal to justify talk about a 'resurrection' at all? The mere fact of an empty tomb; or must it be awestruck reactions to an empty tomb? Post-resurrection appearances? Including appearances to Stephen? And to Paul? Can we list any priorities? Here is a task awaiting someone's attention. Note that whatever we specify must be enough to do justice to 'resurrection', and not just 'resuscitation'. Further, could there be any prior contexts for the word 'resurrection' as for the word 'love'? If only approximate contexts, probably there are some in the Old Testament.

(*b*) We next ask: Does the resurrection-presupposition (grounded in this way) harmonize with other Christian generalizations, and other principles of Christian practice—liturgical and moral? An Affirmative answer would presumably appeal to the existence of the Christian Church, the fact of Sunday observance, and so on.

(*c*) We now need to list any contra-factors, e.g. the rumour that the disciples stole the body; the earthquake; the general scientific quest for regularities; and so on. All these call (as far as may be) for harmonization—but different sorts of harmonization in each case.

(*d*) We must be prepared to reject the resurrection if too many contra-factors appear. But we have no need to specify a point of rejection beforehand.

(*e*) We may come to disbelieve in what have been thought to be, or even in what we ourselves took to be, pro-factors in the post, or we may believe them in the context of psychical research rather than in the context of the world of the exact sciences—and all this without disbelieving in the resurrection, and *that reasonably*. Let me develop the point a little in relation to the model of 'falling in love'. It may be that the look of the eyes which first evoked the love only occurred because of the skilful use of eye-shadow or because of (say) some biochemical leap in sugar concentration on a particular evening. Even so, the loyalty, if it has an already broadened canvas, may remain, and reasonably remain, even though (as in such a case) the original event from which it took its rise proves bogus. So (if this pattern of reasoning be allowed) Christian faith might reasonably remain if some one event or other proved false as a historical fact. But *not all* the events must be proved false without our being converted to infidelity. There, in outline, is the way in which a reasonable belief in the resurrection could be tested and defended on the model supplied by our talking about situations of love and trustworthiness.

As a further indication of how this kind of model can afford us clues to reasonable arguments which link Christian assertions with 'historical facts', let me say a little more about the case of 'love'.

'Love' may be evoked (as we have said) by a smile, a look of the eyes, and so on. But the test of whether our 'falling in love' is or is not reasonable, will be (as we have seen) whether the resulting loyalty and pro-attitude can remain when confronted with a larger and larger picture, and when the empirical canvas broadens. In this connection there is here a subtle and complicating difficulty, namely that it is 'love' which of all personal activities is the one most able of itself to convert contraconsiderations into pro-attitudes. This in fact is what is meant by 'redeeming love'. But complications apart, if a religion takes 'love' as its key concept, its cosmic claims are much more likely to be reasonably substantiated.

My point is that if we allow that such ordinary situations as we have mentioned, such ordinary disclosures as falling in love and recognizing a man's trustworthiness, if we allow that these can be reliable models and patterns of a Christian situation, then we have not only recognized the kind of topic that the gospel writers were trying to write about, we have also got some idea as to how we can distinguish between reliable and spurious arguments, some idea of how we can judge one man's conservatism, or another man's scepticism as reasonable or unreasonable. You will now see (for better or worse) my own attempt to answer the questions I formulated in the heart of the paper. I have suggested that the philosophy of 'disclosures' can provide us with useful clues to the kind of situation to which a Christian appeals; and can also suggest patterns for the kind of reasoning by which talk about these disclosures is justified; patterns by which to judge the reliability of discourse which seeks to connect historical assertions and religious beliefs.

At the end, I have approached a point not far distant from Fr Hebert's position,[19] and both of us would agree with Professor Nineham when he concluded in a recent series of papers in *The Journal of Theological Studies* by remarking:

> The gospels were not means to give us an uninterpreted picture of Jesus' ministry so full and detailed that we could interpret its significance for ourselves. They were meant to admit us to that understanding of, and relationship with, Jesus which was vouchsafed to the apostolic Church. At the same time they make possible sufficient historical knowledge of the person and ministry of Jesus for us to assure ourselves that the early Christians were not making bricks without straw; and also for us to see the sense in which their interpretations were intended and were legitimate and to set about the task of reformulating them in terms of our own needs and experience.[20]

At the same time Professor Nineham is not blind to the practical and pastoral implications of these reflections—nor should we be:

> . . . it is idle (he says) to deny that some real loss is involved

[19] Cf. *Studies Evangelica* II, pp. 65–72.
[20] New Series 11, 1960, p. 263. Professor Nineham also notes the similarity of his views to those expressed in Professor John Knox's *Jesus: Lord and Christ*, New York, 1958.

in our conclusions. If they are right, it is illegitimate to press the details and many of the personal traits, in the stories; yet it is precisely through dwelling on such 'human touches' that many Christians have felt themselves brought most vividly into contact with their Lord. And not only is it illegitimate to press these details in an historical interest, it is surely hazardous to press them for devotional purposes, or at any rate for devotional purposes not directly envisaged by the Evangelists. A question-mark is clearly set against some forms of *imitatio Christi* devotion and also against the practice, which still largely governs the life of the Churches, of quoting individual sayings and incidents from the gospels as precedents. In general it may be said that if our conclusions were to prove justified, they would have signi-ficant implications for devotional and homiletic practice and for moral and ascetic theology, which the Churches for the most part have by no means thought through.

and he continues later:

> Undeniably, in these implications there is much food for thought, particularly perhaps for those who have to deal with congregations and assemblies accustomed to accept unquestion-ingly the precise historical trustworthiness of every detail they read, or hear read, in the gospels.

Perhaps I can end these highly generalized reflections with an example taking us back to the name of one who will always be revered in Oxford scholarship on this matter—the late Dr R. H. Lightfoot. Everyone will recall the conclusion of Lightfoot's *History and Interpretation in the Gospels* and how sceptical this seemed to be to many, and how distressed Lightfoot was that it should seem to be so:

> It seems, then, that the form of the earthly no less than of the heavenly Christ is for the most part hidden from us. For all the inestimable value of the gospels, they yield us little more than a whisper of his voice; we trace in them but the outskirts of his ways. Only when we see him hereafter in his fullness shall we know him also as he was on earth. And perhaps the more we ponder the matter, the more clearly we shall understand the reason for it, and therefore shall not wish it otherwise.

We are now in a position, it seems to me, to give Lightfoot the full appreciation he always deserved. For if what I have been saying is right, it can be *reasonable* to base a full and total personal commitment on what may be no more than 'a whisper' of a man's voice. But our commitment will only be reasonable if we strive continuously (as Lightfoot did) to get clearer and clearer about the spatio-temporal facts and their harmony one with another. Nor, because our commitment may be reasonably based on a few facts, do we reasonably or rightly conclude that it might just as well be based on one at all, or that no 'facts' matter. We return in the end to what we were saying earlier—the Christian faith cannot be content merely with historical facts, nor can it do without them. But no more can love or trustworthiness or any 'existential' human situation, be content to regard persons as no more than their overt behaviour. Neither can it seriously pretend that the love and trustworthiness could still exist if there were no visible behaviour at all.

This leads us to make one final point by transferring this reflection to the Christian case.

For some historical-religious assertions, the historical events are theoretically (at any rate) determinate and clear. This is the case, e.g. of the Virgin Birth (parthenogenesis) and the Cross (crucifixion). The danger here is that a man's belief may be no more than that these events happened; so that he will assent to 'purely historical' assertions and believe that he is making a religious profession. The danger here is that he will measure his theological discourse by logical rules provided by history books, if not worse, by 'scientific history' books.

For other historical-religious assertions, the historical events are problematical, e.g. the ascension and the resurrection. The danger here is that a man's belief may try to ignore or by-pass the historical difficulties; think them of no account, pretending that it does not really matter what happened. This may be a parody of certain Collingwoodians or of certain existentialists, but it is not too wild. The danger then is that (at best) we will assimilate theological discourse to the language of myth (in the ordinary sense) and fabrication. On such a view Enid Blyton's 'Christmas Story', which mixes Big Ears, Santa Claus, angels and Bethlehem, becomes the norm for theological preaching and Christian devotion.

What we need to avoid both dangers is a model for reasoning which makes religious assertions both relate to historical events and yet transcend them, and this, I have hinted, can be found in characteristically personal argumentation. Problems of history and of the gospels are problems which can be matched in the logic of personal relationships, and I have suggested that since the logic of the one can be a clue to the logic of the other, we are not without standards of reasonableness by which to judge between better and worse theological arguments.

APPENDIX
Ian Ramsey in Dialogue

Bibliography

Freedom and Immortality *1*[1]

A REVIEW BY H. D. LEWIS

A philosopher who undertakes to write about religious questions today is apt to find himself balancing on a very slim tightrope. In the abyss below him there lie, on the one hand, his critics, especially empiricist ones, with eager hands outstretched to snatch at him and tear him apart the instant he comes within their reach. He will be their victim as soon as he begins to speak of God as if he were one entity among others and limited by his relations to other finite beings. This is how reliance on the traditional arguments usually leads to disaster. If God is thought of as one member of a causal series, however paramount his place, we find it difficult to show that there is one cause which has this unique position—and if we could find one it would still appear to be less than God. In seeking, however, to avoid this disaster we are apt to topple over, on our other side, into the bottomless abyss of not saying anything at all, or of cancelling what we say by nervous retractions and qualifications. Some religions mind this less than others; some forms of Hinduism, for instance, are content to say that 'the Self is Silence'. Some Western philosophers of late have likewise warned us not to say even that God exists, for that begins the fatal move that brings God within the scope of ordinary discourse. It thus becomes hard to say anything else about God and we are in danger of having an utterly formless and empty religion. Professor Ramsey[1] is well aware of these dangers, and it is a tribute to his skill and theological insight that he manages to keep his balance so well. He does not quite lose his foothold at any stage, but it must also be admitted that he does give his readers some exceedingly anxious moments by leaning so far over on the side of the abyss of silence. That he manages to right himself without toppling right over is a feat of which he may be proud, but one hopes that he will not presume too much upon it.

[1] *Freedom and Immortality.* The Forwood Lectures in the University of Liverpool, 1957. By Ian Ramsey. S.C.M. Press, p. 157.

The present book continues the theme of an earlier work, *On Religious Language*. There it was maintained that religious statements are logically odd and, indeed, inappropriate, but that their proper significance is found in certain disclosure situations where 'the light dawns' without our taking these religious statements at the face value which their form suggests. Varied and lively illustrations of this were offered, but without investigating any particular theme in detail. In his new book Professor Ramsey brings the principles of this earlier study to the closer examination of two themes central in religious thought, namely freedom and immortality, the attention paid to the latter being particularly welcome because, in recent years, philosophers have been very shy of it. An invocation to Kant, who looked to moral experience to remedy the deficiencies of strictly scientific knowledge based on sense experience, gives a firm indication at the start of the procedure to be followed.

Professor Ramsey believes that the usual approach to the problem of freedom is very mistaken. The determinist argues, on the one hand, that we have only an impression of freedom, because we can never be certain that all the factors relevant to some particular case have been noted. But this is a double-edged argument, and the libertarian can also use it to cut the other way by arguing that, as there are many matters unknown to us, we can never show conclusively that any event is inevitable. I am not myself convinced that the traditional debate between determinists and indeterminists has in fact spun as much on this particular merry-go-round as Professor Ramsey supposes, and I believe that the position of the libertarian is not always presented by him in the fairest light. Libertarians have not been nearly as prone as absolute idealists to speak of a 'timeless self' and their view is not usually that 'we are determined by the moral law'. Indeed, some explicit reference to the work of some outstanding libertarian, like C. A. Campbell, is what we should have particularly liked from Professor Ramsey. But granted the dilemma he specifies, what solution are we offered?

The answer turns on certain situations where, it is alleged, 'without any difference in the cause-factors' a person gives some decision 'his personal backing'. Such decisions cannot be 'netted in the language of objects'. 'My behaviour, to me, when deliberate or decisive is objects *and more*.'[2] It is not 'reaction to stimuli'.[3]

[2] p. 28.   [3] p. 29.

The Priest and the Levite in the parable move through 'prescribed behaviour patterns', but the Samaritan is 'moved inwardly', ' "man" meets "man" ', and there is a response to a moral obligation 'which cannot be netted in the language of observables', 'a free decision—a decision which is backed personally—is a response to objects and more'.[4] The 'situation takes on "depth", becoming observables *and more*'.[5] It is obvious that there is blended here with the voice of Kant a resounding echo of modern existentialists, and while we owe them the credit of placing the emphasis in the right quarter, one hesitates to regard them as the soundest guides where clarity and careful thought are required; and I must confess that I am not quite certain how to take Professor Ramsey's meaning at this crucial point. When he says that there is 'no causal determination' 'when there is free will', 'no more behaviour according to a line of least resistance', but that 'we now do it as a duty', one is apt to take the meaning in a plain libertarian sense. But it is not at all certain that this is the intention. The idea seems to be rather that, while there need be no break in the causal story, the 'personal backing' and so on redeems an action in some fashion from being objectionably determined. This I am not able to follow, and it seems to savour of many attempts in recent philosophy to speak with the angels while thinking otherwise. But here I may be doing Professor Ramsey much injustice. The issue turns on just how much force he allows to the 'personal backing': how does it come about and is it efficacious, how precisely do we understand 'the more' which expresses itself in various observable 'directions' but 'cannot be entirely cashed in terms of these observable features alone?'[6]

A subsidiary difficulty concerns the dismissal of behaviour which does not involve the 'free and personal' decision in question as only 'reaction to stimuli', or following automatically a behaviour pattern. We can draw a rough distinction between doing things automatically and doing them deliberately, but our conduct is never quite automatic, unless we are walking in our sleep and so on; and what shall we say of the Priest and the Levite? Were they not in their way acting responsibly or should we exempt them on the grounds that their choice is not free? Many redoubtable defenders of freedom in the past have ended up in the position of holding that only good actions, but never bad ones, are free and

[4] p. 33.   [5] p. 33.   [6] p. 37.

responsible. That accords well with one kind of theology, but not I imagine one that commends itself to Professor Ramsey.

This does not mean that all actions and choices are free in the same sense. To suppose that they are is one of the root causes of confusion in discussions of freedom. My freedom, in making a moral choice, is different from the freedom involved in ordinary voluntary action. But there are wicked as well as good moral choices; and moral choices are not distinguished from others by a personal, 'man meeting man', character of a situation which is not found elsewhere. I may have that situation vis-à-vis an inspired teacher when no moral issue is involved. The 'more' that Professor Ramsey offers us seems to be too much and too little. I am loth also to treat the distinction between personal and impersonal relationships as more than a matter of degree. We never treat other persons solely as objects, any more than our conduct is ever mere 'response to stimuli'.

Some misgiving is caused also by the description of a free decision as 'spatio-temporal and more'. That a choice is not just an occurrence in space is plain. But all our conduct is surely temporal. We may also be said in some senses to transcend time, in memory for instance and in anticipation of the future. But there seems to be nothing here peculiar to important decisions or ethical choice; and while there are many features of human life (and of the life of brutes too) besides spatial or temporal ones, we must beware of presenting this in terms that take us back again to the notion of a timeless self. That would certainly not be Professor Ramsey's wish, he insists that the decision *is* spatio-temporal. But he is liable to misinterpretation when he says that it is 'more'—unless he ventures to be more precise than he seems ready to be about the import of 'the more'.

The linkage of the argument, as outlined hitherto, with religion is established when reference is made to 'disclosure situations other than moral ones'. These are evoked by the 'most diverse stories', such as those 'about causes and existents'. All these evoke something important subjectively which gives the word 'I' its 'appropriate logical placing', and we then find we have to use the word 'God' 'as a sort of objective counterpart to "I" '.[7] But the word God may also predominate and become 'the ultimate category' when it is seen to 'integrate the various words and phrases which are attached

[7] p. 48.

to the diverse routes by which distinctive situations are evoked'.[8]

I have put this as much as possible in Professor Ramsey's own words, because I am not sure that I follow him at every point. He clearly finds a more direct path from certain peculiar situations, such as being confronted by a duty, to God than I am able to tread. God is involved, as I understand it, in the being of anything, although there are situations which evoke the awareness of this more readily than others, for example those which set us thinking about ultimate explanations. I also believe that there are distinctive situations, especially moral ones, in which we acquire more intimate knowledge and experience of God. This I have stressed and made prominent in my own attempt to discuss these subjects, and I much welcome any indication of more explicit logical relationships between such situations and God than I have indicated in my own account of them and of their place in the maturing of our knowledge of God. But I am not very certain what Professor Ramsey offers us here—except at one point.

That point is where he stresses 'the logical kinship between "God" and "I" '. From his articles and other books it is clear that this has central importance for Professor Ramsey. But my own reaction to it is again twofold. It is not from the fact of our being persons, or of anything else distinctive of human life, that we know that God exists, but from any fact whatsoever. But, on the other hand, granted this initial insight, the way we come to know God within the world and experience has very important similarities with the way human persons communicate. In fairness it must be added that Professor Ramsey is as anxious as anyone to induce caution in our talk about God. We must not assimilate God's nature too closely to our own. But it is this very proper caution that seems to reduce him to talking about God as 'the ultimate category', the 'objective counterpart to "I" ', and so forth; and the difficulty I find with this is to know just what is being affirmed beyond the distinctive characteristics of certain finite situations. It is plain that Professor Ramsey does want to affirm more, he is far from wishing to retain religious language for an essentially humanist view—as happens to so many philosophical apologists today. The position, at this point, is not unlike that of prominent idealist writers in whose work Professor Ramsey also takes a close interest. But it is not quite an idealist view that he offers, and

[8] p. 48.

beyond this I, for one, am not able to go until I have grasped better than I have done hitherto what we are to understand by the 'logical kinship between "God" and "I" '. It is to this central topic that I hope Professor Ramsey will return when he writes on these themes again.

One advantage of Professor Ramsey's position—and he naturally seizes upon it—is that it offers a way out of a very trying dilemma. On the one hand there is much that induces us to say that ethics are quite independent of religion—the unbeliever need not be unaware or unmindful of his duty, and there are well-known objections to simply saying that duty or worth are just what God wills or commands. On the other hand, to make ethics wholly independent of religion seems odd. Perhaps then a more subtle view may present an inherent relation of religion and ethics which does not impair the things we most wish to preserve in stressing the autonomy of ethics. There may be some sense in which ethical notions are essentially religious ones; and, in the light of recent work, including that of Professor Ramsey, I am inclined to entertain much higher hopes of this possibility than I used to. But again I am not clear what precisely is the course Professor Ramsey wishes us to take here.

It does not seem enough, at this point, to speak of 'alternative and complementary assertions viewing the same situation through two different language frames'.[9] It is not that these assertions are thought of as 'synonymous substitutes'. Of that we have firm assurance. But in that case what are they? Can we say what they are without a bolder indication of factual differences than Professor Ramsey is disposed to provide? One must make every allowance for all that is said about the 'disclosure situations' in relation to which the argument is meant to be understood, and one can warmly admire the skilful exhibition of the subtle gradation from some of these to those that lie nearest religion. The reader must judge for himself how much is accomplished in this way; and that is what makes the task of the reviewer very hard. Professor Ramsey's procedure is of a type which may make it peculiarly misleading just to expose the main bones. But when every allowance of this sort is made, and with the best will in the world, I cannot be happy with the statement that 'talk of God's punishment becomes a picturesque means of insisting that "God's will" relates to moral

[9] p. 50.

obligations that one way or another are inescapable and will prevail'.[10] Nor does it seem adequate to say that 'we are in fact using such a phrase as "God's will" to give us an alternative description for what confronts us when we are aware of obligation, an alternative description which seeks to do justice to the fact that there are distinctive disclosure-situations other than those in which "Duty" is pegged'.[11] There is no crude identification of religion and morality here. But have we a God transcendent?

The discussion of immortality follows very closely that of freedom—too closely for my liking. The main emphasis is again on the fact that we are 'spatio-temporal and more'. 'Because we are in that sense "free", in that sense we are immortal.'[12] Now if this meant that we could not have immortality without being more than the physical behaviour which ends with the dissolution of the body at death, it would plainly be true. One of the most grievous features of recent philosophy, for any religious view, is the ease with which behaviourist views of the self have been adopted and the notion of the self as a persisting non-material entity abandoned. No one, admittedly, wishes to return to the notion of the self as a quasi-material object attached to the body or mysteriously concealed within it. Perhaps no one has seriously held that view, although it is the view lampooned in discussions of the subject today. But it seems plain to me that, unless we can recover something more akin to the traditional view of the soul or person than the prevailing ideas, it is quite idle to talk of any form of immortality. If a man is no more than his observable behaviour or dispositions to behave, or if he is merely the 'point of view' of his body as some have curiously suggested, there appears to be nothing which could survive his demise.

With this Professor Ramsey would certainly agree; he stresses repeatedly the need to evoke the awareness of ourselves as 'more-than-public-behaviour'. But he is cautious about the way this must be understood. We are warned not to speak of the soul in language which is 'a logical duplicate of language about physical objects'.[13] The soul is not 'a shadowy existent, some kind of counterpart of this body'.[14] But we are also not to 'over-argue' the point.[15] For such language is not 'altogether bogus'.[16] This seems to me very true and important, and there seems to me also to be no more urgent task in contemporary philosophy than to discover proper

[10] p. 52.   [11] p. 53.   [12] p. 66.   [13, 14, 15, 16] p. 105.

H

ways of referring to the self and consciousness without either assimilating them to objects in the external world or eliminating them altogether. Here Professor Ramsey admirably points the way, and his caution is proper and significant.

All the same, one has the suspicion that more is conceded than is necessary to prevailing fashion. Is the self for Professor Ramsey in no sense an entity? And is it enough to refer to distinctive situations in which we are alert, responsible, and sharply aware of personal and moral factors in our situation? Are we not *always* more than spatio-temporal, even in humdrum and routine behaviour? Can we avoid the general epistemological problem of the self by directing attention to the 'existentialist' situations in which we may be said to transcend our normal self and so forth? And are we not in danger here of substituting helpful metaphor for philosophical analysis? At its crudest this might take the form of asserting that I must have a soul because I am sometimes 'soul-ful'. Not that Professor Ramsey lapses into this, but the questions I raise may serve as warning posts to point to the dangers in which we may easily land in Professor Ramsey's tracks unless we walk very circumspectly indeed.

But suppose such perils are averted, how do we now reach belief in immortality? For to have a proper view of the self is only a preliminary, albeit a very important one. And this is where I find Professor Ramsey's procedure least easy to follow. For he comes dangerously near equating immortality itself with this essential prerequisite, as if in being aware of ourselves as more than 'spatio-temporal' we were *ipso facto* immortal—or known to be immortal. That does not seem to me to follow. It would not be inconsistent to hold a firmly non-physical and substantival view of the self and yet wonder whether this self persists without the body —or flatly deny that it does. Some humanists might well accept all that Professor Ramsey has said about the self and our moral and personal relationships and sensitivity and so forth, and yet be quite agnostic and unbelieving in other regards. In other words, a further case has to be made for immortality. Professor Ramsey is however extremely shy of arguments for immortality, and I think he raises telling objections to the sort of arguments he examines—arguments from duty, arguments from psychical research and so on. I should myself not think it impossible for psychical research to prove some kind of survival, but it could not give us all that religious people understand by 'eternal life'; and generally I share Professor Ramsey's suspicion of large *a priori* arguments, such as the argument from duty or from some allegedly indestructible character of soul or personality. At the same time, some case must be made—for the Christian, I submit, in terms (mainly at least) of matters peculiar to the Christian faith. We cannot conclude that because we are persons and responsible beings we are *ipso facto* immortal.

Yet that is what Professor Ramsey comes dangerously close to doing. And this is for him the real force of the traditional arguments. 'It is in so recognising duty as something which transcends the spatio-temporal, that we recognise our own transcendence of the spatio-temporal, our own immortality.'[17] 'In some cases, our awareness of obligation and our awareness of immortality are given together.'[18] 'In short, "immortality" and "unending life" do not tell of some "property" of a "thing" called the soul, or of some existence like our public behaviour now, but going on and on and on. They tell rather of a situation we know *now* which is characteristically distinctive in being more than spatio-temporal.'[19] The Christian does admittedly speak of eternal life as something available to him now, but he certainly does not intend to reduce immortality to a quality of life in the present. I do not suggest that Professor Ramsey wishes to do that, but it is extremely difficult to know what he is affirming which could not be put exhaustively in terms of moral and psychological aspects of the present life. He does stress the sense of wonder and mystery and depth which surrounds the 'special situations' he describes, but even if this does lend these situations a religious character, that will not suffice to establish particular items of religious belief. It would not be inconsistent to believe in God without believing that it is his purpose that we should be immortal—the Hebrews at some stage apparently did so.

A further consequence of Professor Ramsey's view is that the distinction between freedom and immortality tends to be blurred. He writes: 'So to justify "freedom" by appealing to decision-situations which exceed public behaviour, and even to recall one use of nicknames,[20] is, at the same time, to justify belief in immortality. For to do either shows that we are not restricted or

[17] p. 73.   [18] p. 72.   [19] p. 104.
[20] The point of this is clear in the context.

confined to those features of our existence which are in space and
time. Because we are in that sense "free", in that sense we are
"immortal".'[21]

Again it must be borne in mind that 'exceeding public behaviour'
is to be understood, in this book, in a context which leads out to
God as 'the ultimate category'. It involves a 'situation of mystery
and wonder',[22] and again the argument is meant to turn a great
deal on the examples which illustrate it. But for me at least the
procedure as a whole involves too close a merging of issues that
are by no means identical. It is not enough to evoke a sense of
mystery, or a religious view of life in general. Not all mystery is
religious, and there are many religions—and many forms of the
same religion. The apologist must consider what weighs with him
in this or that regard, notwithstanding that his faith may have
close integration and unity. A great deal of recent apologetics
overlook this.

I cannot follow Professor Ramsey into closer detail in a review
that is already very long. But there is one argument in his account
of immortality which I feel I must mention, for it has been given
much prominence elsewhere; and I must admit that, in common
with many of my colleagues, I find it extremely puzzling. It is a
very linguistic argument and turns on the allegedly odd logical
behaviour of the verb 'to die'. A fuller statement of the argument
than Professor Ramsey offers may be found in a paper by Professor
Poteat[23] to which reference is made in the book. Briefly it runs thus.
I can say 'he died', or 'I shall die' just as I can say 'he ran' or 'I
shall run'; but while I can say 'I ran' I cannot say 'I died' or 'I am
dead'. To say 'I died' would be absurd, and the implication of this
presumably is that immortality must not be thought of in terms
of any kind of survival. I have not discovered how immortality
could be understood if it did not involve survival in some form.
We can baptize the terms into different existentialist use if we
wish, and that, it seems to me, is just what Professor Poteat at
least is doing, notwithstanding that his role is that of Christian
philosopher. But setting that aside, what should we make of the
argument itself?

Obviously it would seem absurd for anyone to say 'I am dead'
or, in a similar but not quite identical case, 'I am asleep'. We

---

[21] p. 66.   [22] p. 68.
[23] 'I will die: an analysis', *Philosophical Quarterly*, Jan. 1959.

should treat the statement as a joke. But that is only because my being able to say these things in present circumstances is foolproof evidence that in fact I have not died. But suppose a person does die, and then survives (and one must not rule out the possibility of survival at the start in an argument meant to disprove it), what is there inherently absurd about the possibility of his addressing the words 'I died' to another departed spirit? This holds whatever form of survival we have in mind. We may be thinking of a cycle of rebirth, and then we may suppose someone who remembers his previous lives explaining how he died at the end of one of them at the hands of an assassin, and so on. There may be other arguments against these possibilities, or a lack of evidence for them. But it is not inherently contradictory or logically absurd to suppose that someone could properly refer to his own death—at the very least it is not absurd in the way the present argument supposes. Indeed, it is often maintained that the dead do communicate with the living. The case for this may not be made out, and there may be insuperable difficulties in fact about such communication. But it does not seem true that those who entertain this possibility and investigate it can be shown from the start to be committing a palpable logical or linguistic absurdity. A dead person, as yet only pronounced 'missing', might thus wish to ease the tension of anxious relatives, or serve some other purpose, by letting them know that he was in fact dead. This may not have much bearing on 'eternal life' as the Christian understands it. But certainly means that his case is not ruled out *ab initio* by an alleged linguistic difficulty.

Indeed, this seems so plain to me that I wonder what there can be about the argument that I am overlooking. Of the assertions: 'I am asleep' or 'I am dead', Professor Ramsey says that 'they are assertions which would be falsified on utterance'. This seems to me just not true, least of all in the second case. And if there is something which I have missed about the argument, bandied about as it has been in recent controversies, I should be much relieved to have that pointed out to me. I am also, I fear, naïve enough to find any talk about immortality that does not include a person's survival in some form puzzling in the extreme. I much doubt whether it conforms at all to what most people have in mind in entertaining the hope of immortality, and for that reason I do not think many would consider themselves well served by the sort of assurances of immortality offered in some quarters today.

I must not, in ending, seem unfair to Professor Ramsey. He moves with exceptional subtlety between the extremes of an out-and-out positivist reinterpretation of religion and the cruder forms of theism from which he is very properly anxious to save us. No one who reads this book can fail to have a finer understanding of the elusive character of religious truth and the care with which its problems must be handled at the philosophical level. Nor can he fail to derive delight and instruction from the abundance of homely illustrations and the simplicity and clarity of the author's style. Above all, this book takes us to the heart of the controversies about religion which arise from the course which philosophy has taken of late. Professor Ramsey is thoroughly familiar with the techniques of recent linguistic philosophy, and he has also wide theological knowledge and acute understanding of theological difficulties. If we are unable to accept all his presuppositions, or follow all his arguments, that does not prevent us from being substantially helped by his work, and made to reconsider many of our own presuppositions. No one who wishes to examine the problems of freedom and immortality, as they appear today, can afford to neglect this book; and if I have dwelt mainly on the matters that puzzle me, that is in the hope that when the author turns to these and kindred problems again he will be able to make the darker places plainer and give us not so many moments of anxiously wondering whether he will be able to maintain his balance and foothold on a course that is bound to be so slippery.

Freedom and Immortality 2

SOME FURTHER REFLECTIONS
BY IAN RAMSEY

I am immensely grateful to Professor Lewis for the helpful and constructive criticisms he has brought to bear on my book *Freedom and Immortality* and for the sympathetic and generous treatment which he has given to my views in his recent article.[1] I cannot hope to take up every point he raises, but I have selected three topics around which to make some further comments, and I draw one or two threads together in some concluding remarks.

FREEWILL

Perhaps I ought to say at the start that what I most tried to do in relation to this complex topic was to make clear what I believe is the empirical anchorage of discourse about free will. I tried to say just what sort of situations justify talk about free will, talk about the 'freedom' which belongs to 'responsible moral decision' and so on. Undoubtedly, as Professor Lewis recognizes, I am nervous of phrases such as 'timeless self acting' or 'moral law determining', and while I agree that wise libertarians such as Professor C. A. Campbell do not use these cruder expressions, does not even Professor Campbell use expressions with similar initial difficulties? He says, for example, 'The self is free when it possesses freedom located in the decision to exert (or withhold) moral effort needed to rise to duty when the pressure of its desiring nature is felt to urge it in a contrary direction',[2] and somewhat later he comments: 'Moral decision is an activity directly comprehended only "from the inside", by the agent actually engaged in it'. It is *not* that I see myself *denying* what Professor Campbell talks about in this way. Rather I try (if possible) to say what these situations are in language less open to logical misunderstanding. What sort of situations have such advocates of free will wished—and I think

[1] *The Hibbert Journal*, LIX, pp. 168–78, Jan. 1961.
[2] *On Selfhood and Godhood*. C. A. Campbell, Allen & Unwin, p. 178.

rightly—to defend? My answer is: situations where I give my 'personal backing' to what otherwise I would do 'impersonally'. Professor Lewis then pertinently asks: What do I mean by this phrase 'personal backing' (pp. 169–70)? Obviously, after what I have said, I must not explicate it in terms of a self or a timeless self 'rising to duty' when pressures 'of its desiring nature' would direct it otherwise. I can see that these phrases *may* say what I want to say. But they may also mislead; they may be wrongly construed in terms of some sort of metaphysical statics, and ironically enough then do no justice to the transcendence—indeed mystery—which perhaps all would agree lies behind any claim for free will.

Having in this way ruled out (and I believe on good grounds) the possibility of one kind of answer to Professor Lewis's question, all I can do to explicate the phrase 'personal backing' is to give examples in the hope that the point of the phrase will otherwise strike the reader. All I can do at most is to give examples which will enable the reader to 'see' for himself what there is 'more' about the case where there is a personal backing, than the case where I would be acting impersonally. Let me take three examples, the first of which I mention in my book.[3] This is the case of, I believe, a certain Duke of Newcastle who dreamt he was speaking in the House of Lords and woke to find that he was. What I am appealing to when I talk of 'personal backing' is the significant kind of difference that would make itself known to the Duke of Newcastle at some point when (just having wakened) he discovered that he was after all speaking in the House of Lords, and at that moment decided deliberately and as an act of 'free choice' to continue his speech. That the particular moment could be described in various ways by an observant biologist or psychologist who happened to be a peer present at the debate, I do not doubt. But my interest is not in such scientific specifications of the moment when the Duke decided to continue his speech; my interest is in what happened to the Duke of which he himself was distinctively aware at the moment when he deliberately decided to give his words henceforward his 'personal backing'.

My second example develops one which has been used by various people for various purposes. Suppose on a black night we see flashes across a remote highland valley, and judge them to be

[3] *Freedom and Immortality*, pp. 22–3.

on some distant mountain road. Such flashes may be caused by raindrops shortcircuiting a car lighting set. In such a case the flashes would be highly 'impersonal'. On the other hand they might be caused by a man working 'mechanically', displaying some kind of conditioned reflex. He might be learning to signal Morse, and learning to press a button appropriately—'automatically', we would say—at the sight of some letter of the alphabet. Here again, while the action would now be biologically and psychologically much more complex and certainly much more 'human', it would still be, in my sense, impersonal. But, thirdly, the flashes might be caused by a man deliberately using a car lighting set to call for help in some desperate circumstances which arose for him as a moral challenge to which he felt obliged to respond in this way. In such a case he would know and display 'freedom', the observable features would have a 'personal backing', and we might say that he displayed a 'freedom of choice'[4]—if, for example (as a shepherd), he could have avoided the moral challenge by leaving the crashed car and its injured occupants on the moorland road.

As a third example let us consider a man who is cutting the lawn in a large garden attached to some vast institution, with the regularity normally known only to those who devise problems in junior books of arithmetic. His mower cuts on each journey a strip 21 inches wide and he proceeds up and down with parallel cuttings. He is 'as regular as clockwork', we say. Here is precision behaviour; no disclosure in this case. If he sees a small twig on the lawn he 'instinctively' bends down to pick it up—it is all part of the regular pattern. At one point, however, bending over the machine he espies a shilling—something for which there is no specified

---

[4] It happened that in my discussion of freedom, and in trying to make clearer the empirical anchorage of discourse about free will, I approached the matter by a discussion of predictability rather than by a discussion of choices. I quite agree that a discussion of how we use the word 'choice' would offer another inroad to the problem. But in the end we would (I fear) find ourselves with the same kind of difficulty which I notice in my book surrounds the word 'decision'. There would be two senses of the word, and our problem would be—as in the case of my phrase 'personal backing'—to make clear what there is 'more' about the sense of 'choice' to which the advocate of free will appeals. All we could do would be to tell stories in the hope that the reader would see the point, that the light would dawn, and so on, that he would recognize the situation in which talk about freewill is grounded.

precision behaviour, something which admittedly brings him somewhat to life. He stoops and picks it up and already his thought is on the extra cigarettes or drink. But no more than in the first case is there anything we could call a moral issue. He has just reacted in a certain way to a distinctive change in the environment. Later, however, he notices in the grass, on a bank he is about to cut, a slim knife, the one the police have been searching for in connection with a stabbing which took place in the vicinity some weeks before. Undoubtedly now he 'comes to himself' in response to what is a distinctively moral challenge. Now, for the first time, his behaviour has what I have called his 'personal backing'. Now, for the first time, he displays *characteristically* 'personal' behaviour as contrasted with routine, rule-bound behaviour. I should not strongly complain if someone protested that we normally call a man a person all the time. It is undoubtedly and unfortunately true that the word 'person' has been devalued currency for some while, ever since it was used in notices such as appear on railways and in lifts, when all that is of interest concerns numbers and weights and possible obstruction to traffic, e.g. 'To carry 4 Persons', 'Persons may not . . .'.

Professor Lewis talks of degrees of personality (p. 170). I agree that between impersonal and 'personal' behaviour there is a sequence with many shades and subtleties, and when, in my examples above as well as in my book, I speak of human behaviour in terms of conditioned reflexes, I may be justly accused of over-simplifying the matter. My defence would be that in a few cases I over-played my hand simply to make my antithesis clear. For despite the continuous grading we may find in human behaviour, it does not follow that there are not two end points significantly different in the way I wish to make evident by using words like 'impersonal' and 'personal'. The priest, the Levite, and the Morse code learner may be more 'personal' than I appear to give them credit for being, though the very use of descriptive titles does not normally suggest any high degree of personal characterization about their behaviour. But what I am arguing for as the empirical basis of 'free will' is more than any 'richness of personality'; it is that spontaneous 'realization' of ourselves which comes to us in certain situations, especially those which (as we said) confront us with a moral challenge. These are the situations where we are (as we would say) '*genuinely* alive' and '*distinctively* ourselves', where

I am most *characteristically* myself, the one place where my subjectivity is known, the one place where I am free. In the end, as I
hinted above, I agree with Professor Campbell's talk about 'inside'.
All I have tried to do here and in my book is to make the kind of
situation Professor Campbell has in mind plainer and its significance more apparent than I think traditional ways of talking in
fact make it. Freedom of the will talks of a recognition of my
transcendence in and through an act of will; it talks of mystery,
i.e. what I am more than any and all of my observable behaviour.

Is our action, then, in time? Certainly it relates to temporal
behaviour. *In so far as* my deliberate activity expresses itself in
temporal features, *to that extent* it can be timed and dated. But
when the word 'action' denotes all that happens when I respond
freely to a moral obligation, temporal categories cannot be used
of it *as a whole*. They are logically inappropriate. I cannot emphasize too strongly that for me the phrase 'act of will' labels an
ontological peculiar.

Incidentally, to take up another point which Professor Lewis
makes, nothing which I say means that responsible action is
necessarily good (p. 170). Logically we might 'come alive' in
responding to evil, just as a good man comes alive by being devoted
to a transcendent Duty. We might in this way worship evil; we
might find our 'freedom' in serving the devil. Such indeed would
happen in the case of those who appeal to the maxim 'Evil be
thou my good'. It is not the case that any and all 'freedom' may
also be called 'the service of God' that possibility is deliberately
reserved for cases of '*perfect* freedom'.

IMMORTALITY

Undoubtedly Professor Lewis wishes to talk of this plainly in
terms of survival. Immortality in this way is a going on and on and
on. . . . I am quite ready to admit at the outset that for me the *basic*
meaning of immortality is not a continuous going on and on, but
an assertion of my transcendence, or (negatively) a denial that I
am nothing but what my mortality removes.

The difficulty for me in taking Professor Lewis's sense as basic
is in attaching any clear meaning to this picture of going on and on
and on continuously. How can our existence after death be at all
continuous with this present existence, if only because in terms of
public behaviour such devastating things obviously happen to the

body?[5] Further, where could the continuous behaviour be located? Such questions for me all cluster around, and converge on, what becomes the leading question: with what meaning and on what grounds can we talk of 'personal survival'? I cannot see that we can answer that question at once in terms of a plain 'going on'.

So, as in the case of free will, I try to see what is the basis in fact of belief in immortality. I try to see in this case as in the first what is the empirical anchorage for discourse. Only then and thereafter do I ask how best we can talk further about it, whether it be in terms of a 'future life' or in terms of more complex phrases such as 'second coming', or 'end of history'.

The *basis* for our belief in immortality lies (I try to argue) in a claim that in certain situations—which it is the function of argument for immortality to evoke—we discern ourselves as more than our spatio-temporal behaviour. From this it follows that we cannot talk significantly of 'I'—that word which is most apt to what we discern in this way—as 'beginning' or 'ending', because these are essentially terms which relate only to spatio-temporal patterns. We may talk of 'I', 'beginning', or 'ending' *in so far as* I am a toddler, a schoolboy, a tutor, a father, and so on. But to talk of 'I' beginning, or 'I' ending, is (I would say) just not sense. It is to misuse words, to confound categories, to make a logical blunder.

When we talk of our 'immortality'—just that and no more—we intend (I claim) to call attention to a transcendent situation. If somebody asks: 'And what is immortal?', the old answer might have been 'the soul'. What I suggest as a less misleading answer, and it is *not* one which makes 'the self . . . in no sense an entity' (p. 174), would be: 'What I now know as most distinctively myself'. When further we try to develop a context for immortality, when we talk about 'survival' or 'the end', we are endeavouring to do more and more justice to what is disclosed about ourselves as transcendent in this way.

So much for an outline of my position, which I have tried to formulate in a way that meets by implication certain of the

---

[5] Cp. even such a staunch champion of orthodoxy as Reinhold Niebuhr, who says (admittedly in relation to the more complex Christian claim): 'It is unwise for Christians to claim any knowledge of either the furniture of heaven or the temperature of hell: or to be too certain about any details of the Kingdom of God . . .' *Nature and Destiny of Man*, Vol. II, Chap. X, p. 304.

questions Professor Lewis raises. I think that some at least of the other differences between us can perhaps best be seen in terms of the criticisms which Professor Lewis would bring against Professor Poteat as well as myself, in so far as we both are more impressed than he is with the significance of the assertion 'I am dead' for belief in immortality (p. 176). Professor Lewis would argue that 'I am dead', far from having any difficulty about it, can easily and naturally be asserted in another world in which we live after death.

But whatever may be the case about its utterance in a future existence, my claim is that it is a *this-world* curiosity. Here and now we must either say that it cannot be uttered, or that it is falsified on utterance. But someone may say: what is curious about it on this score? They would say that it is only curious, it is only falsified on utterance, because when we are dead we have no mouth or vocal organs by which to utter it; or (a rather more subtle answer) that when we are dead there is, in Professor Ayer's phrase, no 'this'[6] for 'I' to refer to. But supposing all that is allowed, at least for the sake of argument. Have we then said everything there is to be said about the oddness of 'I am dead'? In so far as 'I am dead' is like 'I am soaked' (by the rain); 'I am melted' (by the sun); 'I am desperate' (without a penny); or 'I am dished' (as the police arrive), none of them could, for the reasons that have so far been given, be uttered after death either. But that reflection reminds us that the whole discussion so far has presupposed that 'I am dead' is logically innocent; that it is in every way like the other assertions I have just given. Now whatever *else* is to be said on the peculiarity of 'I am dead', this much at least is also true. *Part* of its strangeness arises from the fact that 'I'—unlike 'he'—resists total absorption in an impersonal and completely verifiable predicate. Unlike 'he', 'I' resists a predicate which only too easily is associated with 'complete extinction'. Now 'dead', in contrast to any and every other predicate, completely exhausts public behaviour, and part at least of the peculiarity of 'I am dead' is this—that, as a this-worldly assertion, the existence of the predicate seems to deny the possibility of the subject. The utterance only has significance when it is seen as a means of shocking us into a sense of our present transcendence. We begin to know what 'I am dead' means as we let 'dead' do its worst . . . till it reveals what we are above any and every observable verifiable predicate.

[6] *The Problem of Knowledge*, A. J. Ayer, Chap. v(i), p. 211.

So it is that our attitude to 'I am dead' registers our intimation of immortality, and therefore provides us with an 'argument' for immortality, an argument that our present existence is not limited to the spatio-temporal, an argument (if you like) of 'survival'. But again I would emphasize that to give a reliable account of talk about this 'survival' in terms of future life, end, and so on, is no easy matter.

'DISCLOSURES': WHAT DO THEY DISCLOSE?

Admittedly I talk a very great deal in the book and elsewhere about certain situations I call 'disclosures'. What is being affirmed here (asks Professor Lewis) 'beyond the distinctive characteristics of certain finite situations?' (p. 162). Plainly, he is nervous of my ontology, lest everything should be lost in something called a 'situation' so dangerously like (he might think) an 'experience' (cp. e.g. p. 174). For example I argue that 'duty' is to be grounded in a disclosure which may occur, for example, around a group of *prima facie* duties, when a particular duty in particular circumstances is discerned; and I further argue that to talk of duty as 'God's will' is to offer a wider contextual account of the situation which links it with many other kinds of disclosure, for example those given by talk about being, causation, purpose in the universe, and so on.

Now (says Professor Lewis) is this in fact to talk of a transcendent God? (p. 173). In other words, is not the objective reference implied in my account too nebulous?

Let me develop my answer in three points:

(*a*) What more than anything else is important about my talk of disclosures is that it should be regarded as an attempt to indicate the kind of empirical grounding which a phrase or sentence may have when it does not work merely as a plain description. If a word or phrase is not used descriptively, and someone then asks, 'How else could it be used?', what I want to answer is that if it be a phrase from religious language it will have an evocative use, so that we shall only know what it means when *inter alia* a disclosure has occurred.

(*b*) I agree that there is a certain arbitrariness about the way in which we talk about what such a disclosure discloses. To mention some of my favourite examples, we may speak of the object of a disclosure which is reached by means of regular polygons of ever-

increasing sides as a 'circle'.[7] For other disclosures we may speak
of 'persons' being disclosed when they cease to be mere officials;
we may speak of duty, Absolute Value, or God. In this way, *talk*
about the *object* of a disclosure *always* comes within a contextual
setting, from which it will also derive what justification can be
given to it.

(*c*) But because with a limited, restricted route what is disclosed
has some plain evident name, it does not follow that it cannot bear
alternative levels as the context is widened. For such names as we
first give to the objects of disclosures only represents first-stage
talking about those objects. As we broaden the contexts in which
the disclosure-yielding language is set, then some other phrase *as
well* may become currency for what is objectively disclosed. Nor
does this cast any doubt on the basic 'objectivity' which belongs
to the various disclosures, objectivity which only those who have
a naïve belief in 'pure subjectivity' could deny. Further, in saying
what I have done I am not going beyond, and I am certainly far
from denying, the kind of religious language which in fact people
have used when they have talked, as they have talked, of circles,
persons, duties, and so on, in theological terms. Men have worshipped the perfect circle; they have talked of God as the Great
Mathematician; they have talked of logic as an expression of the
will of God. People have also talked of a true marriage as 'made
in heaven'; of duty being 'God's will'. What I try to do is to give
some kind of background to these admittedly curious assertions
which does not make them bogus, vacuous, or just pleasantly
grotesque, or (still less) naïvely descriptive, so that God, for
example, is regarded as a cosmic sergeant-major. So while I agree
that from the standpoint of first stage discourse disclosures disclose 'anything', that does not preclude us from giving wider and
wider interpretations, from supplying supplementary interpretations to characterize the object of the disclosure more reliably, as
the context is progressively extended.

So to a few concluding remarks.

(*i*) Both Professor Lewis and I agree in wishing to give an
account of religious language which does justice to its themes of

[7] It is interesting to recall that this same example was used in a not
dissimilar way by Nicholas of Cusa. See e.g. James Collins, *God in
Modern Philosophy*, p. 6 and Note 8, p. 413, to whom I am indebted for
this point.

transcendence and mystery *inter alia* in situations of duty and so on.

(*ii*) On the whole I am more nervous than Professor Lewis of the language in which to talk appropriately of this mystery.

(*iii*) But I think that Professor Lewis's basic difficulty about my position is that he believes that I do not make the objects disclosed in these situations certain enough, so let me emphasize that I do not appeal to situations so as to avoid questions of ontology and that the situations to which I appeal are certainly *not* finite,[8] for in every disclosure the object can eventually bear the name 'God'. Further, since the paradigm for understanding all disclosures is the disclosure that each of us has of himself in decisive, free, moral action, our certainty about God is at least like the certainty we have of our own existence. This indeed is my defence for bringing together God, Freedom and Immortality, and for moving so easily from the one to the other.[9] That such movement has its dangers I do not deny; but I am sure that it is to be practised if we want to do justice not only to the mystery but to the intelligibility of religious language. So I end, as Professor Lewis began, by agreeing that the task of the philosophical theologian today is that of a tight-rope walker; in fact on this both of us not only agree but even agree with Karl Barth.[10] Which is an eirenic note on which to end!

[8] As Professor Lewis believes they may be. See p. 211 of his article.

[9] See e.g. p. 216, . . . 'too closely for my liking', says Professor Lewis.

[10] See his *Anselm: Fides Quaerens Intellectum* (tr. Ian Robinson), p. 70. 'In the history of theology in all times and developments the *via regia* of divine simplicity and the way of the most incredible deception have always run parallel, separated only by the merest hair's breadth.'

The Intellectual Crisis of British Christianity 1

NINIAN SMART'S ARGUMENT

The situation is shocking and ludicrous. So I hope no one will mind if I am rude about it.

Christianity is in an intellectual crisis in Britain. This has to do, broadly, with philosophy. Why?

Christianity (I think) claims to be true. If so, what are the grounds on which its rests? We can avoid philosophizing directly about them by centring Barth-wise everything on revelation. Barth is, for that reason, respected by philosophers. He does not compromise, and he does not play around with dubitable metaphysics. He challenges precisely because he does not allow the question of natural theology to arise. We can, then, remove the intellectual crisis by following Barth. But a price has to be paid. The great Calvinist distance between heaven and earth can turn into a gap between the Church and 'secular' society. And a man can feel spiritually crushed when he cannot discuss his faith with friends. When, too, they belong to another faith, there is stalemate. Nothing can be said: one can only go on talking. Barth is magnificent, but he is imprisoned. It may be that we should thus be prisoners of the Lord; but there must be those who doubt it. What alternative is open to them?

This is where the ludicrous and tragic nature of our present crisis becomes apparent. The fact is that most of the influential intellectual anodynes—Tillich, Ramsey, van Buren—are lethal.

After the last war, linguistic philosophy boomed, and religious intellectuals became sensitive. You didn't want so much to show that religion is true as that it is meaningful. This was a new version of the Ontological Argument. If 'God' means something, all is well: it is but a small matter to go on to show that he exists. But the intellectuals were sensitive too about empiricism. So we had analyses (or supposed analyses) of religious language which made its meaning look strange. These unrealistic accounts of religious language have proved quite incapable of providing a secret defence of Christianity.

Notoriously, R.B. Braithwaite's empiricist account was atheistic. R.M. Hare's account of the 'blik' makes us ask whether God truly exists, or whether it is just a way we have of looking at the world. And what of the Marxist and Buddhist bliks? Marx would, no doubt like St Thomas Aquinas, be shocked to have his doctrines thus watered down. Bliks may have nothing to do with the truth. It is no wonder that the atheistic Paul van Buren finds so much in the blik-concept. If Christianity becomes thus non-cognitive, it becomes ineffective; for a man cannot rest his life on seeing elephants in the clouds. We can look on the clouds that way: they may look like elephants on a stormy afternoon. But we cannot expect the elephants to descend and haul logs for us.

Besides all which, the blik analysis does not chime in with the way folk use religious utterances. Folk make truth-claims about the transcendent, as if it is a sort of fact that God exists, not unlike the fact that we exist.

Braithwaite and Hare seem to represent a modern trend towards formulating a non-theistic Christianity. A colleague of mine recently said to me: 'My wife is an atheist, but she wants to be an Anglican as well. Is there anything she can read?' 'My dear fellow,' I replied, 'we've got plenty of books showing how the trick can be done.' I reflected sadly that it was difficult to find books on how to be a theist.

Such 'empiricism' culminates in Paul van Buren. For him, a transcendent God is meaningless. The doctrine of creation boils down to an affirmative attitude to the world (in which case most of my atheistic friends believe in the doctrine). He has not yet written *The Secular Meaning of the Covenant*. No doubt it is this: the Jew has a perspective on the world centred on the historical events of the Exodus, and he is gripped by a contagious legalism. Nor has van Buren expounded the secular meaning of Jesus' own faith. There is no Father to forgive van Buren: he knows not what he does. I can't imagine Anthony Flew rushing into the Church from reading van Buren. He no doubt is chuckling: at last these Christians have realized that all this talk of God is empty. Well, if it is, let us abandon Christianity. A Christian atheism can be a new force in the world—except that some folk would not be self-sacrificing just on the grounds of a secular Gospel. In any event, candour is best. If we really are atheists, let us stop the clap-trap about worship and prayer.

Unfair to Paul van Buren? He means well, but he does not mean much. But it may be that there is more in him, for he leans too on Ian Ramsey, and it might seem a bit outrageous to say that Ramsey is an atheist. But let us look at his *Religious Language* more closely. It is a book with a wide circulation. If it is inadequate as an analysis or as an anodyne, it will confirm the fact that the intellectual basis of contemporary British Christianity is in a bad way.

The main function of religious language, for Ramsey, is to evoke a disclosure situation in which the universe comes alive in a personal way. Thus religious language has primarily an engineering function. It engineers insight: it engineers discernment. It whirs until the penny drops. It does this by massive negation (as in negative theology), or by using limiting concepts like 'perfection', or by the use of models and qualifiers ('perfectly good', 'first cause'). The language of religion is like the significant tautology 'I'm I', which somehow shows the self to be more than observables. The objections to all this are manifold.

First and perhaps less importantly, it is only an analysis of theistic language. That is not the only kind of religious language.

Secondly, if the function of religious language is one of evoking a discernment, there is no reason to suppose that it *describes* anything. Swearing, which is notoriously non-descriptive, evokes responses. But some religious language (not of course 'Praise be to God' and the like) is seemingly descriptive. If we take the descriptions away, we take truth away. This is why Ramsey's position, though it so far need not entail atheism, is compatible with it.

Thirdly, Ramsey appears to concede (op. cit., p. 74) that 'God' becomes a word to talk about discernment situations. He writes: 'What we posit is language which claims to talk about what is given and disclosed to us in a certain way.' In short, 'God' becomes a name for penny-dropping experiences. But experiences are not ontologically privileged. If 'God' is about items in the world, theology is only concerned with a small fragment of reality. It is as though someone were to say that 'God' was the name for all patches of blue. Ramsey thus has really dispensed with transcendence. This must be fatal, if religion is to make truth claims, for claims not involving reference to the transcendent will always be claims about bits of the world. God becomes finite and of this world. This is equivalent to a superstitious atheism.

Fourthly, though the universe may come alive in a personal way, it may evoke other reactions, like Buddhist ones. Such different reactions, considered merely as experiences, and without reference to truth-claims, are compatible. Thus if the Ramsey line were generalized by men of other faiths, including atheism, the way would be open to a new psychological syncretism.

Fifthly, as Frederick Ferré has pointed out,[1] Ramsey has not defended himself against the charge of mere subjectivity. It is not enough to reply, as he does, that religious experience is subject-object in form: so are experiences of pink rats. No criteria of objectivity, i.e. truth, are given, beyond the fact that if the religious man goes on talking long enough a penny will drop. Such 'verification' cannot be enough, for, as we have seen, there are alternative ways of talking.

Sixthly, and connectedly, Ramsey's position means the death of argument. The cosmological and teleological arguments come in through the back door, but by the time they reach the dining room they are served up as hash. (I confess to doing something like this in my *Reasons and Faiths*, but in this case curry was added.) But the 'First Cause' penny can only genuinely drop if there are grounds for holding that the existence of the cosmos requires explanation. Otherwise, this sort of natural theology cannot be worked. There are even naughty Thomists who try to substitute intuition for argument in these matters—Dom Illtyd Trethowan for one. The trouble is that either you have an intuition or you don't, and that's that. Truth is different.

Seventhly, Ramsey's thesis about significant tautologies must be wrong. He counts 'God is Love' as one such, like 'I'm I'. Tautologies are fine. They are virginally true: they cannot be violated. But they can have no offspring. They can tell us nothing about the world. The person who repeats 'I'm I' is bombinating. It may be true that there is self-discernment, over and above particular items of consciousness. But if there is such a self, it is as good a claimant for external status as God. We end up with Vedant. Shankara argued exactly in such terms, about the 'self-luminous intuition of the Self'. If the self is something (and I have my doubts), it is

[1] *Language, Logic and God*, p. 141.

something tremendous. Ramsey's God is doubtful; and not every-one has a disclosure. But each man has a self, if anyone does.

For these various reasons, Ramsey's prescription on how we ought to look at religious language is not only compatible with atheism: it implies a kind of atheism, but a superstitious one, in which 'God' is the name for bits of experience. Neither science nor true theology can be done by induction from experience. It is thus no coincidence that Paul van Buren, who has a confessedly non-cognitive approach to religion, i.e. who is a crypto-atheist, should use Ramsey as one of the ingredients in his new recipe.

In a way, linguistic philosophy in these manifestations of it is close to existentialism. There too the world is seen through man's reactions and commitments. This is as though God is waiting to be called into existence by my decisions. This is anthropocentric pride. Though existentialism can give us insights into the meaning of authenticity and freedom, it cannot serve as the *basis* for theology, just as it cannot serve as the basis for a metaphysics. Truth may concern persons as well as things; but truth is objectivity. One needs a genuine ontology.

But Tillich's will not do, because it is itself a farrago of linguistic confusion. If there is one thing that has been learnt from linguistic philosophy (and much too still has to be learnt), it is that loose talk of 'being' is not good enough. Consider a typical Tillich passage:[2]

> In order to be able to ask for something, we must have it partially, otherwise it could not be the object of a question. He who asks both has and has not at the same time. If man is that being who asks the question of being, he had and has not the being for which he asks. He is separated from it while belonging to it. Certainly we belong to being—its power is in us—otherwise we would not be. But we are also separated from it; we do not possess it fully. Our power of being is limited. We are a mixture of being and non-being.

The first sentence seems false: when I ask for an omelette I do not already have a partial omelette. Of course, an omelette has to be possible, or I am an ass to ask; but that is the most favourable interpretation to put on Tillich's words, and it is not good enough. So the second sentence seems false (though if someone says to

[2] *Biblical Religion and the Search for Ultimate Reality*, p. 11.

me 'Do you have or not have?' I should want a bit more specifi-
cation of what it is I am supposed to be having or not having).
The third sentence is obscure. Elsewhere, Tillich interprets the
question of being as 'Why does anything exist at all?' (p. 6, p. 9)
and as the question of 'what it means to *be*' (p. 6). On the first
interpretation, the apodosis of the third sentence seems false. If I
ask whether God created everything else, I do not *have* God. I
might answer in the negative. Still my question would show
interest. (Anthony Flew, for instance, is interested in whether God
exists.) But that can be stated without bringing in the mumbo-
jumbo. On the second interpretation, what man is is a linguistic
philosopher. The answer as to how the verbs 'to be' and 'to exist'
function is complex, and need not detain us here. Or perhaps
Tillich means that people ask about the meaning or purpose of
life. In what sense does anyone at this stage both have and have
not the purpose?

The fourth sentence need not delay us. The fifth sentence
deserves scrutiny, however. So we wouldn't be if the power of
being weren't in us? Obviously: 'Snookfish eats' implies that
snookfish is capable of eating. But though the sentence incorporates
this uninteresting logical point, it also suggests that being is a
peculiar kind of activity. This, to say the least, needs some
extended defence, in view of most of recent philosophy. And it
would be tedious to go on. We conclude that we are a mixture of
being and non-being, a way, no doubt, of saying that we can do
some things and not others. Certainly there are some things Tillich
can't do.

Why then is a man so capable of this obscure ineptitude widely
respected? Partly because here and there he is psychologically
perceptive. Volume Two of the *Systematic Theology* has some
insights. The first volume, though, to anyone with a respect for
philosophy must seem to be rubbish. It is a tragedy that this useless
nonsense has gained currency among theologians—a part result
of the split of the academic world into departments and faculties.
And there are few philosophers willing to take time off to go
through the weary business of exposing Tillich's trivialities. Mr
Heywood Thomas, it is true, has not so long ago published a book
criticizing Tillich from a logical point of view: but unfortunately
he was not incisive. The unfortunate impression has therefore
been created that Tillich is a philosopher to take seriously.

It is a painful matter that professional philosophical competence —the kind of thing a good teacher wants to create in his students— should be flouted in this way by a supposedly distinguished theologian. But he has his excuses. Those who follow him in this country have little excuse. The crypto-atheists have at least paid some attention to clarity and coherence.

There are of course a few good philosophers here who are Christians. But the above trends that I have described are the most influential ones, and they are lethal.

All this means that the dialogue with the humanist is difficult to start. Atheistic Christianity is so like Professor Ronald Hepburn's project of a reconstruction of humanist theology that there can be no dialogue, because no difference. On the other hand, a dialogue cannot start on the basis of Tillich, because no self-respecting philosopher would bother to take such Christianity seriously.

There are two things which hold an intellectual from Christianity—moral disapproval of Christian prescriptions, and difficulties about belief in God. We are here concerned with the latter issue. The way forward in discussion is by reconstructing the concept of a transcendent (and immanent) being. There will still, of course, remain the historical questions and the claims of other faiths: but unless transcendence is taken seriously there can be no truth-claim in Christianity. And a man is not to be split into compartments. Belief is a spring of action.

These points imply something too about theological education. Philosophy should become an integral part of it, where this is not already so. Even Barthianism ('philosophy is a waste of theological time') implies this, for one has to *see* that philosophy is a waste of time, and this is partly a philosophical insight. I am, of course, far from decrying revelation. Theology, obviously, cannot begin without it. It is given. But there are questions about it, especially today, and these need to be faced. Even the thesis that they do not have to be faced has to be faced.

Something also is implied by the present situation. Systematic theology is unavoidable.

When I was teaching at King's College, London, I came across certain practical hardships. Thus I would ask students about the fall—how it was to be interpreted and whether the doctrine as interpreted was true. The trouble was that very few of the students had any view. They were concurrently having the Bible taken to bits, by the brilliant Professor Nineham and others. This was extremely good for them. But it induced scepticism about the possibility of systematic belief. One of them confessed to owning a grubby and intellectually rather disreputable textbook on doctrine. He didn't quite believe it, but it gave him theories. I am sure he was right in one respect. We need the theories. They may be false, but they focus enquiry. The same is true in science. Otherwise, we get into the stamp-collecting syndrome. In short, we need both Nineham and . . .

Exactly.

Biblical theology is obviously not the answer. The texts are just quoted in a less random way. But the point remains—a systematic error can be illuminating and interesting and can help men to crystallize their own system, or non-system. Propositions are indeed heaven-sent, though not in the way we once thought.

(I had one other practical difficulty in London. One of the students did not exist. He signed the register regularly, but by sleuthing I found that he was a fiction, even though he wrote entertaining essays. Evidently he did not have the courage to be.)

By consequence of all this the humanist is liable to encounter a mushy faith, somewhere between Thomism and the Conservative Evangelicals. If this intermediate position is impossible, it is a poor show for ecumenism and, as I believe, for the faith.

The cause of the mushiness is the lack of philosophical competence and insight and the lack of Christian doctrinal coherence. I am not blaming anyone. I am just, as I think, telling the truth. The time has come for a new *summa*, even a second-rate one.

Can we end with a short litany?

'From being, bliks, Braithwaite, and van Buren, good Lord deliver us.

'From "I'm I", alleged logical oddity and penny-dropping, good universe-coming-alive-in-a-personal-way deliver us.

'From looking on freedom as a mere contagion, good affirmative-attitude deliver us.'

('But, Lord, I am worried: these fellows are good, better than I am.' Perhaps the answer is: 'Men can have faith in me, even when they by implication do not believe that I exist. But I shall not tell you whether this is a point for or against Humanism.')

The Intellectual Crisis of British Christianity 2

A REPLY BY IAN RAMSEY

My friend, Professor Ninian Smart, has certainly let off some sparkling fireworks by which to greet the new birth of *Theology* and I hesitate to come forward with a hose of cold water to damp down at least part of the blaze.

But it is perhaps worth recalling that *Religious Language* was written at a time when, to meet attacks on the Christian faith, it was necessary to show (*a*) that religious language should not be read as if it were flat and altogether descriptive like 'Blue copper sulphate turns white on heating', and (*b*) that 'what there is' is not restricted to 'empirical facts' supposed—implicitly if not always explicitly—to be solid, independent, utterly objective sense-data.

So I was concerned in that book to trace some of the logical patterns in religious language when it is not supposed to be transparently descriptive on the one hand nor unintelligible jargon on the other hand; and, further, to argue that whatever we think of sense-data, something at least of 'what there is' is given in disclosures—in this way we are aware of our own existence and of the existence of God. I agree then with Professor Smart that theological propositions—and I would add metaphysical propositions—are heaven sent. Hence my stress on penny-dropping and light dawning where something of 'what there is' constrains language not by being discriminated and labelled, but by declaring itself and making an impact on us.

Is 'God' then a mere name for 'penny-dropping experiences' or what Professor Smart calls alternatively, 'bits of experience' or even 'reactions considered merely as experiences'? Setting aside such expressions as crude over-simplifications, even if intelligible, my answer would be that on the contrary 'God' is a word which talks of what is objectively disclosed in a disclosure of a cosmic kind. Do I then suppose, as Professor Smart suggests, that God might have the objectivity of pink rats? Even allowing for the sake of argument that this possibility is consistent with what I say about disclosures, the question of the objectivity of pink rats is not all that easily settled. None of us, theists or atheists, has objectivity merely for the asking or looking. The very distinction between 'fact' and 'illusion' depends on some background conceptual scheme. Professor Smart, as much as I, allows that all experience is subject-object in structure so that even pink rats have *some* objectivity, *some* objective reference. As Professor Smart will agree, this objectivity happens, however, to be more reliably talked of in terms of (say) the excess of alcohol in the digestive system rather than in terms of animals who eat corn and get chased by fox terriers. To put a wider and very complex point all too briefly, any claim for objectivity stands or falls with the reliability of the conceptual scheme in terms of which the 'object' is talked about; and the claim for objectivity in relation to cosmic disclosures stands or falls on the reliability of what those disclosures enable us to say about God.

What do they enable us to say? Even in *Religious Language* I showed every disclosure arises in some context which is characterized by models, and it is from these models that there arise suggestions for being articulate about God. Our discourse will be the more reliable the more models we have surveyed, and the better we have related the model-based articulation to the world so as to provide what I have called 'empirical fit'. In all this, there arise plenty of possibilities for argument.

Here are admittedly complicated issues, and I agree that in *Religious Language* I hardly faced these questions of reference and criteria. Professor Smart is undoubtedly right to focus attention on this problem of objectivity and reference as being crucial in contemporary philosophical theology. But it will not be solved by rehashing—with or without curry—views of ontology and experience which have already proved only too attractive for 'cultured despisers' like Flew. Meanwhile I have no desire to be a purveyor of anodynes, lethal or other, and I hope that those who are still alive after reading *Religious Language* will perhaps now turn to what I have written further on these points in (say) *Models and Mystery, On Being Sure in Religion*, and even *Science and Religion: Conflict and Synthesis*.[1] Not that I suppose that even now the

[1] Alternatively, they may care to look at a discussion which I had with Professor H. D. Lewis on my *Freedom and Immortality*, cf. p. 207.

matter is altogether satisfactorily worked out, but at least the reasons may become more evident why I consider it to be more exciting than true to call me an atheist. In any case, *Fact, Metaphysics and God* (if not a *Summa*) is still, I am glad to say, on the way.

I agree that my approach certainly means that dialogues with humanists are difficult to start. But I do not see why to make for easy starting we take up positions which also produce quick and disastrous endings, especially when these positions do no justice to the kind of language which religious language—Christian, theist or any other—must be; and if we are theists we must do justice to a God who is not only objective and transcendent, but also related to the world in ways that have been traditionally spoken of in terms of prayer and miracle. At the same time dialogue will not be difficult to start with those humanists, or even with those Christians, who are far from granting to me readily the significance which I attach to disclosures—as the present controversy plainly proves. Further, with a theory of models grounded in cosmic disclosures, dialogues with other religions may be all the more possible—as Professor Smart implies in his fourth and seventh comments which to this extent ill-match his first.

In all this, the irony is that, like Professor Smart, I, too, would say that 'it is *a sort of fact* that God exists, not unlike the fact that we exist' (italics mine); adding though that this 'sort of fact' is disclosure-given, and noting that at this point even Professor Smart seems to be wavering in his loyalty to the purely descriptive. Further, if the self has anything like the same 'eternal status as God', then attention given to self-disclosure—when I come to myself with a conviction that 'I'm I'—may yet provide a possible 'way forward in discussion [towards] reconstructing the concept of a transcendent (and immanent) being'.

So my hope is that readers of a newly-born *Theology* may after all be encouraged to believe that in the present crisis other intellectual labour wards have already opened from which may yet emerge a bonny Theology. If its parents prove in the end to be atheists, no doubt Professor Smart will protest against indiscriminate baptism; but I still cherish the possibility of his being a godfather.

Christian Education *1*

'POST MORTEM DEI'
BY PAUL M. VAN BUREN

The following article is written in response to a request to develop
the implications for Christian education of the approach to and
interpretation of Christian faith represented in my book, *The
Secular Meaning of the Gospel.* I intend neither to summarize nor
defend the argument of that book, but in the light of further
reflection since it was written, I do wish to touch briefly on two
aspects of that interpretation, by way of clarifying the point of
view of this article. Then, after making clear how I intend to use
the term 'Christian education', I shall develop programmatically
the implications of the one for the other.

I

The argument of my book suffers from two major limitations, or
at least there are two problems which beg for fuller and more
careful development. One has to do with metaphysical assumptions, and the other has to do with our interest in the past. A word
addressed to each of these problems may serve to indicate the
approach to be used here.

The argument of my book rests on the acceptance of what could
be called the metaphysics of 'So what?', a way of seeing the world
and of understanding how things are, which seems to be operative
for most of us in the West most of the time. When we ask 'so
what?', in response to something said to us, we are asking for the
implications or consequences of that which has been said, or of
that which is said to be the case. The kinds of responses which we
take to be answers to our question, as opposed to those which strike
us as evasions or nonsense, reveal our operative understandings
of the way things are, of what is 'real' and what matters to us. This
configuration or network of understandings I take to be the 'going'
metaphysical assumption of our culture.

If asked for more precision about the character of this metaphysics, I am willing to answer that it is somewhat empirical, somewhat pragmatic, somewhat relativistic, somewhat naturalistic, but also somewhat aesthetic and somewhat personalistic. My answer is intentionally vague, in order to make clear that the metaphysics in the terms of which I have developed my interpretation of faith is meant to be descriptive. I wish neither to defend nor attack this way of seeing the world and ourselves in it. I do suggest that it is possible to clarify a descriptive metaphysics which is characteristic of our age, and if I have misrepresented it, I should be glad to be corrected. In any case, it is in the terms provided by this framework that I have tried to develop my interpretation of the language of faith. Probably the only case that can be made for relying on this common-sense metaphysics lies in appealing to its descriptive character, for that is the basis of saying that it is more widely shared than are the metaphysical assumptions of, e.g. biblical theology, Thomism or Heidegger. Whether the pattern and presuppositions of our daily thinking ought to be what they seem to be is not a question I have argued. I have assumed that we do see the world in certain ways, that our culture has what can be called a loose metaphysics, and for the purposes of doing theology today, I have proposed that we explore the possibilities of standing on this common ground. If faith has an argument with culture, if it evaluates elements of human life and culture negatively, still it will, on my interpretation, conduct this argument in the terms provided by this common ground.

These remarks indicate that I am looking at metaphysics not as some sort of super-science which might provide us with new information about the 'universe' or 'reality' (cf. J. Heywood Thomas *contra* Tillich). Rather, I am assuming that any and every metaphysics is a proposal, an invitation, to see what we already know in a particular way. Metaphysics does not give us something new to see in any other way than by giving us a new way to see what we have been looking at all along (cf. John Wisdom).

The metaphysical status of Christian faith is odd. Faith would appear to entail a certain way of seeing the world and this would seem to make a contribution to a believer's network of understandings. The terms of that network, however, are shared (in my view of faith) with unbelieving contemporaries. My interpretation of Christian faith, therefore, is an attempt to portray the contribution it makes to a believer's network of understandings, in so far as it does not provide new 'facts,' new information, or assume the presence of entities (such as gods or God) lying beyond the general framework of the descriptive metaphysics of our time and place. An attempt to make sense out of the language of faith and theology in the terms of a contemporary descriptive metaphysics can have no other status than that of an invitation to see the matter in one way, and the double use of the definite article in the title of my book should not be taken as implying that I was attempting or doing more (or less) than that.

II

The second problem lies in the dependence of my interpretation on the past, on the history of Jesus and of Easter. It may be argued, however, that one feature of contemporary secular culture is its almost exclusive concern with contemporaneity: the past is not of great moment to most of us most of the time. Moreover, does not Christian faith qualify an interest in the past, leading us to say, in various ways, that the past is of no avail unless it becomes 'somehow' contemporaneous with the believer? It would have been more honest to the tradition and also to contemporary thought if I had argued that in fact it is not the historical event which becomes an occasion for 'discernment' for the believer, but rather the *story* of the event, or even the image of Jesus which is portrayed by the contemporary church in its preaching and worship.

This present image of the church is one which is constantly changing with the changing cultural context of the church. When Christians today speak of Jesus as a man involved in history and 'the world', they speak out of a context which sees history and society in certain ways which influence the way they see man. Marx and Freud have played their part in defining the image of Jesus as 'the man for others', and the development in the nineteenth century of the Western understanding of man separates a Bonhoeffer, a Barth and a Bishop Robinson from a Luther, a Calvin and a Bishop Jewel. Certainly the contemporary picture of Jesus is also produced by the fact that the contemporary church reads with contemporary eyes the writings of the New Testament, but perhaps a relative and pluralistic appreciation of something like the Catholic conception of historical tradition would help broaden a too naïve dependence upon the past. With these qualifications or clarifications of the empirical and—let us say it—a-theistic interpretation of the language of faith which I have made, let us turn to the subject of 'Christian education'.

III

Education, Christian or otherwise, is a word which may be used in a number of ways. It can be used so broadly, and it frequently is, that it includes within it almost all of life. We do speak of 'the school of life', 'education of the whole man' and 'education for life'. If Christian education means education as sponsored by the Christian churches in this broad sense, everything which the churches and Christians do could be considered as Christian education, including at least preaching, worship, praying, evangelism, missions, discipline, and family life, as well as Sunday School and adult classes. I wish to make it clear that I have no intention of speaking to a subject as broad as that. Instead, *for the purposes of this article, I shall take education to refer to planned programmes of instruction, to what we ordinarily think of when we speak of teachers and students, books and class rooms.* In short, I want to allow for a variety of activities in life, one of which, and only one of which, is education. By taking this narrower use, I acknowledge the pluralism of modern life, within which the activities of the churches are only a part, and within which part, Christian education is taken to be only a part. I exclude from my consideration, for example, the teaching done by a Christian employed to teach in a college or university, not because I deny that his work may also be called 'Christian education', but because I want to focus the problem narrowly. Unless clarity can be gained in the narrow case, I fear confusion will be compounded in the broader cases. My focus, therefore, shall be on Sunday Schools, so-called, adult classes, and similar formal means of instruction which make up part of the planned activities of normal congregations.

The question to which I shall address myself, then, is this: in so far as 'believers' share the common-sense metaphysical commitments of our age, and in so far as their faith functions in the way I have indicated, i.e. within the terms of those metaphysical assumptions (and I am aware, of course, that there are those who would not accept the adequacy of either of these conditions), what are the possibilities and limitations of the teaching work, as distinct from the preaching and worship, of the churches, of religious organizations and their professional or voluntary staff?

Christian education is planned instruction in the service of Christian faith. In that service, the teacher can (1) teach the Christian story, and as a story, (2) clarify the relations between faith and knowledge, and (3) clarify the relations between believing and living. In summary, he can teach 'about' Christian faith in a way comparable to teaching 'about' love.

IV

Near the end of an essay entitled 'The Choice of Comrades', Ignazio Silone compares the spiritual condition of himself and others with a refugee encampment in no-man's land. 'What do you think refugees do from morning to night? They spend most of their time telling one another the story of their lives' (*Encounter*, Vol. III, No. 6, Dec. 1954, p. 28). Christians have continued and have led others to join them through telling and retelling an 'old, old story', which they tell as being in some peculiar way the story also of their own lives. They tell this story and their faith lives off this story. He who performs the work of Christian education serves faith by teaching this story, making it familiar, tracing different ways in which it can be and has been told. He does not *tell* the story itself. That is for pulpit and holy table. He teaches the story as a story.

He teaches the story. It is nothing short of amazing that preachers still use, in whatever way, biblical texts, still make references to biblical passages. What sense can this make to those who do not even know the stories of the Bible? In order that the particular story or the particular form of the whole Christian story which is being told at any one time may be heard with even a fraction of the fullness which the preacher intends, it is necessary that the listeners know the whole range of biblical stories. If they do not learn these stories in Sunday school or Bible class, where shall they learn them? What is Easter without the story of Mary and the Gardener and also the story of the Exodus? What is Christmas without the nativity stories of both Matthew and Luke? What is Christian love without the stories of the Good Samaritan and of Lazarus and the rich man? Stories can be taught and learned. That is the task of Christian education.

Christian education involves the teaching of the stories of Christian faith as stories. If refugees spend most of their time telling the story of their lives, it is because telling stories does something which listing statistics does not. A good story, which as a story serves a certain purpose, may no longer serve that purpose if transposed into a 'record of facts', whatever that may be. If believers are to benefit by hearing the Christian story, it might be well for them to be shown that stories have important functions to perform. Deprive man of his stories, make him unable to tell and hear stories, and you make him by that much a poorer creature.

Men do other things besides telling stories. They also collect facts, as we say, and they also do critical historical investigation, at many different levels. You can collect 'facts', as it were, related in various ways, it may be argued, to the founding of the Plymouth colony. You may attempt to get at the critical historical account of the Pilgrims' lives and times. In addition you can tell the story of the Pilgrim Fathers, having to do with, e.g. the celebration of Thanksgiving Day. The story is not the same as facts and not the same as critical history, but it can do something which neither of the others can. It can give an American a way to tell about the origin of his country and about himself all at once. Stories are appropriate to celebration, and celebration is important to being human. Indeed, stories are one of man's great ways of understanding himself. As Silone continued: 'The stories are anything but amusing, but [refugees] tell them to one another, really, in an effort to make themselves understood.'

He who serves in the work of Christian education serves faith, therefore, by teaching the role which story telling plays in human life, in the hopes of winning a frame of mind that will appreciate stories, not as 'facts', not as 'critical history', but as stories, as one of men's important ways of winning understanding and of being understood.

V

Christian faith finds expression in language. It is expressed in other ways as well, but with respect to faith, as with respect to so many of man's concerns and activities, language is one of the principle ways in which we communicate with one another. Believers, when speaking as believers, have said all sorts of peculiar things. They have said 'Jesus is Lord', 'Glory to God in the Highest', and 'I believe in the Holy Spirit and eternal life'. But believers have spoken as ordinary men, in ways which do not seem particularly to express Christian faith, in saying such things as 'Johnson is President', 'Three cheers for the Yankees', and 'I believe in the graduated income tax and old age pensions'. There seem to be no important relations between these two sets of sentences. Is it because the second set are about concrete things and persons which all of us or many of us care about, whereas the former set have to do with another world? Or put the question another way. I know that Johnson is President. Do I know that Jesus is Lord? In each case, how? In each case, what sort of knowing am I talking about? These questions indicate the task of Christian education in serving faith by clarifying the relation between faith and knowledge.

It is a common-place to say that most church-goers are either wrong or confused about the nature of faith. Some take faith as assent to a group of peculiar assertions, as did the Red Queen when she said she had mastered the art of believing six impossible things before breakfast. Others take faith to be a sort of inner glow that makes you feel good all over. Since the language of faith, traditionally, is so often associated with things which no man has ever seen, it is not surprising if a somewhat empirical age finds faith to be at best a bit fuzzy. All of this is widely known and often decried. Little seems to be done about it. Whatever can be done about it, it is the task of those engaged in Christian education to help untangle the mess so that church-goers might at least have some idea of the logical placing of the language of faith and so have some idea of what faith is and isn't.

One way in which this untangling might begin is by calling people's attention to other areas of human experience which lead to similar linguistic problems of unclarity, misunderstanding and imprecision. If church-goers find religious language puzzling, they ought to take a look at the language of art criticism, to give just one example. If they think that faith is sometimes at its best without verbalization, they should ponder the masses of people who today flood art museums. If one compares aesthetic experience, if there is such, and religious experience, if there is such, if one reflects on the suggestion that museums have replaced or are becoming the contemporary form of cathedrals, they might at least be opened to entertaining a fresh consideration of the workings of religious language.

The privileged status which we seem to have conferred on the natural sciences, however accurately or inaccurately understood, has for many led to an odd association of knowledge with fact, which is, when you come to think of it, exceedingly odd. Be that as it may, it takes a bit of stirring up for most of us today to be reminded that in science itself, in poetry, in doing history, and in philosophy, there are many occasions when language seems to come up against its limits, as it were. That is to say, there are many areas of human experience—think of falling in love—when we have all sorts of difficulties saying what would be appropriate and would do justice to the occasion. Try telling a friend about the painting which came alive for you that afternoon you 'really saw it for the first time' (something you might well say of a painting which you had looked at a dozen times). Try to explain how it is you can recognize a good friend in a crowd. Try to tell your beloved how much you love him or her.

Learning about art and about talking about art is something which is not in principle impossible for contemporary man. Courses in art appreciation can develop a certain sensitivity, can teach one to look with greater care, can lead one by comparison to become aware of the variety of ways in which artists have set problems for themselves and gone about solving those problems. Learning about religion need not be any more difficult, though it may not be any easier, and it may be facilitated by awakening an appreciation for comparable features in other learning games, such as learning about art, about duty, about music, about love. Are these areas in which it seems appropriate to use words such as 'know', 'fact', 'prove'? In some parts, yes, and in most parts, no. If an appreciation for the problems of clarity in these areas were aroused, a great step forward would have been made in leading the horse to water. You can't, we are told, make the horse drink, but it would be helpful if the horse and the water were, so to speak, at least formally introduced to each other, so that the horse may realize that the water is not something you rake into a pile before beginning to consume it.

VI

Those engaged in Christian education can serve Christian faith by clarifying the relation between believing and living. Christians have long insisted that how a man believes effects how he lives. One of them once said that if any man says that he loves God and at the same time hates his brother, he is a liar, and another early believer called Christianity 'the way'. On the other hand, believers frequently disagree about the precise consequences of believing when it comes to specific decisions. This disagreement appears to have led many Christians to conclude that the relationship between believing and living is so vague or general that nothing specific can be said, or even that faith has no concrete ethical consequences at all. We face today some of the painful consequences of this conclusion in the present sorry state of churches in which many believers see no conflict between Christian faith and the practice of racial discrimination.

As a contribution to clearing away confusions in these and similar areas, it could be the task of those involved in Christian education to help identify the ethical assumptions and practices of the society in which we live, assumptions about law, politics, and government, about economics, automation, and technology, about social, economic, and racial groups, and about sex and its relation to the rest of life. If, by the use of the case method and other means designed to keep the problems specific, contemporary attitudes and assumptions of our society could be brought out into the open and identified, one would at least be in a position in which it would be interesting—and possibly exciting—to develop the implications of believing that the Sabbath was made for man, that the neighbour is the occasion for love, and that human personhood is of unsurpassable importance. Clarification of the assumptions of our society and the development of specific implications of Christian faith, with the initiation of reflection on whether and how they are related, is a task which could well be performed under the heading of Christian education.

VII

In conclusion: Christian education involves teaching 'about' Christian faith in a way which is comparable to teaching 'about' love. I should think that most people would agree that you cannot 'teach love', that this combination of words does not go well together. You can love another person, and he may then respond with love, but it would also be rather awkward and inappropriate to say he had then learned 'how to love'. Love can, however, be 'taught about'.

How would you go about teaching about love? You might begin with the literature of love—love stories of ancient and more modern vintage. You might go on to the histories or stories of great lovers, including the reading of their letters. Then you could turn to the poetry of love. Finally, you could add other ways of talking about love—the analyses of anthropologists and psychiatrists—ways which would hardly be those of lovers. The differences between these various kinds of language are worth exploring.

In making this analogy, I do not wish to say that faith is in all respects of the same order as love. Like love, it is a human posture, a commitment, a way of seeing some people and things (but probably not a vision which governs all of man's thinking and activity in every realm of his existence), and it entails certain actions. Unlike love, however, its object is not at hand. Believers have stories to tell, not a photograph to look at. Since the death of God and the rise of the critical historical imagination, Christians have had to find analogies for the object of faith in myth, story and parable. They have always had to do this, but before the death of God they could always pretend that their faith somehow gave them an insight into 'ultimate truth'. Now that God is gone and with him the justification of faith, unjustifiable faith must live by faith alone, and in this sense it is not unlike love. Human love, therefore, provides a helpful analogy to human faith, and in this sense, those engaged in Christian education have the task of teaching 'about' faith.

Christian Education 2

DISCERNMENT, COMMITMENT, AND
COSMIC DISCLOSURE
BY IAN RAMSEY

Like Paul van Buren, I shall not here be concerned directly with the argument of his book, *The Secular Meaning of the Gospel*, but only with his book and article in so far as they have important implications for Christian education. Yet at the outset I must record my judgement that we would be blind if we did not recognize in this book a genuine and serious attempt to find a meeting place between the Gospel and the secular world, and we would be ungracious not to acknowledge the clear, honest and challenging way in which van Buren develops his case.

I will begin from a point of agreement which leads me, however, to what seems to me to be an unnecessary limitation about van Buren's position, and it is a limitation which, as we shall see, has some implications for Christian education.

I share with van Buren and many others the view that metaphysics is not a super-science. The metaphysician is not a recluse shut off from human affairs whose intensive peering discovers a counterpart world. He is not engaged in a remarkable kind of scientific enquiry, remarkable not least in costing virtually nothing. So religious education has not to be thought of in terms of a verbal experiment which produces new facts, in the sense of 'fact' in which it is a fact that there are alligators in Florida. The success of religious education is not measured by the number of facts the students have absorbed. Someone for example who knows in every detail the Arianism of Asterius the Sophist, the theology of the Cappadocian Fathers, the relation of Aristotle to St Thomas Aquinas, of Schlegel to Schleiermacher, may be theologically well-informed, but from a religious point of view he may be quite uneducated.

What religious education must do above all is to create a discernment, and to call forth a commitment. How it does this, and

whether van Buren's recipe is entirely satisfactory and unambiguous, are points I will come to in due course. But I entirely agree
with him in what he singles out as the primary aim and end of
religious education. It must evoke, as I would say, a 'cosmic disclosure'. So, like van Buren, I would say that we are to 'teach
"about" Christian faith in a way comparable to teaching "about"
love'. We certainly have to teach an affirmation, a commitment,
and a commitment which accompanies or follows on an insight.
We have to teach a new way of seeing what we already know, 'a
new way to see that we have been looking at all along'.

But it is at this point that what I believe to be a limitation, or at
least an ambiguity, in van Buren's position begins to make itself
evident. Granted that religious education must teach an affirmation, it seems to me that it must teach this affirmation by teaching
that to which the affirmation is a response. Not that van Buren
would deny this, but I think that the difference between us will
eventually become clearer if we begin to look at the nature of that
which calls forth the response.

I

Let me start from his own illuminating example of teaching about
love. We might talk about love, as he says, in ways characteristic
of anthropologists, and psychologists, and even psychiatrists. But as
van Buren recognizes these ways 'would hardly be those of lovers'.

As I have remarked elsewhere: 'no one puts his arm around his
girl friend and speaks of their relation in terms of available response
alternatives, or reinforcement parameters'.[1] Here indeed would be
talk about love all right, but to someone who wanted to know what
'love' was, who wanted an education in love, it would be a pretty
inadequate syllabus. It would be a dehumanized, 'dehydrated'
love, scarcely worthy of the name. There would be a parallel here
with religious education which concentrated on nothing but 'the
facts'—the canon and text of the Bible, the Christian persecutions
at Rome, Calvin's Ordinances, the Elizabethan Settlement in
England, the Franciscan missions in California.

Now as van Buren sees we would only learn about 'love' more
adequately if we spread ourselves more widely, if we refused to
allow this 'exceedingly odd' 'association of knowledge with fact',

[1] *Models and Mystery*, pp. 27–8.

and read 'love stories of ancient and more modern vintage', 'the histories or stories of great lovers, including the reading of their letters'. We could also 'turn to the poetry of love'. We might add, as van Buren suggests elsewhere in his article, that to learn about love we might also look at appropriate paintings and listen to appropriate music. 'Love' would now be something much more human, and we ourselves would certainly have gained an insight and sympathy if we have been taught to read the stories, and the poems, to look at the art and to listen to the music—appreciatively. Here again is a parallel with religious education. Appreciation of Christian art and architecture, appreciation of Christian music, should be as much part of a Christian education as (say) the letters of a St Paul and a C. S. Lewis, and with the Bible could usefully be associated *The Oxford Book of Christian Verse*.

But in learning about love this way what would be our aim? Would it be to recognize love when we saw it in its fully human setting? Certainly we could test the success of our education in love by seeing how satisfactory it was by that criterion. But I think van Buren would rightly wish to go further. He would presumably hope that by reading the stories and the poetry, looking at the art and listening to the music, our hearts would burn within us, that we would come to see this love as a Good Thing, see it as an ideal, and respond appropriately in loving service. Here would be the parallel to Christian commitment. But this is a response to some sort of objective challenge. What sort of objective challenge?

Let it be granted at once that the behaviour of many 'educated Christians' falls disastrously short of such agepeistic service. So it is that no Christian can afford to despise this view of Christian education. But we then notice that, for better or worse—and no doubt van Buren would say for better—in the case of 'love' it does not matter whether the stories are historically true, or whether the letters or the poetry happen to be about persons who once lived.[2] It is sufficient that they disclose love to us in such a challenging way that we cannot help but acknowledge it and respond, and respond with the same freedom, the same fulfilment of personality as when we respond to duty. Further, it is for van Buren an important point, indeed his crucial point, that the Christian stories could be used in this way, and by anyone, to evoke such a response. Even the secular world can read stories and poetry in this

[2] Though could love be *wholly* invented?

way, look at art and listen to music, and if the readers and lookers
and listeners, recognizing love, then go and do likewise—what
more should anyone want?

My answer to that hypothetical question falls into two parts.
(i) Already, if he has accepted my explication of his views so far,
van Buren has gone beyond a position which some rightly or
wrongly associate with him—For it is not the case that someone
decides all by himself to opt for love, that some kind of deep-set
roving eye scans various possibilities, and chances to rest on one
of them. Christian education on my view is *not* the teaching of 'a
new way of looking at things' where it is supposed that *everything*
except ourselves remains the same. For the 'new way of looking
at things' only occurs when these things themselves generate a
disclosure, and when we respond to what that disclosure objectively
discloses. Even with the least recognition of this fact it would
have to be granted that we only go and do likewise, the 'gospel'
only has any effect on us at all, if the gospel narratives, the history
and the poetry, the art and the music, manage to create some sort
of challenge to which we cannot but respond in a commitment.

On this interpretation van Buren, it seems to me, is creating a
modern version of what in earlier times was called 'natural
religion' and the novelty and originality of van Buren's position
is that he is, on this view, creating a natural religion from the
Gospel. His secular sympathies and his serious Christian concern
lead him to see 'natural religion' not as a first stage on the way to
Christianity: instead he offers his readers a 'natural religion'
derived from Christianity.

But it *is* a 'natural religion'—and its key-idea is love. We may
now repeat our question: What more should anyone want? The
purpose of this section (i) has been to show that they may already
have more than they think. For the loving response presupposes
some sort of objective challenge about the stories, the art, the
music, and so forth. But is there not still more to be said about the
character of this objective challenge? (ii) Undoubtedly many
Christians would claim to be wanting more. For they would say
that this Love, wherever it otherwise occurs, points to and is fulfilled in the cosmic disclosure which occurs around Jesus of
Nazareth who, while having undoubtedly a historical strand,
expresses a transcendence and divinity through it. Their reason
for saying this would be that in various ways whether by a doctrine

of the Messiahship, of the Remnant, or of the cosmic Christ, whether by a doctrine of Christology or Trinitarian doctrine, Christians have talked in a way that spoke of finding in Christ Jesus, a love which was of God. They have claimed that here was a love historically expressed, but having a measure of transcendence. It may be that in elucidating these claims some Christians have talked far too easily about God—ignoring the complex logical rules that, e.g., Trinitarian and Christological doctrine embody: and no one need regret the demise of this sort of God. It may be, too, that they have talked about the transcendent in ways that are metaphysically bungled. But let us not convert their errors into our inadequacies.

There is certainly an objectivity about the 'love' disclosed in Jesus Christ, and an individuation given to it, to which Christian theology—and Christian education—must seek to do justice. It is this element of objectivity and transcendence which I am not sure that van Buren acknowledges or perhaps wishes to acknowledge. Here it seems to me is a fundamental ambiguity in his position.

II

Now whether we believe this transcendent objectivity to be there or not will make a difference to our way of teaching the Christian stories, the history, the art, and the music in such a way that they are fully appreciated. For here we must have second thoughts about the 'facts' that by themselves were so inadequate for proclaiming the Christian message. It is these very facts that must be so talked about that they generate the disclosure of which they remain a part, but only a part. Any story suitably told—whether historically grounded or not—may disclose God. That is only to say that any poem or even fable may be inspiring. A fairy story may encourage us in various ways, so may the story of an imagined friend. But if stories are to have uncompromising usefulness, their topic must be at least as 'real' as ourselves. They must match us: otherwise they will transport us into a fantasy world. The Christian stories must certainly be given a 'secular' interpretation. Too often in the past that has not been the case. But their topic must be at least as 'real' as ourselves and the world we live in—and that means, I would say, that through and by means of their historicity they must express an element of transcendence, however cautiously this has to be expressed. It also means that I myself see rather more in metaphysics than van Buren does, even though neither of us wants metaphysics as a super-science.

In all this, suffering is a crucial issue. If we want a disclosure, the coming alive of some situation, to have any relevance for the world, and we might say in particular for its suffering, that disclosure must itself be centred on actual suffering, or on a story of suffering which has genuine links with the suffering we experience. But if that suffering is to be redeemed, there must be an element of transcendence in both the objective reference of the disclosure and in our own subjective response and commitment. Christian stories must be so told in Christian education that while as a *sine qua non* they lead to disclosures, and while even a secular world may value them for the commitment they create, they also arise out of historical events that not only safeguard the relevance of the theology in terms of which the disclosures are explicated, but ensure also a reference to that element of transcendence without which the good news is less good than it might be.

In practice, indeed, the parallel between knowledge 'about' faith and knowledge 'about' love may go further than van Buren thinks: for a person does not really know love unless, and until, his knowledge about 'love' is fulfilled when he responds to someone who loves him. There is a sense in which our education in swimming and dancing is not complete until we find an occasion to dance or swim: and Christian education will not be complete until on some occasion we discern the actual love in Jesus Christ, whether by word or sacrament, and realize that the love disclosed in Jesus has an objectivity and individuation about it, belongs to the very structure of the universe and is distinctive in being cosmic in its significance. To reveal this element of given-ness and distinctiveness must certainly be part of a Christian education.

I hope I have now made clear both my sympathies with van Buren's position, and yet my suspicions of its possible limitations. I suppose he would say that I am in the end rather too metaphysical for him—even if in the first place it is a chastened metaphysics, developed very much under an awareness of the peculiarly difficult logic of the word 'God' which popular orthodoxy, as well as some sophisticated orthodoxy, has not sufficiently realized, and even if, in the second place, it is grounded in a disclosure.

III

There are three other comments I would like to make by way of underlining what seems to me to be three other important points in van Buren's article.

(i) I am sure that a profitable way of Christian teaching, equally valuable to believers and unbelievers, and of interest to both, is to examine how people with a Christian commitment have talked; and to do this with a view to filtering out their presuppositions. This was of course how the early church found itself starting on the road which led to Chalcedon: but wherever the exercise led, it would always be valuable.

Christian discussion of moral problems—whether contraception or race relations—could always supply grist for the mill; and the same exercises could well be done very profitably with newspaper reports. We might then discover much more clearly Christian and other presuppositions, look for overlapping and so on.

(ii) This leads me to suggest that one area of Christian education might well involve the meeting together of different disciplines in an endeavour to struggle with teasing problems of concern to all, yet for which any one discipline is glaringly inadequate. Universities might well be asked to sponsor, as Christian education, a cooperative venture of understandings such as this where, as van Buren says, men could single out and 'identify the ethical assumptions and practices of the society in which we live, assumptions about law, politics and government, about economics, automation and technology, about social, economic and racial groups, and about sex and its relation to the rest of life'. We might add also: the assumptions of the natural sciences and medicine; and all this with a view to wrestling more reasonably and more profitably with the problems which beset contemporary society.[3]

(iii) I think that van Buren's point about the need for and possibility of bringing illuminating parallels alongside religious language to illuminate its logical peculiarities is of the highest value for Christian education. Art, poetry, the natural sciences—and even novels and popular songs can all be of practical significance in Christian education. Those who sing: 'I love you for a hundred thousand reasons, but most of all I love you 'cos you're

[3] I have written further on this kind of possibility in an article, 'A New Prospect for Theology', in *Theology*, Vol. 67, 1964.

you' are not likely, if they are consistent, to expect religious language to be of the plain 'down-to-earth' kind, or likely to expect reasoning in religion to be of the 'knock-down' compelling kind. They are also likely to have some hunch of that total commitment which is distinctive of the Christian faith, as well as being prepared for logically peculiar ways of talking about it.

What links all these reflections together is an over-all conviction I certainly share with van Buren, viz: that the purpose of Christian education is to make Christian language, of whatever kind it is, 'come alive', evoke a cosmic disclosure, when we 'really understand it for the first time', though we may have looked at it, and said it a thousand times before. We further agree that when Christian language does this it will necessarily have such a suitably complex logic that we shall only head for disaster if we let it be supposed that it is merely fact-reporting like 'The cat is on the mat'. Christian education must evoke disclosures and train us to have an eye for logical peculiarities, and to be suspicious of all too plain and evident grammatical forms. But in doing this, it must also contrive to point its students to that element of objectivity and transcendence without which its topic would be a mere façade, though it might be an interesting, useful, and impressive façade. Yet if van Buren seems to some to concentrate too much on the façade, let us realize that for many of our contemporaries the Christian faith has no visible façade at all. Christian education needs not less of van Buren, but more—and some might say, more of God.

Selected Bibliography

IAN RAMSEY'S WORKS

'The Authority of the Church Today', *Authority and the Church*. London, S.P.C.K., 1965.

'Berkeley and the Possibility of an Empirical Metaphysics', *New Studies in Berkeley's Philosophy*, ed. W. E. Steinkraus. Holt, Rinehart and Winston, 1966.

'Biology and Personality' (*The Philosophical Forum*, XXI, 1964).

'The Challenge of Contemporary Philosophy to Christianity' (*The Modern Churchman*, XLII, 1952).

'The Challenge of the Philosophy of Language' (*London Quarterly and Holborn Review*, CLXXXVI, 1961).

Christian Discourse: Some Logical Explorations. London, O.U.P., 1965.

(ed.) *Christian Ethics and Contemporary Philosophy*. London, S.C.M. Press, 1966. In addition to the Introduction, 'Moral Judgements and God's Commands' and 'Towards a Rehabilitation of Natural Law' by Ramsey.

'Christianity and Language' (*The Philosophical Quarterly*, IV, 1954).

'Contemporary Empiricism' (*The Christian Scholar*, XLIII, No. 3, Fall 1960).

'Discernment, Commitment, and Cosmic Disclosures' (*Religious Education*, LX, No. 1, January–February 1965).

'Empiricism and Religion: A Critique of Ryle's *Concept of Mind*' (*The Christian Scholar*, XXXIX, No. 2, June 1956).

'Ethics and Reason' (*The Church Quarterly Review*, CLVIII, April–June 1957).

'Facts and Disclosures' (*Proceedings of the Aristotelian Society*, 1972).

Freedom and Immortality. London, S.C.M. Press, 1960.

'History and the Gospels: Some Philosophical Reflections' (*Studia Evangelica: III* (Berlin), LXXXVIII, 1964).

'The House which Barth Builds' (Review) (*The Modern Church-man*, New Series, Vol. 7, 1963-4).

Locke, John, *The Reasonableness of Christianity*, with *A Discourse of Miracles*, and part of *A Third Letter Concerning Toleration* edited, abridged, and introduced by I. T. Ramsey, London, A. C. Black, 1958.

'The Logical Character of Resurrection-belief' (*Theology*, LX, No. 443, May 1957).

'A Logical Exploration of Some Christian Doctrines' (*The Chicago Theological Seminary Register*, LIII, No. 5, May 1963).

'Miracles: An Exercise in Logical Mapwork', *The Miracles and the Resurrection*. London, S.P.C.K., 1964.

Models and Mystery. London, O.U.P., 1964.

'Models and Mystery', Discussion: R. B. Braithwaite, Joan Miller, Ted Bastin; Reply by Ian Ramsey (*Theoria to Theory*, I, 1967).

Models for Divine Activity (Zenos Lectures 1966), London, S.C.M. Press, 1973.

'A New Prospect in Theological Studies' (*Theology*, Vol. 67, 1964).

'On Being Articulate About the Gospel' (*The Chicago Theological Seminary Register*, LIII, No. 5, May 1963).

On Being Sure in Religion. London, Athlone Press, 1963.

'On Understanding Mystery' (*The Chicago Theological Seminary Register*, LIII, No. 5, May 1963).

'Paradox in Religion' (*The Proceedings of the Aristotelian Society*, Supplementary Vol. XXXIII, 1959).

'The Paradox of Omnipotence' (*Mind*, LXV, No. 258, April 1956).

'A Personal God', *Prospect for Theology*, ed. F. G. Healey. Welwyn, Nisbet, 1966.

Personality and Science, ed. Ian T. Ramsey and Ruth Porter, London, Churchill Livingstone, 1971. Includes Introduction, Epilogue, and 'Human Personality', by Ramsey.

'Persons and Funerals: What Do Person Words Mean?' (*Hibbert Journal*, LIV, June 1956).

'Polanyi and J. L. Austin', *Intellect and Hope. Essays in the Thought of Michael Polanyi*, ed. T. A. Langford and W. H. Poteat. Duke University Press, 1968.

(ed.). *Prospect for Metaphysics*. New York, The Philosophical Library, 1961. Includes 'On the Possibility and Purpose of a Metaphysical Theology' by Ramsey.

'Religion and Empiricism: III' (*The Cambridge Review*, LXXVII, 1956).

'Religion and Science: A Philosopher's Approach' (*The Church Quarterly Review*, CLXII, January–March 1961).

Religion and Science: Conflict and Synthesis. London, S.P.C.K., 1964.

Religious Language. New York, Macmillan, 1963.

Review of Maclagan, *The Theological Frontier of Ethics.* London, 1961 (*Mind* 72, 1963).

Review of Matson, *The Existence of God.* New York, 1965 (*The Journal of Philosophy* 64, 1967).

'Some Further Reflections on *Freedom and Immortality*' (*The Hibbert Journal*, LIX, July 1961).

'The Systematic Elusiveness of "I" ' (*The Philosophical Quarterly*, V, No. 20, July 1955).

'Talking About God: Models, Ancient and Modern', *Myth and Symbol.* Ed. F. W. Dillistone. London, S.P.C.K., 1966.

'Towards the Relevant in Theological Language' (*The Modern Churchman*, VIII, September 1964).

Words About God. New York, Harper and Row, 1971.

KING ALFRED'S COLLEGE
LIBRARY